JAPAN AND THE UNITED STATES
1853-1921

JAPAN AND
THE UNITED STATES
1853-1921

BY

PAYSON J. TREAT

BOSTON AND NEW YORK
HOUGHTON MIFFLIN COMPANY
The Riverside Press Cambridge

1921

PREFACE

WITH the exception of the first chapter, the present volume consists of twelve lectures prepared for delivery at four of the leading Japanese universities in the fall of 1921. The purpose of these lectures was to present a brief survey of the relations between the United States and Japan from the beginning of their intercourse to the present time. They therefore omit many interesting events in the domestic history of Japan and in her relations with other Powers, while, on the other hand, they discuss questions in which the United States was not directly concerned, but which have had an influence upon the formation of public opinion in that country. The importance of public opinion in determining international relations is now well understood, and in this survey an attempt has been made to account for the prevailing views of the Japanese and American peoples toward each other at different times in the period.

For the past fifteen years my university duties have been solely concerned with the investigation and teaching of the modern history of the Far East. In that time I have made two visits to Eastern Asia, to check up my studies by observation. These historical investigations should have helped me to understand the causes of many of the present conditions in the Far East, and to avoid some of the errors into which one may fall who confines his studies to a single country without considering contemporary movements in other lands. If these pages help, in any degree, the readers on both sides of the Pacific to understand better the point of view of their neighbors, I shall feel richly repaid.

PAYSON J. TREAT

STANFORD UNIVERSITY, CALIFORNIA
August 23, 1921

CONTENTS

JAPAN AND THE UNITED STATES
1853-1921
∴

CHAPTER I

THE HERITAGE OF NEW JAPAN

AFTER more than two centuries of strict seclusion, the Empire of Japan entered again into relations with the outer world, under the terms of a treaty negotiated by Commodore Matthew C. Perry, the special envoy of the United States. To understand the origin and development of these new relations, which eventually resulted in the admission of Japan to the family of nations and finally to a place among the five great allied and associated powers in the World War, some consideration should be given to the conditions which prevailed in the Island Empire in the middle of the nineteenth century, in the twilight days of Old Japan.

The empire consisted of three islands of fair size, and countless smaller ones lying off their shores — Honshiu, or Hondo, with an area of about 87,000 square miles, Kyushiu, with 14,000, and Shikoku, with 7000. The total area of the main islands of Old Japan was only 107,730 square miles, or two thirds the area of the State of California. To the north Japanese influence prevailed on the island of Hokkaido, and Japanese fishermen were scattered along the Kurile Islands and on the coast of Saghalien, while far to the south the Ryukyu Islands were a dependency of the feudal fief of Satsuma. But in these outlying regions Japanese control was nominal rather than real.

The islands lay off the eastern coast of Asia. At the narrowest point the straits between Kyushiu and Korea were only about one hundred and twenty-five miles wide, while in the middle distance rose the island of Tsushima, a Japanese fief. Far to the north the island of Saghalien lay so near the coast that for many years it was considered, by European navigators, to be a part of the mainland. Thus the empire lay near enough to the continent to come under the cultural influences of the civilizations which developed there, but remote enough to maintain its independence against the great war lords of China. The Japanese can proudly boast that their realm has never known a conqueror's rule, although twice the Mongols sent their armadas against it.

Lying to the east of Asia, the islands look out on the broad Pacific, and their best ports are on its waters. Thus they were destined to have intimate relations with western America as soon as civilized states arose upon its shores. From Yokohama to San Francisco is some 4800 miles. From the American point of view Japan stood at the portals of Asia, while viewed from Europe she was at the end of a long voyage, beyond India, Malaysia, and the China ports.

And though public policy had destroyed the old commerce of the land, yet the natural advantages challenged comparison with the great industrial and commercial state of the West. The islands of Japan, off the eastern coast of densely peopled Asia, possessed many of the physical features which served to make Great Britain the leading industrial and commercial power of western Europe.

THE HERITAGE OF NEW JAPAN

The islands of Old Japan lay in the temperate zone. The climate was favorable and stimulating. Extremes of heat and cold were moderated by the surrounding waters, and by the warm current which flowed up from the southern seas. On the western side the cold winds from Asia produced a more rigorous winter. The soil was excellent, although limited in amount because of the mountain masses of the interior. Perhaps one sixth of the area was arable, but its richness, the ample rains in the growing season, and the mild climate rewarded the husbandmen. Farm labor in Old Japan was abundant, and intensive cultivation was carried to a high degree, but the limited amount of food crops was supplemented by great quantities of fish and sea-food. The fishermen of Old Japan were to man the merchant and battle ships of the new age.

In every landscape a mountain loomed. The backbone of every island was a mountain range, and spurs tumbled down toward the sea. Many of these peaks were of volcanic origin, and about fifty were still active. Fujiyama, the sacred mountain, a perfect volcanic cone, reared its snow-covered crest 12,467 feet above the sea. These ranges served to isolate the different groups of people. To pass from the east to the west coast was not easy, and in feudal days the passes were strongly guarded lest people leave their clan without permission. And down the flanks of the mountains poured many rivers. Short in length, rapid in flow as they tumbled down to the sea, subject to flood when torrential rains were falling, they were of little service in transportation, but of great value for rice irrigation. And in recent days their power has been harnessed to turn a thousand dynamos.

It was a country of great natural beauty — the rugged coast-line, with gnarled pine-trees clinging to the crags; the island-dotted bays; the forest-covered mountains; the

3

shaded streams; the temple groves. The very beauty of
the land developed a love of beauty in the people. Even
the human habitations seemed to blend in the scene — the
thatched roofs, the weathered shrines, the moss-grown
castle walls. And this land the people loved with passion-
ate devotion. They made holiday when the cherry was in
blossom, and they viewed with rapture the wistaria, iris,
azalea, chrysanthemum, and autumn-tinted maple. Their
temples were reared in places of beauty, and wayside
shrines or simple *torii* marked the choice scenes along the
road.

Concerning the racial origins of no great people do we
know so little with exactness as of the Japanese. Many
are the theories which have been advanced, slight is the
evidence by which some of them are supported. On some
points there is now a general agreement, and these will
serve every purpose of this sketch. The earliest inhabitants were probably a primitive people known as Ainu.
Concerning their racial origin there is much speculation.
There is some reason for believing that they represented
a very early type of white men, and that they entered
Japan from the north and gradually occupied all the islands. At a later period the islands were invaded by Mongolian peoples from Asia, by way of Korea, and about the
same time other invaders appeared from the south, of
Malayan origin. Before the dawn of history the new-
comers had driven the Ainu back, out of Kyushiu and
Shikoku, and the battle-line was drawn in the northern
part of Honshiu. These successful warriors we call the
Japanese. The greater part of them seem to have come
from the continent, but the influence of the southern
group seems to have been far greater than their numbers.
And these conquerors no doubt took the women of the
vanquished as wives and thus introduced an Ainu strain

4

into the Japanese blood. The Japanese to-day are, like all the other great peoples of the world, a mixed race. The predominant characteristics are Mongolian in spite of the possible proto-Caucasian element. But this racial mixture occurred at so remote a time, certainly long before the Christian era, that we are justified in speaking of the product as a Japanese race. In historic times some immigration from Korea and China took place, but the numbers were small, and in time the assimilation was complete. This racial unity, omitting, of course, the relatively few Ainu, in spite of diversity in origin, made the Japanese almost unique among the great peoples of Asia and Europe. The melting-pot had functioned successfully in these isolated islands, but it had long since lacked ingredients. In 1854 the population was estimated at about 30,000,000.

The Japanese were also fortunate in the possession of a common spoken language, with certain dialectic differences. The language difficulties which prevailed in China and India did not exist in Japan. The written language was based upon Chinese ideographs, with certain abbreviations of the clumsier characters, known as *kana*. "The genius of man," attests Captain Brinkley, "has never invented any machinery so perfect for converting thoughts into sounds." The Chinese had advanced in civilization much more rapidly than their kinsmen who had settled in Korea and Japan. From China this culture passed into Korea, and from there into Japan. Between the latter countries intercourse began about the Christian era, but developed slowly. After 250 A.D. the relations became more intimate, and by 300 many new ideas had been introduced from Korea, while some adventurous Chinese emigrants had gone directly to Japan. Then began the period in which Japan drew heavily upon the cultural stores of the older Chinese civilization. The process at first was one of imitation, then adaptation to meet their peculiar needs, and finally assimilation, until a Japanese culture emerged. This assimilation of Chinese civilization, however, did not turn the Japanese into Chinese, for it was adaptation rather than imitation. And this process has been repeated in the last fifty years, when Japan drew upon the accumulated stores of Western civilization. By imitation, adaptation, and assimilation she profited through everything which the West had to offer, without losing her own peculiar culture.

From China, therefore, came letters and literature. The first scribes in Japan were emigrants from Korea or China, and their descendants. Later the Japanese learned how to use the Chinese ideographs, but pronounced them differently, and finally they added their own abbreviations. At first the Chinese classics were studied, "The Thousand Characters" and the "Analects of Confucius," and later the Buddhist scriptures. The oldest Japanese books to come down to us are two chronicles, the Kojiki, completed in 712, and the Nihongi, in 720 A.D. A century later the Japanese had developed more and more writers of their own, and, when the classical period came to a full flower about 1000, there were many Japanese poems, short stories, dramas, and histories in circulation. Some of the most brilliant of these classical authors were women.

Chinese philosophy and ethics, the works of Confucius, Mencius, and their commentators, profoundly influenced Japanese thought. Chinese science and medicine became the basis for Japanese study of these subjects. And Japanese art owes a profound debt to Chinese masters. Religious paintings and images were introduced with the Buddhist religion, and temple architecture came in at the same time. Chinese artists instructed Japanese pupils, and some of the latter crossed over to China for further study, and they and their pupils developed the several schools of Japanese art which delight the connoisseur of to-day.

Applied art, in the form of ceramics, lacquering, metal-working, silk-weaving, and embroidering, steadily improved, until the artisans of Old Japan were famous the world over.

Printing, the art preservative of all the arts, was introduced in the middle of the eighth century. The earliest examples were single sheets, printed from a graven block. The first printed book dates from 1088, about the time when the Normans were establishing themselves in Britain. A copy of this book is extant. The Chinese characters required a very extensive font of movable type, so it was not until 1593 that the first book was printed with such type in Japan, a century and a half after their use in Europe. Even then, it was some years before movable type supplanted the wood-blocks. But the ability to read these books was confined to a few. Education, in Old Japan, was enjoyed by the privileged classes; the children of the common people rarely enjoyed it.

The homogeneity in race and culture was reënforced by religious harmony. The ancient, indigenous religion was Shinto, the Way of the Gods. This was not a religion in the strict sense of the word. It possessed no moral code, no system of philosophy, no creed, no sacred books. It was a ritual of observances, in which the people propitiated the gods, good and evil, the deified ancestors of the Imperial House, and the national heroes. Its rites enjoined prayers to the gods, of thanksgiving, supplication, penance, and praise, and bodily purification to remove all contamination. Three things it stressed: loyalty to the sovereign, reverence for ancestors, and filial piety.

On the side of morals, Shinto was enriched by Buddhism, and on the side of ethics and philosophy by the writings of Confucius and the Chinese sages.

Buddhism was an alien faith. It had entered China from India, the land of its birth. About 375 A.D. it was introduced into Korea, and soon afterwards it must have reached Japan, but it was probably two hundred years later before the new faith received royal support. It appealed first to the courtiers and nobles, and later it reached down to the people. On the side of religion it brought a clear moral code. It set off good from evil, and promised rewards for right living and terrible penalties for evildoing. On the cultural side, the Buddhist priests, many of whom came from China or studied in China, became the media for the spread of the superior Chinese civilization among the people. The temples became schools. And when the priests compromised with the old Shinto faith, by identifying the old gods and heroes as the patron deities of Buddhism, it became possible for the people to be both loyal Shintoists and devout Buddhists at the same time. Thus a Shinto shrine frequently stood within the enclosure of a Buddhist temple, the Shinto deity being regarded as the patron of the alien faith. Shinto stressed patriotism and loyalty, Buddhism stressed a calm trust in fate, a stoic composure in the presence of danger or of death itself. Each reënforced the other.

For a time the Christian faith had been preached in Japan. Between 1549 and 1612, Portuguese and Spanish missionaries carried on a vigorous and successful propaganda. At first the faith spread rapidly, especially in western Japan, where many of the common people, as well as some of the warrior class, were enrolled in the church. But for several reasons, primarily the fear of the political menace involved in the spread of the Western faith, the missionaries were banished, then the faith was proscribed, and rigorous measures were taken to drive the converts back to their old allegiances. This was the reason for the expulsion of all foreigners save the Dutch and Chinese, and the adoption of a policy of strict seclusion. But from time to time missionaries returned to minister to their flocks, and in remote districts the faith was preserved through the years in spite of persecution. In the early days of New Japan the Western world was amazed to learn that several thousand Japanese Christians still kept the faith.

The political organization of Old Japan was unique at the time when it came again into contact with the West. For six hundred and seventy-five years Japan possessed a dual form of government. The Mikado (Tenno), Lord of Heaven, was the descendant of the original ruling family. The origin of the Imperial House is lost in the mists of antiquity, but the present Emperor is said to be the one hundred and twenty-second to ascend the throne, and of the sixty-ninth generation from the mythical first Emperor, Jimmu (660 B.C.). The Emperor, however, soon ceased to rule directly, and in his place the duties of government passed to noblemen at the court. Later, a family of court nobles, the Fujiwara, controlled the administration, in the Emperor's name, from 670 to 1156. These courtiers, in turn, were replaced by one of the great military families, which had gained strength during the constant struggles on the frontier, and from that time the control of the Emperor was the prize for which the military chieftains struggled. A great general, Yoritomo, received, in 1192, the title of Shogun (General), and from that time on a Shogun acted as administrative head of the state, but always in the Emperor's name.

Three military families held the Shogunate for the next six hundred and seventy-five years. When the rulers were strong, the country enjoyed peace, for the Shoguns held the lesser war lords in subjection. But when the Shogunate weakened, the generals struggled among themselves, each trying to acquire strength enough to challenge the power of the Shogun himself. So for two hundred and fifty years Japan was "a weltering mass of feudal atoms," until three great generals, Nobunaga, Hideyoshi, and Ieyasu, beat the feudal lords into submission, and the last of them founded the Tokugawa Shogunate, which held power from 1603 until 1867.

In this period the Emperor reigned in his old capital at Kyoto, surrounded by the court nobles (*kuge*), the descendants of the ancient nobility. But no real power was in the Emperor's hands. The Shogun, in his capital at Yedo, three hundred and thirty miles away, ruled Japan in the Emperor's name. He granted an allowance for the maintenance of the Court, and stationed one of his retainers to live in Kyoto to see that no mischief was wrought by the nobles there.

Ieyasu, who was not only a great general, but a greater administrator, so perfected the old feudal system that Japan enjoyed perfect internal peace for over two hundred years. This was a remarkable record, especially in the seventeenth and eighteenth centuries when Europe, America, and Asia were deluged with blood. It is, of course, the answer at hand to the charge that the Japanese are excessively fond of war. Their history contains many a gory page, but the Great Peace of more than two centuries proves them to have been duly appreciative of the blessings which it conferred.

The power of the Shogun was based upon his extensive domains and his large body of immediate retainers and faithful lords. These gave a sanction to the acts which he performed as representative of the Emperor. The rest of the land was divided among some two hundred and sixty feudal lords, known as *daimyo*. Some of these lords had been rich and powerful before Ieyasu rose to power. Others had accepted his leadership promptly, and had become his vassals. The old lords (*tozama daimyo*) were allowed to hold their estates, although some lost part of their domains, but Ieyasu carefully provided that loyal lords (*fudai daimyo*) held the principal seaports and controlled the strategic mountain passes, and generally held estates interspersed among the old rivals, who might perhaps try to unite against the new Shogun. In western Japan were the fiefs of most of the doubtful lords, and it was their descendants who united to overthrow the Tokugawa Shogunate in 1868.

The administrative posts in the Shogunate were all held by hereditary retainers; no position could be occupied by one of the old chieftains. And all the lords, great and small, had to spend part of their time at Yedo, under the eyes of the Shogun, and had to leave their families there always, as a hostage for their good behavior. Thus every *daimyo* had a mansion, or *yashiki*, in Yedo, and these residences, with the quarters for guards and retainers, set in handsome gardens, and the thousands of warriors and servants who occupied them, made Yedo the magnificent metropolis of the realm. And the *daimyo* processions along the great highways, as the lords went up to Yedo or returned to their fiefs, were striking incidents in the life of Old Japan.

Within their feudal domains, which varied in size from a few square miles to great fiefs comprising one or more provinces, the *daimyo* had complete administrative power. They had their own courts and codes of law, they levied and collected taxes, they had their own armed forces of *samurai*. They were responsible to the Shogun for military assistance in time of war, and, in general, they were expected to rule discreetly in their domains. For bad government or for disloyalty they would be punished by the Shogun; they might lose their fief or be removed to one of lesser income. But they did not have to furnish any money to him. If they became too rich, and thus might make trouble, they would be entrusted with the great honor of building a castle or a palace for the Shogun, or of making some costly public improvement which would use up most of their surplus. Such a system functioned satisfactorily enough as long as Japan remained in seclusion. But when the nation came into relations with the strong powers of the West, the dual government and the feudal decentralization had to give way to a strong and centralized government.

During the Great Peace the social orders crystallized. In the former days of constant feudal warfare, a man could carve a place for himself with his sword. Hideyoshi, the greatest of Japanese generals, was the son of a wood-chopper, but he rose from the ranks as a common soldier to be the greatest of the generals, the ruler of several provinces, the most powerful personage in Japan, and, had he been of noble birth, he could have won the title of Shogun. But in days of peace such opportunities did not exist.

The social order was divided into four classes: the court nobles, the warriors, the commoners, and the degraded class. The nobles were the descendants of the ancient nobility; rich in honors they were poor in purse, and they served in the Imperial Court at Kyoto. The warrior class was ranked by the Shogun, then came the feudal lords, or *daimyo*, of various rank and power, then the immediate retainers of the Shogun, and finally the *samurai*, or hereditary warriors, attached to the various lords. In the old days of war these *samurai* were constantly in service, but during the long peace they lived in ease, supported by pensions of money, rice, or land, engaged in military exercises, in the civil administration of the fiefs, or in honorable but non-military vocations. They were versed in the Chinese classics, and they favored the Zen sect of Buddhism, which appealed especially to the warrior. In all there were some five hundred thousand *samurai* families.

First in the ranks of the commoners stood the farmers. They produced the food which maintained the whole population of the land and paid the bulk of the taxes. In some parts of the land the *samurai* considered it no disgrace to till the land, and thus become warrior-farmers. Below them stood the artisans. They, too, produced something. In the days of peace the industrial arts were brought to a high state of perfection, for the Shogun and the *daimyo* encouraged the artists and artisans, the silk-weavers, the metal-workers, the porcelain-makers, and peace gave the lords the income which might be used in rewarding these skillful craftsmen. But at the bottom ranked the merchants. Old Japan had little use for the man who produced nothing himself and made his living out of distributing the products of the labor of others. The small tradesmen were looked down upon with contempt, but the great merchants of Yedo and Osaka were treated with respect because of their wealth, which was often in demand by the Shogunate and the feudal lords.

Lowest of all were the degraded classes, whose blood was thought to be polluted: those who came in contact with unclean things, such as dead bodies, the beggars, the professional entertainers, and many others who practiced occupations by no means esteemed dishonorable in the West.

For two centuries Japan had been practically a hermit nation. In order to avoid the political dangers which seemed to accompany Christian propaganda, especially in the seventeenth century, that religion had been proscribed, the Spaniards had been expelled, then all Japanese were forbidden to leave the country under pain of death, and finally, in 1638, the Portuguese were excluded, after almost one hundred years of intercourse. Only the Chinese and the Dutch, who were not interested in religious activities, were allowed to trade at one port, Nagasaki, under the most rigid regulations. This policy of exclusion and seclusion cut Japan off from contact with the rest of the world. It certainly enabled her to enjoy long years of peace, for intercourse with China, Korea, and the European possessions in Asia would probably have resulted in friction and war. But it also caused the Japanese to give up any commercial development, so that in 1854 she had no ships large enough to sail overseas. And it caused her to remain almost stationary during the wonderful years when Europe and America were learning the marvels of applied science. The application of steam power to machinery, in industry and transportation, gave the West a great advantage over Japan, China, and the rest of Asia. In the nineteenth century Europe and America were building railway lines and steamships, and great factories, where steam took the place of wind or water power and of human labor. And they were improving the instruments of destruction as well.

The free intercourse between Western nations permitted all of them to enjoy the discoveries or improvements of any one, and thus the progressive states of the West moved steadily forward, each benefiting through all that the others had learned. But Japan stood aloof. A hint of these wonderful inventions came into the country through the Dutch ships. Open-minded scholars learned all that they could about the progress of the West, but few dared advocate the introduction of the new ideas in Japan. The ruling classes were well satisfied with conditions as they were, and the scholars looked up to China as the fountain head of knowledge. So in the middle of the nineteenth century Old Japan lived in the past. The time for readjustment to the new age was at hand.

CHAPTER II

PEACE AND FRIENDSHIP

THE diplomatic relations between the United States and Japan cover a period of just seventy-five years — a brief span in the history of international intercourse. And this period in turn may be divided into three fairly well-defined phases, each with a distinct central theme and each set apart by a great event in the history of the Island Empire. Thus the first phase deals with the establishment of friendship and commercial intercourse between the two countries. It covers the whole period of troubled relations which ended only with the restoration of the Emperor, in 1868. The second phase covers the struggle of Japan to win admission to the family of nations and to maintain her place there. It might properly close with the revision of the treaties in 1894, although I believe the war with Russia lies within this middle period. It would be difficult to conceive of intercourse between two countries so different in race and culture conducted in a more creditable manner than that which prevailed in these thirty-seven years.

And, finally, comes the phase since the Russian war, from which Japan emerged as a world power with enlarged interests and responsibilities on the continent of Asia; a period in which contacts increased, and with contact came friction; a period in which popular opinion was moulded by more or less reliable information; and a period in which wise statesmanship has been in demand on both sides of the Pacific.

American interest in Japan had been slight until the

middle of the nineteenth century. Japan had been closed to all foreign intercourse, save that of the Dutch and Chinese at Nagasaki, since 1638. And two years earlier an edict had forbidden, under pain of death, the emigration of Japanese. No commerce could develop until the exclusion edicts were repealed and the ports of Japan again opened. Fortunately for Japan, her islands lay out of the track of the usual voyages from Europe and America to Canton, in China, so there were few attempts to engage in trade with Japan. American ships, chartered by the Dutch Government, carried on the trade between Nagasaki and Batavia during the Napoleonic Wars, and British ships performed this service while Java was held by Britain, 1811–16, but otherwise there is no record of foreign ships trading with Japan save the Dutch ships at Nagasaki, which after 1790 were limited to one a year.

In the early nineteenth century, Russia was the European power most interested in Japan. In the very year that Japan adopted a policy of exclusion (1638), the Russians had raised their standard on the Pacific, at Okhotsk, and during the next two centuries they had consolidated their control until they were ready to move down upon the Amur region of China and the island of Saghalien, claimed by Japan. Russian explorers had already passed down the Kurile Islands toward Hokkaido. In the eighteenth century Russian ships visited the main island (Honshiu), and their activity in the north caused the Shogunate to take active measures to defend the island of Hokkaido, while raids upon Saghalien and some of the Kurile Islands early in the nineteenth century further alarmed the Japanese, who now realized that they must prepare to enforce their exclusion laws.

If the isles of Japan lay out of the course of ships in the China trade, they were brought within the field of foreign maritime operations when British and American whalers began to frequent the North Pacific about 1820. On the rocky, fog-banked coast of the northern islands not a few whalers came to grief, and all of these ships would have welcomed a port of refuge there where wood and water and provisions might be obtained. America's first interest in Japan grew out of the operations of her stout-hearted whalers.

In 1832, and again in 1835, Mr. Edmund Roberts, American Minister to Siam and Muscat, was furnished with letters to the Emperor of Japan and instructed to visit Japan to enter into negotiations for the opening of commercial relations. Unhappily his death at Macao, in 1836, prevented this first attempt of the United States to open official relations with Japan.

Early in 1845, Mr. Zadock Pratt, a member of the House of Representatives from New York, submitted a resolution which recommended "that immediate measures be taken for effecting commercial arrangements with the empire of Japan and the kingdom of Corea." Although the resolution was laid upon the table, yet within a few months the commander of the East Indies squadron, Commodore James Biddle, was instructed to take the utmost care to ascertain if the ports of Japan were accessible. The American Commissioner to China, Mr. A. H. Everett, had been given letters of credence to Japan, and if he desired to visit that country Biddle was to accompany him with his squadron, but should he decline to do so, then the Commodore might make the attempt himself, "yet not in such a manner as to excite a hostile feeling; or a distrust of the Government of the United States."

These instructions resulted in the first official attempt to establish official intercourse between the United States and Japan. Commodore Biddle, with two ships of war, arrived in the Bay of Yedo on July 20, 1846. A Japanese officer was told that the Commodore had come to see if Japan had opened her ports as China had done, and to fix the terms of trade by treaty. As Biddle refused to surrender the ships' guns and the muskets and swords of the crew, as was required of the Dutch at Nagasaki, the ships were surrounded by small guard-boats. The Japanese refused to accept copies in Chinese of the first British, American, and French treaties with China, and it was only after protest that enough water could be secured for the ships. On the 27th, an "explanatory edict" was delivered to Biddle. The document was unsigned and unsealed, and its purpose was to explain why foreign trade would not be permitted. From time immemorial, it asserted, the country had refused to trade with foreigners. No distinction was made between nations and all were treated alike. The Dutch trade at Nagasaki was not to be regarded as furnishing a precedent, for the trade there was small and the whole affair of no importance. "We are aware," it continued, "that our customs are in this respect different from those of some other nations, but every nation has a right to manage its affairs in its own way." So permission to trade was positively refused, and Biddle was earnestly advised to depart and not to appear again upon that coast. When Biddle tried to enter the Japanese junk, to receive the edict, a seaman, misunderstanding the situation, pushed him back into his own boat. Biddle took no offense at this, as every atonement expected was made and the man punished. But a report circulated abroad that the American officer had suffered a personal indignity.

From this time events moved more rapidly. Interest now centered in the fate of certain American seamen, some shipwrecked men and others deserters, who had been arrested by the Japanese, and, according to their exclusion laws, had been held in confinement until they could be sent to Nagasaki for repatriation by means of the annual Dutch merchant ship. Such was the fate of the survivors of the American whaler *Lawrence*, wrecked on May 27, 1846, off the Hokkaido. Eight survivors reached land, and one of these was afterwards killed while attempting to escape. The remaining seven were detained for seventeen months before they were finally sent away from Nagasaki on a Dutch ship.

Early in 1849, the Dutch Consul at Canton advised the American Commissioner that fifteen seamen were detained at Nagasaki, as they had arrived there too late to be sent away in the Dutch ship of 1848. Mr. Davis communicated this news to Commodore Geisinger, in command of the East Indies squadron, and the latter promptly dispatched Commodore Glynn, in the *Preble*, to Nagasaki. In his sailing instructions Glynn was told to proceed to Nagasaki and obtain the release of the seamen. If the release was refused without orders from Yedo, then Glynn was to proceed there, and "make a firm, temperate, and respectful demand of that court for the immediate release and surrender to you of the above-mentioned prisoners." "In your correspondence or intercourse with the Japanese," Glynn was instructed, "your conduct will be conciliatory, but firm. You will be careful not to violate the laws or customs of the country, or by any means prejudice the success of any pacific policy our government may be inclined to pursue. Nevertheless, you may be placed in situations and circumstances which cannot be foreseen, and on which special instructions cannot be given you in anticipation. In all such cases, every confidence is reposed in your discretion and ability to guard the interests as well as the honor of your country." And, in conclusion, he was reminded that "the protection of our valuable whaling fleet and the encouragement of the whale fisheries are objects of deep interest to our government," and he was told to be prompt to aid and promote these objects.

Glynn's voyage was completely successful. The seamen proved to be thirteen survivors of fifteen deserters from the ship *Lagoda*, who had been under arrest since they landed on the Hokkaido in June, 1848, and Ranald McDonald, who had been set ashore, at his own request, about the same time, from the whaler *Plymouth*. In securing the release of the seamen, Glynn had broken through the strict regulations regarding shipwrecked seamen. An American officer had dealt directly with Japanese officials, American seamen had been restored to an American ship rather than by a Dutch or Chinese vessel, and the transaction had taken place presumably without reference to Yedo.

The account of the treatment of the men of the *Lawrence* and *Lagoda* created an unfavorable impression in some quarters in the United States. In each case the men had been kept in close confinement for months, at times even in bamboo cages, and they had been punished for attempting to escape. Furthermore, according to the laws dealing with the proscribed Christian religion, they had been compelled to trample upon a crucifix. All this was contrary to the American idea of the way in which helpless mariners should be treated, and it caused some to believe that a serious effort should be made to compel the Japanese to deal more humanely with shipwrecked seamen. As a matter of fact the Japanese treated the seamen as well as could be expected in view of the stern exclusion edicts, and the real kindliness of the Japanese peasant folk was clearly brought out in their treatment of shipwrecked men in later years, after the repeal of the exclusion laws.

Just at this time a new reason for American interest in Japan appeared. It was due to the raising of the American flag at the Golden Gate and the annexation of California. Then direct voyages were made from San Francisco to Shanghai and Canton, and these brought American ships within the waters of Japan. And promptly the desire arose to establish a steamship line to the Orient, but this would require coaling stations along the way, and one of these would have to be on one of the Japanese islands. This was the dominant reason in the decision to send out a second naval expedition to Japan. California thus became linked with Japan at the very dawn of international intercourse.

Commodore Aulick, who was placed in command of the East India squadron in 1851, was instructed to visit Japan and secure, if possible, a treaty of amity and commerce, including the right to obtain coal, the opening of one or more ports for commerce, and protection for shipwrecked seamen and property. By some oversight the letter to the Emperor, drafted by Daniel Webster, failed to mention the protection of seamen as one of the desiderata. On his arrival at Hongkong, Aulick found a letter of recall, for the administration had determined to entrust this delicate mission to Commodore Matthew Calbraith Perry.

According to his instructions, the object of Perry's expedition was to secure protection for shipwrecked American seamen and property, permission to secure supplies (especially coal), and the opening of one or more ports for commerce. These objects were to be obtained by argument and persuasion, but in any event American citizens wrecked on the coasts of Japan must be treated with humanity or the offenders would be severely chastised. The mission was to be of a pacific character, and Perry was to use force only in self-defense, and he was, furthermore, to be "courteous and conciliatory, but, at the same time, firm and decided. He will, therefore, submit with patience and forbearance to acts of discourtesy to which he may be subjected, by a people whose usages it will not do to test by our standards of propriety, but, at the same time, will be careful to do nothing that will compromit, in their eyes, his own dignity, or that of the country. He will, on the contrary, do everything to impress them with a just sense of the power and greatness of this country, and to satisfy them that its past forbearance has been the result, not of timidity, but of a desire to be on friendly terms with them."

To create this sense of the power and greatness of the United States, the five ships of the East India squadron were to be reënforced by eight additional ships. During the nine months which elapsed before the first of these was ready for sea, Perry busied himself in gathering all available information which might bear upon his mission. To this thorough preparation the success of the expedition was in large part due.

On the 8th of July, 1853, with only four ships of war, Perry anchored off the town of Uraga, at the entrance to the Bay of Yedo. The Japanese had been advised of this American mission by the Dutch at Nagasaki, yet its appearance caused consternation. According to law, the ships should have been sent away, and, if they would not go, then the armed forces of the Shogun and the feudal lords (*daimyo*) should have repulsed them. Yet there were influential officials at the Shogun's Court who realized the danger of precipitating hostilities with a power represented by such destructive armaments. And Perry's wise conduct gave them support in their temporizing proposals. On his first visit, Perry remained for only ten days. He impressed the Japanese with the strength of his squadron, containing the largest vessels and the first steamships ever seen in Japanese waters, and, perhaps of equal importance, with his own good-will. In dealing with the Japanese officials he was dignified, firm, and fearless. He insisted upon receiving the treatment due the representative of a great power, and he so far succeeded that, contrary to all precedent, the President's letter was honorably received by two high officials. Then he sailed away to allow the Japanese ample time for the consideration of so revolutionary a proposal as the abrogation of their exclusion laws, as well as to await the arrival of additional ships from home with the gifts selected for presentation to the sovereign and his officials.

After leaving Japan, Perry returned to Hongkong and Macao, visiting the Ryukyu (Loochoo) Islands on the voyage. If the American merchants and the American Commissioner in China could have had their way, Perry would have remained constantly on the China coast, for all foreign interests seemed in jeopardy during the Taiping Rebellion; but the Commodore was confident that a portion of his squadron could protect the few Americans there, while the larger part was engaged in carrying out his important mission to Japan. Learning that both French and Russian squadrons were planning to visit Japan, Perry hastened his departure from Hongkong, sailing on the 14th of January, 1854.

At Ryukyu, where the squadron rendezvoused, Perry received a letter from the Governor-General of Netherlands India advising him of the death of the Shogun shortly after he had left Uraga, and transmitting the re-

PEACE AND FRIENDSHIP

quest of the Japanese officials that he postpone his promised visit until the period of mourning had expired. The Commodore decided, however, to proceed to Japan. On February 13th, the squadron, now consisting of seven vessels, anchored in the Bay of Yedo. Two other ships joined the fleet later, and eight were present when the treaty was signed on March 31st.

During Perry's absence, the American request for friendship, commerce, supplies, and the protection of shipwrecked seamen had been seriously considered by the Shogun's officials. Without question the Shogun could have dealt with this matter on his own responsibility, reporting his decision to the Mikado for his formal approval. But the steady weakening of the Shogunate during the past fifty years had undermined its old fearlessness and readiness to accept responsibility. A few of the high officials at Yedo realized the necessity and wisdom of modifying the old exclusion laws, but the bulk of the feudal lords and their retainers were stanch conservatives, and this was made clear when the unusual step was taken of transmitting the President's letter to the Mikado and the *daimyo* for their consideration. The Imperial Court promptly instructed the Shogun to drive the Americans away, and the senior Prince of Mito, one of the ablest and strongest *daimyo* in the land, though nominally in retirement, led the opposition of the feudal lords to any dealings with the foreigners. At first orders were issued to strengthen the defenses of the coast and of Yedo, troops were drilled and cannon cast. But in November orders were issued that if the Americans returned, they were to be received peacefully.

The Shogun's Cabinet had, therefore, decided to give a favorable reply to the American requests. So on Perry's second visit the negotiations were carried on with the utmost friendliness and the conduct of the American officers and men was above reproach. There were, of course, differences of opinion to be harmonized, but these were satisfactorily arranged. The Japanese, for example, wished to have the negotiations take place at Uraga or Kamakura, but Perry objected to both places because of the unfavorable harbors, and suggested Yedo, the capital, as the proper place. By a compromise the little village of Yokohama, some eighteen miles from Yedo, was agreed upon. There Perry landed three times, with proper ceremonial, to discuss details with the Shogun's commissioners. A reply to the President's letter was presented, which granted all the requests—kind treatment of shipwrecked men, the furnishing of provisions, supplies, and coal, and the opening of Nagasaki, which was a port "in the southern part of the empire," as the President had desired. Perry naturally wished to have these concessions protected by a formal treaty, rather than stand as national law subject to modification or repeal at any time. He tried, therefore, to use the American treaty of 1844 with China as a basis for discussion, but the Japanese promptly replied that they were not ready for the establishment of such extensive commercial relations. Perry insisted upon a treaty, and even went so far as to suggest that the President would be satisfied with nothing less, and that a failure to secure it might necessitate the sending of more ships amd men from America with, perhaps, more stringent instructions. This strong statement aroused the indignation of Dr. S. Wells Williams, an American missionary to China, who served as first interpreter of the expedition. Yet Perry was right in desiring a formal treaty, and his views prevailed.

During the progress of the negotiations, gifts were exchanged, and those from the United States included two telegraph instruments, a miniature locomotive, tender, cars, and rails, books, weapons, tools and implements, wines and spirits, and many other objects of interest to the Japanese. All of which they carefully studied as evidence of the material strength and wealth of the Western nations.

Finally, on the 31st of March, a treaty of peace and amity was signed, the text being in English and Japanese, with translations in Dutch and Chinese.

This epoch-making treaty, which brought to an end the long period of Japan's seclusion, consisted of twelve articles. First of all, it established a "perfect, permanent, and universal peace, and a sincere and cordial amity" between the United States and Japan. The other clauses covered the concession of the American requests. The port of Shimoda was to be opened for supplies at once (Perry had refused to consider Nagasaki), and Hakodate (near the whaling-grounds) a year later. Shipwrecked Americans were to be well treated; trade was permitted under temporary Japanese regulations and through the agency of Japanese officers; and an American consul or agent might be sent to Shimoda after eighteen months, provided either government deemed it necessary. The "most favored nation" clause, which would automatically confer on Americans any privileges granted to other powers, was included, and in additional regulations, signed at Shimoda on June 17th, a crude form of extraterritoriality was provided.

In comparison with the customary treaties of commerce of the period, this was but a beginning. But in the light of Japanese history for the past two hundred years, and in view of the repeated enforcement of the exclusion laws against Russians, British, and French in the last few decades, it was a great achievement. Without the use of force, Perry had won far more than one might well expect.

It has been customary, in many quarters, to consider this treaty as having been imposed by force upon the Japanese. It has even been said that Perry threatened to open hostilities if his demands were refused. There is no evidence which can support such views. A naval officer was entrusted with this mission because of its dependence upon a fleet for possible success. A strong squadron was placed at Perry's disposal because of the hostile nature of the exclusion laws, and the necessity for defense in case of attack. The ships entered the Bay of Yedo cleared for action, with every man at his post, yet Perry was under the strictest orders to resort to force only in self-defense. These orders, given in his sailing instructions, were repeated again and again in later dispatches. If Perry had taken the offensive, — and there is not the slightest reason to believe that he ever considered doing so, — he would have violated the injunctions of the President and of his immediate superior, the Secretary of the Navy. He was engaged in a pacific mission, success was to be obtained by argument and persuasion, and, if he failed, then only was he to warn the Japanese that future acts of cruelty to American seamen would be severely repaid.

The presence of the powerful ships, and especially the steamships, must have made a profound impression upon the Japanese officials. This evidence of the progress of the West, brought to the very doors of the Shogun's capital, certainly supported the arguments of those who favored the opening of the country. But, if there had not been enlightened men in the councils of the Shogunate, there is every reason to believe that the ignorant conservatives would have carried the day and an attempt would have been made to repulse Perry on his second visit.

PEACE AND FRIENDSHIP

For his success in negotiating this great treaty, much credit is due to the Commodore himself. He was certainly wise, patient, dignified, and determined. Courteous in dealing with the Japanese officials, he insisted upon the respect due his rank and the importance of his mission. And he convinced the Japanese who came in contact with him of his real good-will toward their nation and people. On this point the testimony of the missionary, S. Wells Williams, is of decisive value.

But Perry's wisdom and the impressive strength of his squadron would have counted for little had there not been Japanese in high places who could appreciate the one and rightly interpret the other. These were men who had kept in touch, as best they could, with the progress of the world by means of information which seeped into the country through the Dutch trading-post at Nagasaki. They knew something of Western science and politics, something of the amazing advances made in the West since the days of steam, and they knew how China, the great Middle Kingdom of the East, had been battered to her knees by only one of the maritime powers. And the steady advance of Russia from the north aroused interest in foreign relations. Such feudal lords as Abe, Hotta, and Ii Naosuke were powerful forces working for the success of Perry's mission.

Having altered their laws in favor of the Americans, the Japanese were quite willing to grant equal terms to all who applied. The Crimean War was now raging in Europe, and the fleets of Britain, France, and Russia desired ports of refuge and supply in Japan. Admiral Stirling, with an English squadron of four ships, appeared at Nagasaki on September 7, 1854. Without difficulty a treaty was negotiated which covered most of the points in Perry's treaty, while the "most favored nation" clause applied to the others. Nagasaki and Hakodate were to be opened to British ships for supplies, and ships in distress might visit other ports. Two months later, Vice-Admiral Poutiatine, with one ship, visited Shimoda and asked for a treaty on behalf of Russia. This was his fourth visit to Japan, and before Perry's success he had been able to accomplish nothing. But now, even though he lost his only vessel in a great tidal wave, the Japanese signed a treaty, similar to those which had preceded it; Shimoda, Hakodate, and Nagasaki were opened to Russian ships, and the full principle of extraterritoriality was granted — every person who shall have committed a crime should be arrested, but he should be tried only according to the laws of his own country.

At Nagasaki the Dutch were still laboring under the ancient regulations which made residence at their trading-post a virtual imprisonment. On November 9, 1855, a preliminary convention was signed, which was supplanted by a treaty on January 30, 1856; the only important difference between the two documents being the withdrawal of the privilege previously given the Dutch to lease the land at Deshima (the trading-post) and purchase the dwellings and warehouses there. The terms of this treaty indicate the strict regulations under which the Dutch had carried on their trade, and which were now removed in large part.

The Japanese, therefore, granted every formal request for a treaty, but when a French vessel arrived at Shimoda, in 1855, they would have nothing to do with it, as France had not asked for and secured a treaty. Two Japanese shipwrecked seamen, whom the French would return to their native land, were finally transferred to an American ship, and permitted to land from her.

Although the Shogun's Government had decided to set

aside the ancient seclusion edicts, it did not follow that its course was generally approved. The opposition which had developed between the first and second visits of Perry was still unconvinced. In general, the people at the open ports treated the occasional foreign seamen with kindness and courtesy. Many of the strangers were impressed by the eagerness of the Japanese to learn about all the new and strange things which the Westerners possessed. Perry's ships, at anchor in the Bay of Yedo, had been a great technical museum which the Japanese, who were permitted on board, studied thoroughly. They were not only interested in seeing all that was new and strange; they wanted to know how the guns and engines and various devices worked. The brass howitzers presented by Perry were used as models for a hundred which were promptly cast. And the Japanese quickly mastered the principle of the steam engine, but the magnetic telegraph proved too hard for them at first.

At the open ports, friendly relations were soon established. But in the interior, at the seats of many of the feudal lords, dwelt those who knew little or nothing directly about the foreigners, and who felt keenly the mistake, if not the cowardice, of abandoning the old laws which had given Japan freedom from foreign interference for over two hundred years.

Some of the doubting officials and lords had been impressed by one clause of the President's letter: "If your Imperial Majesty is not satisfied that it would be safe altogether to abrogate the ancient laws which forbid foreign trade, they might be suspended for five or ten years, so as to try the experiment. If it does not prove as beneficial as was hoped, the ancient laws can be restored. The United States often limit their treaties with foreign States to a few years, and then renew them or not, as they please." They were willing, therefore, to give the new arrangement a fair trial, but, in later years, many of them remembered this proposal and insisted that Japan might fairly restore the old edicts.

Criticism was, for a time, quieted when, in February, 1855, the Mikado gave his approval to the treaties of 1854 and 1855 with the United States, Great Britain, and Russia. But this proved to be only a lull in the storm, and any attempt to enlarge the privileges already conceded to foreigners would certainly arouse embittered protest.

CHAPTER III

COMMERCIAL INTERCOURSE

In accordance with the terms of Perry's treaty, the United States Government determined to send a consul to reside at Shimoda. He was not only to concern himself with the protection of American citizens who might frequent that port, but he was also to endeavor to secure an audience with the Shogun, and, if possible, convince the officials of the wisdom of further enlarging the commercial intercourse between the two nations. In the choice of Townsend Harris, of New York, the American Government was most fortunate, and the Japanese have much to be thankful for that a man of his fine character should have been selected to inaugurate the new treaty relations.

When he arrived in Japan, Townsend Harris was in his fifty-second year. His early life had been spent as a merchant in New York City, where he had taken an interest in public affairs and had served as president of the Board of Education. From 1848 to 1855 he had engaged actively in the Far Eastern trade, and he was familiar with the coast and peoples of eastern Asia, Malaysia, and the Pacific Islands. In August, 1855, he was appointed consul at Shimoda, and was commissioned to negotiate a treaty with Siam on his way to his post. The latter mission was easily performed, for the Siamese were quite willing to grant to the Americans a treaty similar to the British convention of 1855. On August 21, 1856, the steam frigate *San Jacinto* entered the harbor of Shimoda bearing the first resident representative of the United States in Japan.

Much depended upon the character and personality of the first consul. He was dealing with a strange people, concerning whose laws and customs little was really known in the West. Differing in training and culture as the two peoples did, it was essential that the representatives of each should try to understand the point of view and the procedure of the other. An understanding must be arrived at, and only a sympathetic mind and a real desire to reconcile differences could avail much. Townsend Harris entered upon his service with an open mind and a kindly disposition. After his first interview with the local officials, he recorded in his journal: "We were all much pleased with the appearance and manners of the Japanese. I repeat that they are superior to any people east of the Cape of Good Hope." And, in spite of early disagreements and apparent signs of duplicity and bad faith, he was able to the end of his residence in Japan to retain the good impression he had first received. Few Westerners, during those troubled years, approached the problems of honorable intercourse between such widely different peoples with so sincere a desire to understand, and thus to make allowances, as did Townsend Harris.

At first the Japanese did not wish to receive him. The Japanese text of the treaty read that a consul might be appointed if *both* nations deemed it necessary. The American text read *either* government, and this had been understood during Perry's negotiations. They also assured him that Shimoda was still in ruins since the disastrous earthquake of the preceding year, and they begged him to go away and return in about a year. But Harris had no intention of leaving, and he was soon installed in a temple as a residence. Then came four months of unsatisfactory relations, during which, however, Harris so impressed the officials that finally

34

friendly relations were established, which steadily improved. As they gained confidence in Harris and found that he spoke the truth and kept faith, their dealings became more straightforward. Within a year he was able to negotiate a new convention, signed on June 17, 1857. which, among other terms, opened the port of Nagasaki for supplies, permitted Americans to reside at Shimoda and Hakodate, provided for the exchange of coins by weight, and granted extraterritoriality to the Americans. Four months later, the Dutch agent signed a new treaty which removed more of the old restrictions upon Dutch commerce, but also provided for a temporary import duty of thirty-five per cent, forbade the introduction of opium into Japan, and secured the right of the Netherlanders to practice "their own or the Christian religion" within their buildings or burying-places. Under the "most favored nation" clause the rights gained by one country were automatically extended to the other treaty powers. Thus Harris had gained the right of residence at the open ports and the right to exchange coins by weight, while the Dutch had gained toleration for their religion and a conventional tariff. The introduction of the anti-opium clause in the Dutch treaty was a valuable service to Japan, and the Russians accepted it in their supplementary treaty of October 24, 1857. It has been suggested that the Dutch and Russians were perhaps as much interested in depriving British trade of its leading export (if Japanese trade should develop as Chinese trade had done) as they were in protecting Japan from this dangerous drug.

For almost a year Harris had tried to secure permission to go up to Yedo and there present to the Shogun his letter of credence from the President. At the capital there was much opposition to any further relations with the foreigners, beyond the limited intercourse granted in the early treaties. But once again the liberal officials carried the day, in spite of bitter opposition, and Harris was advised that he would be escorted to Yedo in a most honorable manner, there to have an audience with the Shogun. In November, 1857, the party set out from Shimoda, consisting of officials, armed retainers and transport-coolies, about three hundred and fifty in all. The journey of one hundred and eighty miles was performed in seven days, and on the 30th, the American flag was, for the first time, carried through the streets of the Shogun's capital. After a week of hospitality and the exchange of courtesies, the American Consul was received in honorable state by the Shogun. While princes of the blood and members of the Great Council were prostrate on their faces, Harris stood erect, and, after the three bows of respect, he addressed the Shogun. Not since the English envoy, Captain Saris, had been received in 1613, had a foreign representative been accorded so honorable an audience. In this respect the Japanese were far wiser and more considerate than the Chinese. The latter, down until the early nineties, had tried to insist upon the kowtow, the nine times prostration, of the foreign envoys in the presence of the Emperor. But the Japanese had held that only the forms of respect customary in the West would be expected.

The friendly reception in Yedo, and the satisfactory nature of the audience, encouraged Harris to proceed to the real object of his mission, the negotiation of an adequate treaty of commerce. This, he knew, must be won through argument and persuasion — there were no "black ships" to give point to his remarks. Fortunately, in Lord Hotta, the Minister for Foreign Affairs, he was dealing with one of the most enlightened of the Shogun's

officials, whose interest in Western affairs had antedated
the coming of Perry. Then began a series of conferences
in which Harris tried to explain to his hosts the state of
affairs in the outer world, and especially in the Far East,
as well as to give them an introduction to the principles
of international intercourse. In order to drive home his
arguments, that Japan should receive foreign ministers
at the capital and establish free commerce with all
nations, he stressed the aggressive conduct of England,
Russia, and France in the Far East, and expressed the
opinion that, as soon as the war with China was over,
the fleets of Britain and France would sail to Japan to
demand enlarged treaty rights. If Japan would negotiate such a treaty with him, alone and unsupported, her
honor would be unimpaired, and the militant powers of
Europe would be satisfied. These arguments had great
weight with the Japanese representatives, but the actual
negotiations moved slowly until Harris threatened to
return to Shimoda if nothing were done. This resulted in
the announcement, in the middle of January, that the
Shogun had assented to the principles of a commercial
treaty, and that two commissioners would be appointed
to arrange the details. For a month the negotiations
proceeded, twenty sessions were held, and point after
point was argued exhaustively. Some articles which
Harris feared would be objected to were accepted with
little difficulty, while the opening of additional ports
occasioned repeated interviews. Finally, when the treaty
was ready for signature, the protests of hostile *daimyo*
in the castle caused a delay until the approval of the
Mikado, at Kyoto, might be obtained. The Shogun's
representatives had no doubt that this would be secured
as a matter of course, and Harris was told that the Government "had determined not to receive any objections

37

from the Mikado." With this understanding the treaty was completed, but signature was postponed for sixty days, until April 21st. Harris in the meantime returned to Shimoda to await the result of the reference of the draft to Kyoto.

This was the first treaty of commerce negotiated by Japan since she had withdrawn into seclusion in the early seventeenth century. And its terms were so satisfactory that it became the model for all the treaties negotiated with Japan until the revision of the treaties in 1894. It provided for free commerce at the open ports, without the interference of Japanese officials. Kanagawa, Niigata, and Hiogo were to be opened for commerce, and Yedo and Osaka to residence, while Shimoda, which had proven of little importance, was to be closed. Each country might station diplomatic agents at the capital of the other, and consuls at the open ports. Other clauses forbade the importation of opium; permitted the circulation of foreign coins in Japan, weight for weight; defined American extraterritorial rights in civil as well as criminal cases; granted to Americans the free exercise of their religion and the right to build houses of worship; and provided for the revision of its terms after July 4, 1872, on the desire of either government. An interesting clause, which in modified form may be found in American treaties with China and Korea, stated that "the President of the United States, at the request of the Japanese Government, will act as a friendly mediator in such matters of difference as may arise between the Government of Japan and any European power."

In the commercial regulations which accompanied the treaty, a conventional tariff was established. The temporary tariff under the Dutch and Russian conventions of 1857 called for a thirty-five per cent import duty. The

COMMERCIAL INTERCOURSE

Japanese commissioners believed that a twelve and a half per cent duty on imports and exports would be wise. But Harris persuaded them to adopt a sliding scale. Thus, roughly, gold and silver, wearing apparel, household furniture, and books not designed for sale would be on the free list; certain raw materials would pay five per cent import duty; intoxicating liquors would pay thirty-five per cent; and all other articles, including almost all Western manufactured goods, would pay twenty per cent. On exports a duty of five per cent would be levied, and all duties might be revised in 1864 if the Japanese Government desired.

The significance of the Harris treaty lay in the new concessions granted by the Shogunate, and in its codification of various articles of the earlier treaties. The important new features were the right of residence of a minister at Yedo; the opening of new ports and cities; the right to lease land and erect buildings; the provision for free commerce; and the establishment of a regular tariff. The extraterritorial article, the ban upon opium, the free exercise of their religion — all these had been previously conceded.

Harris, of course, could not foresee that the right to export gold and silver coin might work to the detriment of the Japanese. Nor that the conventional tariff, so fairly framed in his treaty, might be altered by later negotiators until Japan was bound hard and fast by treaty stipulations. Nor that the revision of the treaty, which he believed would come as a matter of course in 1872, would be delayed in spite of every Japanese effort for twenty-two years.

The treaty was not signed in April, as all had anticipated. The first envoys of the Shogun to the Mikado, in February, to seek the latter's approval of the treaty terms,

39

failed completely. The next month the Foreign Minister himself, Lord Hotta, went up to Kyoto, and made a brilliant plea for imperial endorsement. But the anti-foreign, anti-Shogunate forces were too strong, and the imperial reply denounced the foreign policy of the Shogunate and demanded that the opinions of the three Tokugawa houses and of the *daimyo* be consulted before the imperial sanction was again sought. For the first time since its inauguration the Tokugawa Shogunate had failed to secure the approval of the Mikado when requested. This was a most serious situation. And it was further complicated by a bitter controversy which was raging within the Yedo castle over the appointment of an heir to the dying Shogun. In this emergency Lord Ii Naosuke, Kamon-no-kami, was appointed *tairo* or regent.

Throughout May, Harris waited impatiently for the return of Lord Hotta from Kyoto. When he realized the significance of the Mikado's approval, he is said to have threatened to go himself to Kyoto to conclude the treaty there. But when he learned of Hotta's failure, he consented to postpone again the signing until September 4th. In this interval Lord Ii hoped that he might settle the dispute over the heirship and also win the tardy approval of the Court.

As to the heir, the wishes of the Shogun were respected, and Iemochi, son of the Lord of Kii, was chosen. This further inflamed the supporters of Mito, who sought the appointment of his son, Yoshinobu, adopted by the Hitotsubashi family. Many of the great feudatories, including the *daimyo* of Satsuma and Echizen, and Lord Hotta, recently the Prime Minister, had supported Yoshinobu. This unfortunate controversy served to divide the councils of the Shogunate at a time when the rise of imperial independence threatened its ancient privileges.

COMMERCIAL INTERCOURSE

Lord Ii was not, however, to have the respite he desired in order to bring the Kyoto Court to terms. On July 23d, a United States ship arrived at Shimoda with news that, in June, China had been forced to sign new treaties with Great Britain and France, under pressure of their ships and men, and with Russia and the United States. And it was reported that the victorious allies were about to proceed to Japan with their fleets. Harris believed no time was to be lost. He at once proceeded to Kanagawa and sent word to Lord Hotta that the treaty should be signed at once, before the fleets arrived, so that Japan might grant, peacefully and with honor, the treaty terms which China had been forced to yield.

This news created consternation at the capital. A special conference of the high officials was summoned, and a majority favored the immediate signing of the treaty. Lord Ii, the Regent, pleaded for delay until the imperial approval could be obtained. But, outvoted in the Council, he yielded to the arguments of his colleagues, and took upon himself the responsibility for completing the treaty. That night the two commissioners visited Harris on the S.S. *Powhatan;* and, early on the morning of July 29th, the treaty was signed.

This was a momentous act. From one point of view it freed the Shogunate from further demands by the European diplomats, who would soon appear. But from the Japanese viewpoint it furnished an explanation for all the domestic and foreign complications of the next seven years. The treaty had been signed without the approval of the Emperor. That robbed it of sanctity in the days when the Emperor's power was being steadily augmented. It gave a rallying cry to the Jo-i, or anti-foreign party, of "Honor the Emperor and expel the barbarians." And it placed the Shogunate in the embarrassing position of trying to keep its plighted faith to the foreigners in spite of the patriotic opposition of loyal Japanese. But there can be little question to-day that Lord Ii and his advisers acted wisely in assuming this great responsibility. The success of the European intervention in China would probably have occasioned a strong effort to secure similar terms from Japan. If the Imperial Court had continued to forbid further concessions, then hostilities might easily have followed. ¡ And if concessions had been won through the presence of imposing armaments, the new intercourse would have been inaugurated under conditions which would have rankled in the breast of every imperial supporter. It was far better that the master treaty of the new intercourse should have been drafted by a wise friend of Japan, and gained through reason rather than by a show of force.

Within a few weeks the representatives of Russia and Great Britain arrived from China, to be followed a little later by the envoy of France. From Nagasaki came the Dutch agent, also seeking a new treaty. So four treaties were promptly completed, all based upon Harris's draft. Lord Elgin, in the British treaty, fixed the date of operation at July 1, instead of July 4, 1859, and secured the listing of cotton and woolen manufactured goods in the five per cent duty class. This was the first modification in the tariff, but, of course, all foreign merchants would enjoy the concession.

The new treaties, granting concessions far more liberal than those of 1854, would go into effect on July 1, 1859. Before that date the Shogunate must, if possible, secure the Mikado's approval. In fact, shortly after the Harris treaty was signed, an imperial order had been received from Kyoto summoning one of the high Yedo officials to report and explain the foreign situation. In October,

Lord Ii sent one of the cabinet, Lord Manabe, not only to gain the Emperor's approval, but also to strike at the anti-Shogunate propaganda which had grown bolder at the Imperial Court. The seriousness of the domestic situation is made clear by the modified terms of the Shogun's request. Instead of seeking the imperial approval of the treaties, as Hotta had done, because the time had come for the abandonment of the old exclusion laws, Lord Manabe argued that the treaties were only temporary evils, which could not be avoided; that the Shogunate did not desire to cultivate friendly relations with the foreign powers, but that, as soon as adequate armaments might be prepared, the barbarians would be expelled. This representation was typical of the policy of the Shogunate during the next six years. It was a policy of expediency; it sought to temporize, in the hope that time would justify its conduct. On the one hand it would try to satisfy the encroaching foreigners, and on the other it would try to bring about an eventual recognition of the wisdom of the new intercourse.

Yet an endorsement of this compromise proposal was not easily obtained. For more than three months Lord Manabe reasoned with the high officials in Kyoto until, in February, 1859, the imperial answer was handed down. This approved the resolution of the Shogun's Government to keep the foreigners at a distance and eventually to restore the old law of exclusion, and it authorized the Shogun to take temporary measures to this effect. At the time this was considered a great victory for Yedo, for it indicated an understanding between the two courts. But in effect it placed the Shogunate in an increasingly embarrassing position as the years went by, for the question was bound to be raised by its opponents — Has not the time come for the expulsion of the foreigners and the restoration of the ancient laws of the land?

Under these conditions, which were not understood by the foreigners at the time, the inauguration of the new treaties was bound to be involved in difficulties. Of the diplomats who had signed the treaties of 1858, Townsend Harris was the only one who remained at his post and endeavored to secure their full enforcement. From China came Rutherford Alcock, the first British Consul-General and later Minister, while France sent M. de Bellecourt. The foreign representatives were, of course, determined to see that the treaty stipulations were fulfilled in letter and spirit, while the Shogunate, in view of the serious controversy raging within the country, naturally sought to grant no more than the minimum engagements. Occasions for controversy promptly arose, and dispute followed dispute throughout the next six years. In dealing with these matters, the policy and conduct of Townsend Harris was in marked contrast to that of his colleagues. His knowledge of Japanese affairs caused him to realize the difficult situation in which the Shogun's officials were placed, and his sense of fair play led him to make allowances for acts over which they had little, if any, control. He was far more concerned with the development of satisfactory relations between Japan and the foreign powers in the future, than in the immediate enforcement of every clause of the new treaty.

The first question of treaty interpretation to be raised was concerned with the port of Kanagawa. This city, on the Bay of Yedo, lay on the great highway, the Tokaido, which ran from Kyoto to Yedo, and along which passed the *daimyo* processions as the feudal lords of the West proceeded to and from their fiefs and the capital. For this reason, lest the *samurai* of hostile lords might attack the unwelcome foreigners, Lord Ii had decided to create a new port at Yokohama, three miles from Kanagawa, where the Perry treaty had been signed. Both Harris and Alcock protested against this move, as designed to segregate the foreigners after the fashion of the Dutch at Deshima, but Ii had made such satisfactory provisions for foreign trade at the new port that the merchants willingly located there in spite of the diplomats' disapproval. To Lord Ii is due the credit for the development of Yokohama as one of the great ports of commerce of the world.

At the same time the currency question was raised. This was due to the fact that Japanese silver coins had a token value far greater than their intrinsic value, while silver and gold coins stood at the ratio of five to one, instead of fifteen to one as in the West. The Japanese tried to introduce a new coin which might be exchanged for the Mexican dollar, with a reduced token value, and they also tried to prevent the exportation of their gold coins, at a great profit to the foreign merchants. Their acts were probably in violation of the treaty, yet they were necessary to meet the unexpected effects of international commerce. Great quantities of gold coin were exported, and an immediate effect of the demand for silk and other export goods was to raise prices in Japan, which the opponents of foreign relations cited as one of the evils of the new régime.

In spite, however, of the widely diffused hostility to foreigners, the new commerce steadily throve. The merchants at Yokohama prospered, and the foreign representatives were established in temporary temple quarters at Yedo. Certain unfortunate incidents occurred, but these were surprisingly few when one considers what was being worked out. The people of a hermit empire had opened some of their ports to the merchants and seafaring men

of the Western world. In Japan there were those who
bitterly resented the change, and among the foreigners
were others who failed to realize that the good name of
Western civilization depended largely upon their individual conduct. If a few foreigners lost their lives during these
days of adjustment, it is also true that many Japanese
suffered at the hands of rude and uncontrolled Westerners.
In the first eighteen months five Westerners and two
Asiatics in their employ were cut down by Japanese sword-
men. On August 25th, a Russian officer and a seaman of
Commodore Popoff's squadron were assassinated in Yokohama. This fleet accompanied Count Muravieff-Amursky, who sought to secure the cession to Russia of the
island of Saghalien. Due reparation was made, but no
indemnity was granted. On November 5th, a Chinese in
the employ of the French consular agent was struck down.
On January 30, 1860, the Japanese interpreter of the
British legation, Denkichi, was murdered in Yedo, and
on February 26th, two Dutch merchant captains were
brutally murdered in Yokohama. In every one of these
cases the crime was probably occasioned by some act
either of the victims or of some other foreigner. But the
difficulty of protecting foreign lives was made very clear
when, on March 24th, the Regent himself, Lord Ii, was
assassinated at the very entrance of the Shogun's palace.
Seventeen of the assassins were former *samurai* (*ronin*)
of Mito, and the reasons which they gave were Lord Ii's
foreign policy and his high-handed conduct at the time
of the appointment of the Shogun's heir.

It was about this time that, after several postpone-
ments, the first Japanese mission to a foreign country
sailed from Yokohama on the U.S. S.S. *Powhatan* to exchange at Washington the ratified copies of the treaty of
1858. In command of the Japanese steamer, *Kanrin*

Maru, was Captain Katsu, better known as Count Katsu Awa, the organizer of the modern Japanese navy. And in the envoy's suite was Fukuzawa Yukichi, who became one of the great leaders of New Japan, founder of the *Jiji Shimpo* newspaper and of the Keiogijuku University. The mission was cordially received by President Buchanan at Washington. The ratified texts were exchanged, and, after a tour of the Eastern States, the envoys returned to Japan with all manner of examples of American products and manufactures. The information brought home by the keen observers in this party must have contributed much to a better understanding of the Western world on the part of the Yedo administration.

The experience of the first year had convinced Harris and his colleagues that it would be unwise to carry out the treaty stipulation for the opening of Yedo to foreign residence on January 1, 1862. The Shogunate officials went even further; they soon asked that the opening of the new ports of Hiogo and Niigata be also postponed.

Early in 1861, the anti-foreign forces became bolder. In January, the Yedo officials warned Harris that a large band of Mito *ronin* was on its way to burn Yokohama. The Shogun's officials took every military precaution, and the attack was not made. But a few days later, the assassination of another foreigner almost precipitated a crisis. This time the victim was an American citizen, Mr. Heusken, who had accompanied Harris to Japan, as his interpreter, in 1856. During his residence in Japan he had mastered the language, and had not only proven of great service to the American Minister, but had been employed by Lord Elgin in 1858, and was at the time assisting Count Eulenburg, who was negotiating a treaty for Prussia. Mr. Heusken was assassinated by a small band of *ronin* as he was returning from the Prussian legation on a dark and rainy night. So far as could be ascertained, the only explanation of this crime was the fact that he was a foreigner, and hostile *ronin* had seized the opportunity to destroy him. Mr. Harris did not hesitate to point out that Heusken had lost his life through his failure to heed the repeated warnings given to foreigners in Yedo.

The immediate result of this assassination was the decision of the foreign representatives, with the exception of Mr. Harris, to withdraw to Yokohama and to remain there, under the protection of the fleet, until the Government had given satisfaction for past breaches of the treaty and guarantees for the security of life and property in the future. Mr. Harris disagreed thoroughly with his colleagues. He asserted the belief that the Shogunate had tried honestly to carry out the treaties, but they had many difficulties to contend with. They had taken measures of precaution for the protection of all foreigners, but it was out of their power to prevent such murders as that of Mr. Heusken, who had failed to observe the counsels and remonstrances which they had given. He himself felt perfectly safe in Yedo so long as he complied with the conditions which the circumstances imposed. But he would not leave Yedo, for if the ministers retired, they might never return. Instead he recommended that they unite in urging upon the Government more vigorous measures, and trust to its good faith to carry them out. In these views he was at variance with Mr. Alcock, and a sharp exchange of notes occurred, in one of which he pointed out the impossibility of demanding of the then Japanese Government the same observances and the same prompt administration of justice as prevailed in the West, while to hold it responsible for the isolated acts of private individuals he believed wholly unsustained by any international law. And in closing he added: "I had hoped that the page of future history might record the great fact that in one spot in the Eastern world the advent of Christian civilization did not bring with it its usual attendants of rapine and bloodshed; this fond hope, I fear, is to be disappointed. I would sooner see all the treaties with this country torn up, and Japan return to its old state of isolation, than witness the horrors of war inflicted on this peaceful people and happy land."

So Harris stood alone. His colleagues retired to Yokohama, but he remained, without molestation, in Yedo. Early in March, the British and French representatives returned to their legations, after having secured the promise of the Government to protect them. But in this crisis Harris was right. And it was demonstrated a little later when, after an attack upon the British legation, Alcock did not deem it wise to repeat the withdrawal to Yokohama. The Japanese officials appreciated warmly the confidence displayed by Harris during these eventful days, and it would be of interest to speculate as to what might have happened if the American representative had joined his colleagues in these, and even more drastic, measures. The officials assured Harris that they would make every effort to arrest and punish the assassins, and they willingly paid $10,000 for the support of Heusken's widowed mother.

The murder of Heusken came near to causing serious complications in another quarter. When the news reached Washington, Mr. Seward, Secretary of State, addressed a circular note to the Ministers of Prussia, Great Britain, France, Russia, and Holland, proposing a joint naval demonstration in Japanese waters. Not only should no concession be granted in the postponement of the opening of Yedo, but the powers should coöperate to demand satisfaction for the murder of Heusken, and punish with signal vigor any insult or injury to foreigners in Yedo after its opening. From every point of view this was an amazing proposal. It was a traditional policy of the United States not to engage in joint operations of this kind. During the last European war in China, the United States had refused to coöperate with Great Britain and France. And, in view of the fact that the Civil War had begun, that the blockade of the Southern ports had been declared, it was surprising, to say the least, that any Federal ships of war could be spared to proceed to Japan. The best interpretation of this note seems to be that it was an attempt, during these critical days in Washington, to secure the coöperation of the European powers in a project which might appeal to their interests, lest they become involved in relations with the infant Confederacy. Happily, a later dispatch from Mr. Harris caused the proposal to be abandoned. Instead, the American Minister was given discretionary powers to consent not only to postponing the opening of Yedo, but also of Osaka, Hiogo, and Niigata.

In July, Mr. Harris requested his Government to recall him on the ground of impaired health and advancing years. This request was approved, with profound regret, and his successor was appointed. When the Shogunate learned that he was to be recalled, it addressed a letter to Seward testifying to his ability, knowledge of the country, and friendly attitude, and begging that he be allowed to remain. And this expression of esteem was renewed when Harris took his audience of leave on April 25, 1862.

For almost six years, Townsend Harris had represented his Government as the first Consul and Minister to Japan. In those years he had not only watched over

American interests with wisdom and diligence, but he had also acted as friend and counselor of the people to whom he was accredited. He had won the confidence of the local officials at Shimoda, and that gained for him the admission to Yedo and the honorable audience with the Shogun. He had impressed the high officials with his fairness and good faith, and that made possible the negotiation of his master treaty of commerce. He had tried to understand the difficulties under which the responsible officials labored, and he never failed to coöperate with them in every reasonable measure. And he did not expect too much of Japan in those early days of international relations. Certainly he would not hold a government responsible for the lawless acts of uncontrolled individuals. For the gossip of the treaty ports he had only contempt, unless it could be supported from sources on which he could rely, and he was as indignant at foreign misconduct as he was at the crimes of lawless *ronin*. When he realized that the treaties called for too rapid an increase in Western contacts, he was the first to advocate the postponement of the opening of the additional ports. And his good works lived after him. The Japanese received with honor his successor, and Mr. Pruyn, in turn, tried to maintain the wise policy of his predecessor. Happy, indeed, were both the United States and Japan in the services of this wise, just, and understanding diplomat in these critical years.

CHAPTER IV

THE TREATIES IN JEOPARDY

ACCORDING to American political theory, the successor of Townsend Harris was an active member of the recently organized Republican Party, which had won its first national victory in the election of Abraham Lincoln as President in 1860. Mr. Robert Hewson Pruyn, of Albany, New York, was a graduate of Rutgers College and for many years a prominent lawyer in his native city. He had served in the State Assembly, having been Speaker of that body, and was among the loyal supporters of Mr. Seward, the new Secretary of State. It was on Mr. Seward's strong personal request that Mr. Pruyn accepted the difficult and remote post at Yedo.

Again the United States was fortunate in the appointment of a representative who tried to understand the complex situation in Japan and who acted wisely and in moderation in spite of the threatening development. During his three years of service, Mr. Pruyn witnessed the culmination of the movement to cancel the treaties and drive the foreigners from Japan. Yet he never lost faith in the willingness of the Shogun's Government to keep its treaty engagements. And his position was a difficult one because of the terrible civil war in which his country was engaged at home. Not only were American interests in the Orient deprived of all but the slightest naval protection, — for frequently there were no American ships of war in Japanese waters, — but American prestige was at a low ebb, especially among the European representatives. In these days the influence of the British

52

chargé or minister, supported by ships of the line and a garrison in Yokohama, was supreme. And the close co-operation of France and Britain, a survival of the Crimean alliance, gave their representatives a dominant voice in the counsels of the foreign ministers, especially after the return of Sir Rutherford Alcock, in 1864, who was the senior, in point of experience, of all the diplomatic agents in Japan.

Day by day the political situation within the empire became more threatening for the foreigners. In Harris's time, the opposition to the foreigners had been led by one of the great Tokugawa princes, the ex-Prince of Mito, and he was, of course, loyal to the Shogunate. But after his death, in September, 1861, the leadership passed to the great *daimyo* of western Japan, to the Lords of Satsuma, Choshiu, and Tosa, and they were hostile to the Shogunate and the Tokugawa family. The rapidly increasing power of the Imperial Court at Kyoto was due to the support of *daimyo* who opposed the Shogunate as well as to those who opposed the latter's foreign policy. Thus foreign relations became apparently involved, beyond extrication, with the domestic political situation. The Yedo officials understood the wisdom of keeping the treaty engagements, but they realized that the treaties might be the occasion for a civil war in which the Shogunate itself would be threatened. Early in 1863, two of the Yedo officials informed Mr. Pruyn that war was threatening between the Shogun and the western *daimyo* who were influencing the Mikado, and asked what would be the action of the United States in such a crisis. To this query Mr. Pruyn replied that his Government would certainly render all moral support and all material support justified by international law, and that he believed, if the Tycoon asked for aid on the ground that the object of the hostile *daimyo* was to drive out the foreigners, all the treaty powers would be justified in giving it, in self-defense. The officials had supposed that this would be the attitude of Russia and the United States, but they had feared the other European powers might act otherwise.

On the night of June 26, 1862, the British legation, in Yedo, was invaded by a single Japanese swordsman, who struck down two of the British sentries and then committed suicide. The authorities made ample reparation, punishing the *daimyo* in charge of the Japanese troops on guard, imprisoning some of the men on duty that night, and offering an indemnity of $3000. But, on the theory that the Government had been aware of the projected attack, and that the *daimyo* had connived in it, Lord Russell demanded an indemnity of £10,000 in gold, and severe punishment for the *daimyo* if guilty.

Two months later came the attack upon foreigners which proved to be the most serious, in its results, of all the blood-stained episodes of these troubled years. On the 14th of September, four British subjects, riding on the Tokaido near Yokohama, were attacked by troops in the train of the father of the *daimyo* of Satsuma. One of them, Mr. Richardson, was fatally wounded, two other men were severely injured, and only the woman in the party escaped unharmed. This was thought to be a part of the general hostility to foreigners, and immediate demands for strong punitive measures went up from the Yokohama residents. Although the facts are still in dispute, it is evident that the horsemen were lacking in the respect due, according to Japanese custom, to a great lord, and, had they been Japanese, would have been summarily punished, although they should not have been fatally injured. In other words, the attack was spontaneous and not premeditated, and the assailants did not know, or care, whether Englishmen or other foreigners were involved, and certainly did not realize that one of the persons was a woman.

From the Shogun's point of view the outrage was especially embarrassing because it was done by the retainers of Saburo Shimadzu, father of the *daimyo* of Satsuma, and the active head of the pro-Mikado faction at Kyoto. Shimadzu had recently come up to Yedo as escort for a court noble who bore the imperial command that Osaka and Yedo must not be opened and that Kanagawa (Yokohama) must be closed, and also that the Shogun must report at Kyoto to take counsel for the expulsion of the barbarians, and reorganize his administration under anti-foreign *daimyo*. Under these circumstances a demand for the punishment of Shimadzu could not be accepted, while any unusual reparation would further inflame the anti-foreign *daimyo*. The steady weakening of the Yedo administration was manifest in its acceptance of the imperial commands. Not since 1634 had a Shogun gone up to Kyoto, and then the mission had been one of respect. In two centuries no Shogun had been commanded to attend the Imperial Court, and the acceptance of this summons may well be considered the beginning of the downfall of the Tokugawa Shogunate. But as compliance was not at once forthcoming, a second imperial mission was sent to Yedo in December, escorted by the Lord of Tosa, demanding that the Shogun appear in Kyoto in the spring and assume the leadership of the clans in the expulsion of the barbarians.

Six months elapsed between the death of Richardson and the arrival of the British demands, for such were the delays in communication between Japan and Europe in those days. If the incident could have been settled by cable in a few days, it would have been far easier for the

Shogunate, but in the six months which had passed, its power had steadily weakened and it was now standing on the defensive, under orders from the Mikado to achieve the impossible, while the strongest of the treaty powers insisted upon heavy penalties which, if not enforced, might lead to open war.

Lord Russell held that in the Richardson affair both the Shogun and the *daimyo* of Satsuma were guilty — the Shogun, because he had not punished the murderers, who were known; and the *daimyo*, because his retainers had committed the crime and had not been punished; from the Shogun, therefore, a formal apology was demanded and the payment of £100,000 as a penalty; from Satsuma, the trial and execution of the chief offenders, in the presence of British naval officers, and the payment of £25,000 to the relatives of the victim and to those who had escaped. A failure to grant this redress would result in measures of reprisal or blockade by the naval forces, while Satsuma would be blockaded or bombarded, and some Western steamships there seized until satisfaction was obtained.

The British Chargé, Colonel Neale, does not seem to have been in complete sympathy with these demands. He pointed out, in reply, that there was no proof that either outrage — the second attack on the legation or the murder of Richardson — had been perpetrated with the knowledge or acquiescence of the Shogun's Government, and that, except for these incidents and the first attack on the legation, "no hostile or defiant conduct has been exhibited towards us by the Japanese Government during the course of our relations with this country." He would, therefore, try to secure redress without coercion, and even in that case he would direct the hardest blows against Satsuma, whose punishment, he believed, would afford

56

satisfaction to the Yedo Government. In this incident, and in several others in the following years, the unfortunate effects of delayed communications was apparent. Lord Russell would never have issued these instructions had he understood the situation in Japan at the time they arrived, and in later incidents actions took place in Japan which violated instructions on the way from the home governments.

The French Minister and naval commander had received instructions to act in full accord with the British policy. But Mr. Pruyn believed that the demands were uncalled for, and would be presented at a most unfortunate time, when they would serve further to weaken the influence of the Shogun in the Kyoto councils. He furthermore used all his influence to prevent or to delay the opening of reprisals and he personally besought the British and French representatives to grant an extension to the ultimatum. To the Japanese, he recommended compliance with the demand, in order to prevent a far larger demand later, and, should they not consent, he recommended an attempt at arbitration by the President of the United States, the Emperor of Russia, or even by the British Government.

When the British demands were presented on April 6th, the Shogun was on his way to Kyoto. The arrival of the news there caused a notification to the *daimyo* to prepare for war, for the demands could not be granted. This additional foreign complication so aroused the anti-foreign forces, that, on his first conference with the Mikado, the Shogun accepted the imperial commands to expel the barbarians, by peaceful negotiations, if possible, but if not, then they were to be swept away. This decision, however, failed to fix a definite date for the expulsion, and thus it failed to satisfy the extremists. On the 5th of June, a second conference was held, and then the fateful date for the expulsion was decreed. On the 25th of June, the foreigners were to be expelled, and the *daimyo* were instructed to prepare to defend their coasts, and, should invaders arrive, sweep them away.

Ignorant of these ominous decisions at Kyoto, the European representatives at Yokohama prepared for the enforcement of the ultimatum. The first time limit expired on April 26th, and, as we have seen, Mr. Pruyn had urged an extension, acting on the clause in Harris's treaty which stated that the United States would act as a friendly mediator in matters of difference between Japan and the European powers. Colonel Neale refused his request, but later extended the ultimatum until May 11th, in the hope that the Shogun might return to Yedo by that time. Again Mr. Pruyn warned the British representative of the unwisdom of commencing coercive measures which might result in the destruction of all foreign interests in Japan. A few days later the ultimatum was further extended to May 23d, and about the same time the British and French representatives offered their naval forces to the Shogun for use against the hostile *daimyo*. This indicated a curious state of affairs. The combined fleets, prepared to punish the Shogun for offenses of which he could hardly have been held responsible, were also offered for his assistance against the hostile *daimyo* who had brought about his discomfiture. On the 23d, when the ultimatum was about to expire, the Shogun's officials declined the offer of the foreign fleets, and promised to pay the £110,000, at some future day, for to pay it then would precipitate civil war.

At this juncture the burning of the American legation in Yedo seemed to be another step in the expulsion of the resident foreigners. The Yedo officials always maintained that the fire was accidental, and Mr. Pruyn accepted this interpretation.

On June 14th, a formal agreement was signed to pay the indemnities demanded of the Shogun, in weekly installments by July 30th, and an offer was made to pay as well the £25,000 levied on Satsuma. The latter offer was refused by Colonel Neale. But before the first payment was due, the Japanese announced that it would not be made, because of orders from the Mikado, which, if disregarded, might cost the Shogun, in Kyoto, his life. This gave Colonel Neale no alternative but to place the matter in the admiral's hands for coercive measures. But on that day the French Minister learned of the Kyoto decision to expel the foreigners. Mr. Pruyn at once took this up with the Governors for Foreign Affairs, and was told that, although the Shogun had been compelled to accept these orders, the officials at Yedo knew that they could not be executed, and the Shogun, who had made the treaties, really wished to observe them. The next day Mr. Pruyn was informed that the indemnity would be paid on the 24th, and that Ogasawara, the Foreign Minister, desired to meet with all the foreign representatives at Yokohama, before he went up to Kyoto to convince the Mikado of the error of his decision. The French Minister, later, was informed that the purpose of the conference was to notify the representatives of the decree of expulsion, and to request them to leave, but at the same time to assure them that nothing would be done pending negotiations which might cover a long period.

Early on the morning of June 24th, the indemnity of £110,000 was paid to the British Chargé, and later in the day a formal communication was presented to each of the foreign ministers.

"I have received orders from his Majesty the Tycoon,

now residing at Kyoto, and who received orders from the Mikado, to cause the opened ports to be closed and the foreigners [subjects] of the treaty powers to be removed, as our people will have no intercourse with them; hence negotiations on this subject will afterwards take place with your excellency."

This notification apparently meant the end of the intercourse between the Western powers and Japan which had been inaugurated by Perry and enlarged by Harris. It was the logical outcome of President Fillmore's proposal that the ancient laws might be suspended for five or ten years, and then restored if foreign intercourse did not prove as beneficial as was hoped. It was but the conclusion of the years of grace allowed the Shogun in 1858, when his administration had adopted a policy of temporizing with the foreigners. The time had come, in the opinion of the Imperial Court and the *daimyo* who supported it, when foreign intercourse must come to an end. Yet the representatives of the treaty powers did not receive this notification with the alarm which it might have occasioned. They were confident that the Shogun's Government had accepted the orders under duress and that it had no intention of resorting to drastic measures. In any case they had no intention of discussing the proposal, and each warned the Japanese that the treaties would have to be observed and that the lives and property of foreigners would be adequately defended.

It was at this critical time that Mr. Pruyn submitted to his Government a proposal which showed a wise understanding of the real situation. It was none other than that the United States should propose a joint naval demonstration at Osaka, only twenty miles from Kyoto, to be supported, if necessary, by a land force, for the purpose of securing the Mikado's ratification of the treaties. For until this ratification was obtained, the position of the foreigners would always be precarious, and their presence would occasion intrigues, and perhaps civil war. In this dispatch Mr. Pruyn pointed out the fundamental weakness of the foreign treaties, and the way in which it could be removed. And as a matter of fact, his plan was subsequently followed with complete success.

In spite of the expulsion decree, the foreigners were safely guarded by the troops of the Shogun. At Yokohama, Nagasaki, and Hakodate, the only open ports, the Shogun's administration was in power, and adequate measures of protection were employed. Moreover, according to the system which had prevailed since the days of Ieyasu, the enforcement of the imperial decree was in the hands of the Shogun alone. No *daimyo* could act on his own responsibility. But in these days of change the old order was threatened on all sides, and one of the leaders of the Mikado's party determined to act on his own initiative. The *daimyo* of Choshiu, Lord Mori, put into effect the expulsion decree at the first opportunity. In the early morning of June 26th (the day after expulsion was to have been enforced), the little American steamer *Pembroke* was fired upon by two of Choshiu's armed vessels at the entrance of the Straits of Shimonoseki. On July 8th, a French gunboat was fired upon by the ships and batteries there, and on the 11th, a Netherlands steam sloop was attacked. Choshiu, to the best of his ability, was carrying out the imperial orders, and foreign vessels henceforth avoided the straits.

Mr. Pruyn first learned of the attack from one of the Yedo officials, and the news was confirmed by a letter from the ship's owners. He learned that the attacking vessels belonged to Choshiu, and he gave warning that ample satisfaction for the insult to the American flag would be demanded. The officials were unwilling to approve an American punitive expedition, and begged that nothing be done until the Shogun's Government had acted in the matter.

It happened that at this time an American ship of war, the *Wyoming*, was in the harbor of Yokohama, a rare occurrence during the Civil War days. Commander McDougal suggested to Mr. Pruyn that the *Wyoming* proceed to Shimonoseki to seize or destroy the hostile vessels. The American Minister approved, not only for the protection of American interests, but also in order that Choshiu's success might not encourage the hostile *daimyo*, while he believed the Shogun's Government would welcome any punishment of the leader of the anti-foreign and anti-Tycoon forces. The *Wyoming*, therefore, promptly proceeded to Shimonoseki, where, in spite of a brisk bombardment by the shore batteries, it succeeded in sinking an armed steamer and a brig. The Americans lost four seamen killed and seven wounded (one of whom died later). The first blow in defense of treaty rights had been struck by the United States. But not against the Government of Japan. The Government, recognized by the foreign powers, was that of the Shogun. It had disapproved of the acts of Choshiu, and it should have punished them. But the inability of the Shogun to coerce the hostile *daimyo* had led to the decision of Great Britain to deal directly with Satsuma, and it led the United States Minister and, a few days later, the French Minister, to send forces directly against Choshiu. And in each case it was felt that the punishment of the western *daimyo* would serve to strengthen the Shogun, who was responsible for the maintenance of the treaties.

The attack on the ships of the United States, France, and Holland caused the agreement of the four representatives, including that of Great Britain, that the straits should be opened and that a combined fleet should take action, unless the Shogun could himself punish Choshiu. This marked the beginning of four-power coöperation, instead of that of Britain and France.

In August, the British fleet proceeded to Kagoshima, in Satsuma, to present the demands in the Richardson case. When Satsuma refused to negotiate directly with the foreigners, the admiral seized three of the clan's steamers, as he had been instructed. This caused the shore batteries to open fire upon the squadron, which was immediately returned. Fires started by the shells, and fanned by a heavy gale, raged through the town, and when the fleet departed it was believed that the entire settlement had been destroyed. But it had not obtained the indemnity nor witnessed the punishment of the assassins. Demands were again made upon the Shogun to order Satsuma to make amends, lest the fleet return and continue its hostilities. But in December, two envoys of Satsuma arrived in Yokohama, ready to pay the indemnity and to promise to continue the search for the assassins. It is of interest to note that the Satsuma delegates requested the good offices of Colonel Neale in the purchase of a ship of war in England. After this experience with the foreigners the Satsuma clan was no longer outwardly anti-foreign, and it sought foreign armaments in preparation for the inevitable clash with the Shogun.

During the summer, the hostile faction at Kyoto continued to urge immediate action against the foreigners. But with the punishment of Satsuma in August, and the expulsion of Choshiu from Kyoto, on the ground that he had conspired to seize the Mikado's person and make himself dictator of the empire, the anti-foreign forces were weakened. This was reflected in the new proposal made to the foreign ministers in October, to the effect that Yokohama be closed to trade, in order to quiet the rising tide of foreign opposition. Mr. Pruyn and the Dutch Minister, to whom the proposal was first made, replied that their Governments would never consent to it, and Pruyn went further and advised the officials to withdraw the order of expulsion transmitted in June. This advice was promptly followed, and, on November 11th, the Shogun's Government notified all the foreign representatives that its former opinion had changed and that it was desirable that the letter of June 24th be returned. But it did not give up the idea of removing the chief cause of friction at Yokohama. It turned again to the American Minister for advice as to how a mission would be received if it sought the closing of that port. Although Mr. Pruyn could hold out no hope of success, he assured the officials that the envoys would be listened to patiently and the proposal carefully considered. Such a mission set forth in February, with the prime purpose of expressing regret for the murder of two French officers in October, but actually to sound the European powers on the closing of Yokohama.

With the settlement of the Richardson affair and the withdrawal of the notice of the expulsion, the strained relations of the summer of 1863 were greatly relieved. The only outstanding question was that of the conduct of Choshiu at Shimonoseki, but as foreign shipping avoided the straits no harm could result, and no great good would be accomplished in forcing their opening. The British Government did not believe in strong measures, and the fleet was to be used only for defensive purposes. In fact, in order to prevent trouble, the British Minister was authorized to issue an order in council prohibiting British vessels from entering the straits or other waters where their presence might lead to disturbances or acts of violence.

In March, 1864, Sir Rutherford Alcock returned to his post after an absence of two years at home. He was the senior member of the diplomatic corps, and he was supported by a strong fleet. His views naturally had great weight with his colleagues and with the Japanese officials. He promptly came to the conclusion that the end of conciliation and forbearance by the treaty powers had been reached, and that only after measures of a hostile and decisive character had been resorted to would the Government realize that the treaty powers insisted upon the observance of all the rights conferred by the treaties. He thus set about securing the approval of his views by the other foreign ministers, with complete success. In his opinion the blow should fall upon Choshiu, and his punishment would impress all the hostile *daimyo*. The British Government did not approve of his proposals, and, instead, instructed him to act according to the views expressed by Mr. Pruyn somewhat earlier; that is, to give encouragement to the Shogun's ministers and the friendly *daimyo*, to arrange with the Japanese for the protection of Yokohama, to keep a strong squadron in Japanese waters for defensive purposes, and to establish an understanding among the four treaty powers for the protection of their common interests. And Alcock was positively enjoined not to undertake any military operations whatever in the interior of Japan, and to use the naval forces solely for defense of British lives and property. Mr. Seward also endorsed these moderate views of Lord Russell. But before these instructions could reach Japan, the Shimonoseki expedition had been launched.

The purpose of this expedition was to punish Choshiu for closing the straits, and thus warn all the hostile *daimyo* of the results of a conflict with the foreigners. The joint expedition was agreed upon by the four foreign ministers on May 25, 1864. When Lord Russell learned of it, he at once recalled Alcock, and instructed him not to attack Choshiu. After unsatisfactory negotiations with the Shogunate, the decision was reached, on July 5th, to open the straits if the Government failed to do so within twenty days. This action was postponed in order to permit two young *samurai* of Choshiu, Shunske Ito and Bunda Inouye (later Prince Ito and Marquis Inouye), to proceed to Choshiu, in a British ship of war, with letters of advice and warning to their *daimyo*. On the failure of this mission, the Shogun was again given twenty days to settle the Choshiu difficulty. And the point was made clear that should force be used at Shimonoseki, its purpose was primarily to strengthen the hands of the Shogun against the hostile party.

On the 28th and 29th of August, the joint expedition set sail from Yokohama. As the only American ship of war in Japanese waters was a sailing ship, which would have been useless in the proposed operations, a little American merchant steamer was chartered, on which one gun was mounted. Its purpose was to carry the American flag into action and manifest the unity among the powers. The British supplied nine ships, the Dutch four, the French three, and the United States one. On September 5th, the forcing of the straits was commenced, and on the three following days the batteries were silenced and destroyed. On the 14th, an agreement was reached with the representative of the lord, whereby the straits would be open in the future, no new forts would be built or the old ones repaired, and a ransom would be paid for the town of Shimonoseki and the whole expenses of the expedition defrayed.

THE TREATIES IN JEOPARDY

This was the second and last occasion on which an American ship took part in hostile actions in Japan. The conduct of Mr. Pruyn was approved by his Government, and, on news of the success of the expedition, Lord Russell approved what Alcock had done, although his instructions to proceed home remained effective.

The punishment of Choshiu so strengthened the Shogun that his officials informed the foreign ministers that they would no longer have to temporize and equivocate in dealing with foreign affairs, that they would abandon even the pretense of closing Yokohama, and that they would send an envoy to Kyoto to secure, if possible, the Mikado's acceptance and ratification of the treaties.

Rather than have the foreign powers deal directly with a rebellious *daimyo*, the Shogunate agreed to assume itself the payment of the expenses and indemnities of the Shimonoseki expedition. The terms were fixed in the convention of October 22d, the preamble of which acknowledged the necessity of the allied operations and the liability of the Tycoon, on whom devolved the duty of chastising the rebellious lord. The amount payable was fixed at $3,000,000, to cover all claims for indemnities, ransom, or expenses, but, if the Shogun preferred to offer the opening of Shimonoseki or some other eligible port in the Inland Sea instead of the indemnity, the powers would have the option of accepting the port or insisting upon the money payment. Nothing was said in the convention about the Mikado's ratification of the treaties, nor was the method of dividing the indemnity among the powers defined.

In April following, the Shogunate announced that it would pay the full indemnity rather than open a port on the Inland Sea, but asked for a delay in meeting the second payment. The American and British Ministers had preferred the opening of a port to the payment of an indemnity, but, if the Shogun preferred the latter, there was no ground for objection. In reporting the request for a delay in making the payments, Mr. Winchester, the British Chargé, suggested that a counter-proposition be made, to the effect that half or two thirds of the indemnity would be waived in return for the prompt opening of Hiogo, the written ratification of the treaties by the Mikado, and the reduction of the tariff to a uniform rate of five per cent.

The Japanese request opened the subject again, and an exchange of views took place between the four governments concerned. France, however, favored the payment of the indemnity in full, rather than any reduction on the terms suggested by Mr. Winchester. But just at this time the new British Minister, Sir Harry Parkes, arrived in Japan. A man of masterful personality, with twenty-four years of eventful experience in China, he was easily able to dominate his colleagues, especially in the absence of Mr. Pruyn, who had returned home on leave. Acting under instructions to ascertain the real state of affairs, in conjunction with his three colleagues and in communication with the Shogun's Council, he summoned the foreign ministers to a conference. He was easily able to persuade them, in spite of the French instructions, to support the British proposal for the remission of part of the indemnity in return for the three concessions. The negotiations, he proposed, should be carried on at Osaka, for the Shogun and most of the Great Council were then at Kyoto. This resulted in the joint expedition to Osaka, in which five British, three French ships, and one Dutch ship took part. As no American ship was available, the American chargé was invited to sail on a British vessel.

On the 4th of November, the fleet arrived off Hiogo.

Negotiations were at once opened. The foreign terms were stated, and the Shogun's envoy was convinced that they must be met. But a delay was requested in order to convince the Mikado of the wisdom of ratifying the treaties. A ten-day interval was granted, but, when news arrived that the conservative party seemed to be in control at Kyoto, a scarcely veiled ultimatum was sent in to the effect that if a reply was not submitted within the ten days its absence would denote a formal refusal, "and we shall, in that case, be free to act as we may judge convenient."

This statement, supported by the strong fleet, carried the day, and, on November 24th, some of the Shogun's officials visited the flagship to report that the Mikado had ratified the treaties, and that the Shogun had agreed to the reduction of the tariff, but rather than advance the opening of Hiogo and Osaka, he would pay the indemnity in full at the stated times.

In this way the Mikado's ratification of the treaties of 1858 was finally secured. It was an act of weighty import. Up to this time, the opponents of the foreigners had a dangerous weapon at hand, for they denounced the treaties as lacking in validity. And the foreigners, in turn, were forced to rely on the Shogun alone, who had made and maintained the treaties. But with the Mikado's approval of the treaties, foreign affairs became freed from the internal complications. The anti-Tokugawa *daimyo* no longer needed to be hostile to foreigners, from whom they hoped to secure the armaments needed in any clash with the Shogunate. And the foreigners could, in the near future, free themselves from the waning fortunes of the Shogun and enter into direct relations with the victorious imperial party. If the civil war had come before this ratification was secured, there is reason to believe that the treaty powers, or some of them, in self-defense would have come to the support of the Shogun against the imperial supporters, as the British and French proposed in 1863, and as the French Minister advocated in 1868.

In these years when the treaties were threatened by the Kyoto partisans, American interests in Japan were bound to stand or fall with those of the other treaty powers. The American Minister was instructed to consult with his colleagues and work in harmony with them, but the American naval force was only to be used in self-defense. The action of the American ships at Shimonoseki, if of doubtful validity according to international precedents, was justified by the unsettled conditions in Japan. But with the Shogun's representatives Mr. Pruyn seems always to have been on friendly terms. He appreciated the heavy difficulties under which they labored, and he constantly counseled moderation on the part of his colleagues. When, for example, he learned that the American steamer *Monitor* was fired upon, in 1864, from Choshiu batteries, he made no claim for indemnity because the ship had no right to enter a closed port. But for the attack on the *Pembroke* $11,200 was paid by the Shogun before the joint expedition sailed to Shimonoseki. It is of interest to note that Mr. Pruyn introduced the principle of arbitration to the Japanese when he secured an agreement that, if certain claims for damages were not paid, the question would be submitted to the decision of the Emperor of Russia. Fortunately there was no necessity for the reference, but the principle then accepted was acted upon in the *Maria Luz* case in 1873.

CHAPTER V

THE RESTORATION OF THE EMPEROR

THE ratification of the treaties by the Mikado, in November, 1865, not only placed the foreigners in Japan in a secure position, but also strengthened, for the time being, the power of the Shogun. His conduct of foreign affairs had been approved by the Emperor, and the great occasion for criticism on the part of hostile *daimyo* had been removed. They did not cease their opposition to the Shogunate, however; they merely had to alter the basis for its continuance. The Mikado's sanction was notified to all the *daimyo* and *hatamoto*, and Sir Harry Parkes took occasion to transmit it directly to the Choshiu authorities as he passed through the Straits of Shimonoseki on his way to Shanghai. They assured him that the Mikado's ratification was of great importance. The Yedo administration was also more indebted than ever to the foreign powers for the support which they had given it in these critical days. In 1863, the British fleet had severely punished Satsuma; in 1864, the allied squadron had humbled Choshiu; and the following year the naval demonstration at Osaka had won the Mikado's approval of all the treaties.

The anti-foreign party was at this time divided in councils. The Choshiu clansmen had been ordered out of Kyoto in the fall of 1863 because of the allegation that they had tried to seize the Mikado and thus control the imperial councils. The next summer a party of Choshiu *samurai* tried to invade the capital, drive out the Shogun's supporters, and seize the palace, but the attempt was defeated by troops loyal to the Shogun with the strong support of Satsuma forces. Thus Choshiu and Satsuma, formerly the leading anti-Shogunate *daimyo*, were estranged, and Choshiu was in disgrace and subject to punishment by the Shogun for the indignity offered the Emperor. It was under these circumstances that the allied fleets destroyed the batteries at Shimonoseki, thus making easy the projected punitive expedition there of the Shogun's forces. So when, a few months later, the invading forces arrived near the borders of the fief, an offer of complete submission was received, and the leaders of the Kyoto assault were put to death by their own clansmen. But this submission was not approved by all the Choshiu *samurai*. The hostile forces were well organized and they soon were in control of the fief. The leaders of the party of submission were put to death, and the clan again stood forth in opposition to the Shogun. But at this critical time, when one clan defied the feudal forces of the military lord of Japan, a good understanding was arrived at with the great clan of Satsuma, which was to strengthen the position of Choshiu and restore the unity of action of the great western lords. The Shogun, learning of the *coup d'état* in Choshiu, determined to take the field himself to punish the unruly clansmen, but among his advisors there was much doubt as to the wisdom of this course. During the summer and fall of 1865, the troops were assembling around Kyoto, and the Shogun and his Cabinet were there, which gave the excuse for the naval demonstration at Osaka, presumably for the purpose of discussing the state of affairs with the Shogun and his councilors.

Early in 1866, the feudal levies of the Shogun took the field. The Shogun was determined to punish and crush the house of Mori, nominally for its attack upon Kyoto, but actually because of its long hostility to the Tokugawa Shogunate. And the Choshiu clan determined to fight to the bitter end because of its hatred of the Shogun. But foreign affairs entered little into this dispute. Both sides were eager to secure foreign munitions, and foreign merchant ships, in violation of the treaties, put in at Choshiu ports and did a thriving trade in ships, guns, and ammunition. An opinion expressed by Mr. Portman, the American Chargé, at this time is of interest: "It is hard to say on which side is the greater reluctance of submitting this question to the arbitrament of the sword. Strong efforts were made to make Japan a great naval and military power and to infuse a martial spirit into the people; but as yet these efforts do not appear to have been very successful; its predilections are decidedly in favor of negotiating, and it is quite likely, therefore, that negotiations, with force in the background, will be carried on for some time, and until the Prince of Choshiu shall have succeeded in obtaining better terms than the Tycoon is supposed to have offered thus far." The penalty later assessed by the Shogun, with the approval of the Imperial Court, called for the forfeiture of a large amount of land, the retirement and confinement of the *daimyo* and his son, and the extinction of the families of the three leading anti-Shogunate advisers. Such demands could not be granted, and the issue was to be joined on the battle-field.

These operations would take place in western Japan, far away from Yedo, where the relations between the Shogun's representatives and the foreign ministers were increasingly friendly. In April, the Government issued a new proclamation to the effect that all subjects might trade freely at the open ports, that steam and sailing vessels might be purchased, but ships of war and munitions could be bought only after obtaining permission from the Shogun's customs officials. In May, the interesting announcement was made that the old seclusion laws would be modified, and that Japanese provided with a proper passport might visit the treaty powers. Up to this time only official missions had been permitted to leave Japan, but a few young men, at the risk of their lives, had managed to escape from the country and visit the Western lands.

During these days negotiations were in progress at Yedo for the revision of the tariff, as promised by the Shogun at Osaka in November, 1865. The conventional, or treaty-made, tariff had developed in the following manner. The treaty powers, following their experience in China, had desired to fix the rate of import and export duties in the treaties in order that the Japanese Government might not, by domestic legislation, place such burdens upon commerce that foreign trade would be curtailed or destroyed. Thus the Dutch treaty of October 16, 1857, had fixed a temporary duty of thirty-five per cent on imports. The American treaty of 1858 divided imports into four classes, certain articles were to be free of duty, a few were to pay five per cent, intoxicating liquors paid thirty-five per cent, and all other articles, including practically all manufactured goods, would pay twenty per cent. These rates might be revised after July 1, 1864, if the Japanese Government desired it. In the British treaty, negotiated a few months later, cotton and woolen manufactured goods were removed from the twenty to the five per cent class, but the Japanese refused to reduce the rate on wines when the French envoy later desired it. In 1862, when the Japanese envoys secured the consent of the British Government to the postponement of the opening of Hiogo, Niigata, Yedo, and Osaka until January 1, 1868, they promised to represent to the Shogun the wisdom and expediency of placing glassware in the five per cent class, of establishing bonded warehouses, and of opening the island of Tsushima to trade. (The purpose of the latter proposal was to forestall the attempted Russian occupation of that strategic island.) The United States, which had been the first to accept in principle the proposal to postpone the opening of the new ports and cities, had failed to give its formal consent pending an agreement as to the concessions to be granted in return. In January, 1863, the terms had been practically agreed upon, but no formal arrangement had been completed. Finally, when the Shogunate was about to send a mission abroad in 1864 to ask for the closing of Yokohama, it realized the necessity of securing the adhesion of the United States to the agreement to postpone the opening of the other ports. So, on January 28, 1864, a convention was signed in which the duty on a number of manufactured goods, as well as wines and spirits, was reduced to five per cent. The approval of the United States to the extension of the time for opening the cities and ports was then proclaimed. It should be said that the enumerated articles did not especially favor American exports. Glass and glassware were included, as Lord Russell had desired in 1862, and Mr. Pruyn reported that he had included wines and spirits in order not to appear unfriendly to France. A few days later, the Japanese themselves reduced to six per cent the rate on a number of other articles, but, as it was a statutory measure, these rates might be restored at any time. The French convention, signed on June 18, 1864, by the mission which had sought to secure consent of the treaty powers to the closing of the port of Yokohama, and also to express regret to France for the murder of two French officers, included the reduction of the rates as granted

JAPAN AND THE UNITED STATES

to the United States and as announced in January; this
being a conventional agreement the latter rates could
not be restored without the consent of both the parties.

In 1864, therefore, the tariff as worked out by Townsend Harris had been very considerably modified. Most
of the imports had been removed from the twenty to the
five per cent class. And these changes were based upon
separate conventions with Great Britain, the United
States, and France, although they applied to all the
treaty powers. The commercial states naturally desired
to have all the duties as low as possible, and the uniform
rate of five per cent was suggested by the British Chargé
early in 1865. It was this proposal which eventually was
among the matters conceded by the Shogun at Osaka in
November of that year.

The convention of June 25, 1866, for the revision of the
tariff was signed by delegates of the Shogun and by the
representatives of the United States, France, Great
Britain, and the Netherlands. In drafting its terms the
influence of Sir Harry Parkes was supreme, because of his
long experience in Far Eastern diplomacy and his masterful personality. The new rates were to take the place of
the original tariffs of 1858 and the subsequent special conventions and arrangements. The new schedule fixed the
import duties at approximately five per cent. Specific
duties, now for the first time used, were quoted on eighty-
nine articles, and five per cent ad valorem fixed on all
other articles, except a few on the free list, and opium,
which was prohibited. And the export duty was fixed, in
the same way, at five per cent by specific and ad valorem
duties. In the case of the specific export duty on tea and
silk, this might be revised if claimed by either party after
two years, on the basis of five per cent of the average
value of these articles during the preceding three years.

76

THE RESTORATION OF THE EMPEROR

And the ad valorem duty on timber might be changed to a specific one if desired after six months. But, as the new rates were merely a substitute for the rates of 1858, they might be revised after July 1, 1872, according to the terms for the revision of the original treaties.

These details regarding the history of the Japanese conventional tariff have been narrated because the rates as established in 1866 remained in force long after the promised date of revision. These were the low rates which at the same time deprived the Japanese Government of much-needed customs revenue and also hampered the development of Japanese manufactures in competition with the wares of the West. During the long struggle for treaty revision, the Japanese often condemned the ignorance and the weakness of the Shogunate for assuming such harmful obligations. It is true that the reduction was granted under pressure, but, in view of the generally understood provision that new rates might be established in 1872, the disability was considered to be only a temporary one. No Japanese foresaw in 1866, it may be safely said, that these rates would continue in force for twenty-eight years.

In addition to rewriting the tariff, the convention of 1866 was broadened to include several matters which had been the subject of discussion and even of agreement in the past. Thus warehouses were to be established at the open ports, as advocated by Lord Russell in 1862; the right of Japanese to trade at the open ports and to buy ships, and the right to go abroad became treaty rights; a free mint was to be established to alleviate the currency difficulties; and no tax or transit duties were to be levied on goods sent to the open ports, except the usual road tolls. This convention, therefore, was of great significance in the development of foreign commerce; its satisfactory conclusion indicated the good relations existing between the Shogunate and the maritime powers; and in taking part in these joint negotiations the acting representative of the United States was following the long-standing instructions to coöperate with his colleagues peacefully in every matter in which foreign rights were involved.

When Mr. Pruyn, the second American Minister, left Yedo in 1865 on a well-earned leave of absence, he fully expected to return to his post, but a combination of personal reasons caused him to decide to retire from the diplomatic service. During his three years in Japan he had seen the rise and wane of the anti-foreign agitation. Yet he had never failed to distinguish between the Shogun's administration, which tried faithfully to keep the treaties, and the hostile faction at Kyoto which sought to attack the Shogun through his foreign policy. He had been sympathetic in his endeavor to understand the troubled state of Japanese politics, and he had advocated moderate measures no matter how serious the provocation might seem to be. His dispatches to his own Government were ably prepared and served to keep the Department of State well informed of the changing conditions in Japan. His successor was again chosen from the State of New York. General R. B. Van Valkenburgh had been a member of Congress for a number of years and had served with distinction in the Civil War. He was by training and disposition well suited to carry on the American policy toward Japan, which had been formulated so well by Townsend Harris. On August 12, 1866, he arrived at his post.

One of General Van Valkenburgh's first official acts was to warn American citizens not to visit the scene of the Choshiu military operations or to enlist in the armies of the rebels. The punitive expedition of the Shogun, planned in 1865, had been delayed a full year. It was not until August that the Shogun's trained troops and the feudal levies of the *daimyo* began to attack Choshiu. But by that time the clansmen had secured an ample supply of foreign arms and ammunition, and had drilled many of their troops according to Western methods. In the engagements which followed, the Choshiu troops generally had the advantage. A contemporary historian describes the opposing forces as follows: "In this campaign the Eastern troops wore armor and surcoats, and their weapons were swords and spears, while the Choshiu men, clad in light, short-sleeved garments, and dispensing with their swords, were chiefly armed with muskets. Their drill, too, was excellent. In fact the Choshiu clan had gained a great deal of experience in the year 1863, which they had turned to account in remodeling their military system. This enabled them on each occasion to beat the Eastern army, which at no period was able to gain a footing on the Choshiu territory." There must be a few veterans still living, in this day of airships, submarines, and tanks, who fought as young men in suits of armor, with sword and spear!

On September 20th, the Shogun, Iemochi, died at Osaka. A cessation of hostilities during the fifty days of mourning was proclaimed, and at its expiration peace was brought about. The failure of the Shogun's forces against Choshiu greatly weakened the Shogunate; its treasury was almost empty and its prestige destroyed when a single clan could successfully oppose its military power.

The successor of Iemochi, as head of the Tokugawa family, was Yoshinobu, usually called Keiki by the Japanese and known to foreigners as Lord Hitotsubashi. He had been a claimant to the Shogunate in 1858, and had been set aside in favor of Iemochi. His father, Nariaki, the old Lord of Mito, had been the leader of the early anti-foreign *daimyo*, and Keiki was imbued with these ideas. So when, in 1863, at the time that the Imperial Court was most hostile to foreigners, the Shogun was compelled to appoint Keiki as guardian, it was believed that the latter would inaugurate a strong policy in place of the temporizing one of the past. But the experience gained during this regency convinced him of the folly of trying to carry out the demands of the Court, and he did not hesitate to report that the expulsion decreed in 1863 could not be carried out. As the leading Tokugawa official during the latter part of Iemochi's Shogunate, and later as Shogun himself, he tried to keep faith with the treaty powers in spite of the bitter criticism which such a course involved. On January 10, 1867, Keiki was invested with the office of Shogun at Kyoto.

For about five years no foreign representative had been received in audience by the Shogun, but Keiki promptly invited all the envoys to visit Osaka for that purpose. Before this could be carried out, the death of the Mikado, Komei, on February 3d, was announced. His successor was the young Prince Mutsuhito, whose long and wise reign saw the rise of New Japan.

During the fifty days of mourning no official functions could take place, and at its close no indication was received that the postponed audience would be granted. Under these circumstances the four foreign representatives, after consultation, decided to proceed to Osaka to discuss the necessary regulations for the opening of the ports and cities on January 1, 1868. The Yedo officials had no objection to this course. They assured the ministers that the ports would be opened at the specified time and that an audience with the Shogun would be promptly granted. In April, the four envoys sailed to Osaka. There, on May 2d, the ministers of Great Britain, France, and Holland were officially received by the Shogun, and General Van Valkenburgh was granted a private audience on the 3d and an official reception on the 4th. During these ceremonies the most cordial relations prevailed. At the audience, General Van Valkenburgh was given a seat at the Shogun's right hand, and at the dinner, in foreign style, which followed, the Shogun was present. The American Minister was strongly impressed with these indications of the wonderful progress which had been made in foreign intercourse with Japan. The Shogun he described as a man "thirty-one years of age and of extremely prepossessing appearance. There is much about him which stamps him as a gentleman; such simple dignity and such an air of perfect breeding, only equaled by his intelligence, which is as superior as it is unassuming. Our conversation ran principally on our army and navy matters, and the manner in which it was conducted on his part showed that he was well conversant with the subject."

The arrangements necessary for the opening of Hiogo (Kobe) and Osaka were promptly agreed upon. The Japanese officials acted with the greatest liberality, and sites for the foreign settlements, unsurpassed for convenience, were granted. The American Minister returned to Yedo inspired with perfect confidence for the future.

In June and July, General Van Valkenburgh visited the west coast of Japan to investigate the possibilities of commerce there. On arriving at Nagasaki, he learned of the arrest of some sixty-five Japanese Christians, descendants of the converts of the seventeenth century who had kept the faith in spite of the severe measures of repression of the Shogunate and *daimyo*. His effort to induce the local officials to release the unfortunate prisoners was unsuccessful, and on his return to Yedo he pointed out to the Japanese Ministers for Foreign Affairs the serious results which news of this religious intolerance would have upon the attitude of the Western powers toward the Shogun, at a time when it stood in such need of sympathetic support. Mr. Seward, the Secretary of State, approved General Van Valkenburgh's conduct, and instructed him to confer with his colleagues and, with their concurrence, appeal to the Government to repeal and abrogate the laws against Christianity. The prisoners at Nagasaki were promptly released, after the French Minister had promised that French missionaries would refrain from propaganda in the interior, but the laws were not rescinded.

On the 28th of October, the American Minister received a copy of a proclamation issued at Kyoto on the 18th to the effect that Keiki had on that day assumed the title of Kubosama, or Shogun. This was taken to be a sign of the consolidation of his power, for he was a representative of the junior branch of the Tokugawa House, and there had been great reluctance on the part of some of the great *daimyo* to the continuation of the Shogunate. It was also considered a favorable omen for the continued improvement of foreign political and commercial relations with Japan, for abundant evidence existed of an earnest intention to carry out the treaties in good faith. Under these circumstances the foreign representatives were amazed to be informed, on November 16th, that "the Tycoon has hereafter no authority to confer or make arrangements with reference to any of the internal affairs of Japan." The notice was first presented to the American Minister, and later his colleagues were informed. On the next morning, two of the Yedo officials visited General Van Valkenburgh and explained that the

THE RESTORATION OF THE EMPEROR

Tycoon had surrendered all his power and authority into the hands of the Mikado, but that he was still charged with the conduct of foreign affairs, and would continue to be so until some further arrangement was made by the Mikado, on the advice of the Grand Council of *daimyo*. About the same time the foreign ministers secured copies of some of the important state papers issued at Kyoto in this connection — the communication of the Shogun to his feudatories advocating the restoration of authority to the Imperial Court, for "our intercourse with foreign powers becomes daily more extensive, and our foreign policy cannot be pursued unless directed by the whole power of the country," and requesting their opinion on the advisability of this course; the acceptance, on November 5th, of the Shogun's resignation by the Mikado; and the request of the Shogun that a council of *daimyo* and clansmen be summoned. In these and other documents, the importance of foreign relations was stressed. What the foreigners did not know was that in October the *daimyo* of Tosa had sent up a memorial to the Shogun advocating his resignation, so that the whole power might lie in the Emperor's hands, and "Japan may take its stand as the equal of all other countries." It was this advice and the pressure of Satsuma which caused the Shogun to take this unprecedented step. As a boy he had been taught to respect a precept of his clan that loyalty knows no blood relationship. If ever the interests of the Imperial House and the Tokugawa family should clash, then he must sacrifice his family to his loyalty to the sovereign.

With the internal situations produced by this fundamental change in the government of Japan, we are not concerned. Our interest lies in its effect upon foreign relations. The envoys at Yedo dealt, as usual, with the

Shogun's officials. An arrangement was satisfactorily arrived at for postponing the opening of Yedo, for residence, until April 1, 1868, and for the opening, at the same date, of the ports of Niigata and Ebisuminato on the west coast. Hiogo and Osaka were to be opened on January 1st, and, although the preliminary arrangements had been completed, yet, on account of the new conditions and in view of the long-standing hostility of the Imperial Court to the opening of these places, the foreign ministers determined to be present in case any difficulties should arise. On December 23d, General Van Valkenburgh arrived at Hiogo, where eventually six American ships and eight British were assembled. In addition to the representatives of the four powers which had coöperated in Japan in the past, the ministers of Italy and Prussia were also present. Thus the foreign envoys happened to be near Kyoto during the stirring days when the Shogun was forced to withdraw from the capital and the imperial power was completely restored. Many complications were avoided by this fortunate circumstance. It was easy to deal directly with the Mikado's representatives, whereas if the envoys had been at Yedo the recognition of the Mikado's power might have been delayed, with serious results.

Hiogo and Osaka were opened, as agreed upon, on January 1st. But on January 3d came the *coup d'état* at Kyoto which placed the city in control of the troops of Satsuma, Tosa, Geishu, and other anti-Shogunate *daimyo*. A decree was issued in the Mikado's name accepting the resignation of the Shogun and abolishing the office. Keiki retired from Kyoto to Osaka, where, on January 8th, he received the ministers of Great Britain and France, and on the 10th the six foreign envoys in a body. To Sir Harry Parkes and M. Roches the Shogun explained the course of events, stating that he had resigned the governing power on the understanding that an assembly of *daimyo* should be called to decide in what manner and by whom the government should be carried on in the future. On this understanding the Mikado accepted the resignation, but now the hostile lords had seized the gates of the palace, secured control of the Emperor, and demanded the Shogun's resignation and the surrender of the bulk of his estates. And he added, further, "as to who is the sovereign of Japan, it is a question on which no one in Japan can entertain a doubt. The Mikado is the sovereign. My object from the first has been to take the will of the nation as to the future government. If the nation should decide that I ought to resign my powers, I am prepared to resign them for the good of my country." This statement outlined perfectly the course which Keiki later adopted. In an address presented by the diplomatic body at the audience on the 10th, an expression of high esteem and gratitude to the Shogun was offered for his success in securing the faithful execution of the treaties, but the foreign representatives were determined to stand aloof from the present dissensions. That the sympathy of the foreign ministers at this time was with the Shogun is evident. He and his house had loyally maintained the treaties in the face of the opposition of Kyoto. And among the leaders of the party in power there were *daimyo* who had the reputation, at least, of being hostile to foreigners. But from the first there was no intention of becoming involved in the strife which seemed imminent. By this time the ministers understood perfectly that the Mikado was the supreme ruler of Japan, and their personal sympathy for the Shogun did not blind them to their duty.

For about three weeks the Shogun remained at Osaka,

where daily conferences were held between the Japanese and foreign officials regarding land regulations at Osaka and Hiogo. On January 23d, General Van Valkenburgh enjoyed a private and social interview with the Shogun. His authority to deal with foreign affairs was still unquestioned. But on January 26th, in response to an invitation from the Mikado, the Shogun set out for Kyoto. On the way his troops were attacked by forces of Satsuma and other hostile clans, and for four days a rear-guard action was fought, until finally the Shogun's troops were forced back into Osaka. Early on the morning of the 31st, the Shogun and some of his high officials took refuge on the U.S. S.S. *Iroquois* for a few hours, until they could be taken off by one of his frigates and conveyed to Yedo. The power of the Shogun in western Japan had been broken. He was a fugitive, and civil war seemed inevitable.

With the retirement of the Shogun, the officials at Hiogo and Osaka announced that they could no longer protect foreign interests. On February 3d, the governor and all the officials left Hiogo, and no government existed. But the next day the advance guard of the imperial troops entered the city. Two Frenchmen, who tried to cross in front of the procession, were wounded, and the commander ordered his troops to fire upon all foreigners. Four of the foreign ministers were under fire, and the guards of American, British, and French sailors and marines replied. This was an unfortunate way in which to inaugurate relations with the Imperial Government. The allied commanders seized four Japanese steamers in the harbor, to prevent further mischief, and preparations were made to defend the foreign settlement. On the 8th a representative of the Emperor arrived at Hiogo. The six foreign ministers met him in a body. He presented each with a letter to his sovereign announcing the resignation of the Shogun and the return of the supreme authority in both internal and external affairs to the Emperor. He then assured the envoys that the Mikado would disapprove of the acts of the Bizen troops, and that demands for reparation would be considered. He furthermore offered to assume the entire protection of the foreigners at Hiogo, if the foreign troops were withdrawn, and guaranteed that there would be no further outrages. The impression created by Higashikuze was so favorable that the ministers agreed to withdraw their troops and surrender the ships which had been seized. At a second interview, on the 10th, the envoy assured the foreign representatives that foreigners would be protected in all the territories occupied by the Mikado, and that the treaties would be faithfully executed by his Government. Further conferences took place, each of a highly satisfactory nature. The reparation demanded for the attack by the Bizen troops was granted. Customs officials were appointed for Hiogo, one of them being Shunske Ito and another Tozo Terashima. On the 14th, a formal letter was presented to the effect that the Emperor had assumed the treaty-making power and that all engagements hitherto existing would be observed. Prince Yoshiakira was appointed chief administrator of foreign affairs, and three assistants were designated.

By these prompt actions the Imperial Government had set at rest any doubts in the minds of the envoys that it would respect the treaty engagements. Although the French Minister expressed more active sympathy with the ex-Shogun than any of his colleagues, yet the diplomatic body agreed informally to preserve neutrality, to deal only with the Mikado or such *de facto* government as held the open ports, and to act conjointly for the general and common interests.

JAPAN AND THE UNITED STATES

This good understanding was not impaired even though, on March 8th, eleven French sailors were killed by Tosa troops at Sakai, near Osaka. For this crime there was no provocation, and an indemnity and the execution of the guilty men were promptly promised.

On the night of this unfortunate tragedy, and while discussing it with General Van Valkenburgh, the Japanese commissioners extended to him a verbal invitation to visit the Mikado at Kyoto. Nothing could have indicated more clearly the attitude of the new Government than this amazing invitation. That the Mikado, whose face had been seen by only à few of the highest officials in the land, should receive in audience the representatives of the once-hated barbarians, seemed unbelievable. Yet this course had been advocated by six of the great *daimyo* who now controlled the Imperial Government. The memorial of the ex-*daimyo* of Echizen, and Tosa, and the Lords of Choshiu, Satsuma, Aki, and Higo, presented on February 29th, had been favorably received. General Van Valkenburgh did not immediately act upon this invitation, for he was about to proceed to Yedo. The French and Dutch representatives were received at Kyoto on March 23d, but, as Sir Harry Parkes was on his way to the palace, his party was attacked by two assailants armed with their deadly two-handed swords. Ten Englishmen and one Japanese were wounded before the two fanatics were cut down, one falling by the hand of Shojiro Goto. The personal regret of the Mikado was promptly expressed, and Sir Harry expressed his entire satisfaction with the good faith of the Government. Three days later he was received with due ceremony. Soon after an imperial edict was issued denouncing acts of violence against foreigners, and threatening punishment in proportion to the gravity of the offense, while in the case of *samurai* their names

88

would be erased from the rolls — a punishment more grievous than death itself.

The opponents of the ex-Shogun, who were now in control of the imperial councils, determined to send a punitive expedition against him, in the Emperor's name. Although his first impulse was to defend his rights against the hostile *daimyo*, Keiki soon decided not to oppose the imperial will and instructed his retainers not to resist the advancing troops. But some of the *daimyo* of eastern Japan, indignant at the treatment which their master had received, determined to defend his rights, even though he refused to lead them. This resulted in the fighting of 1868 and 1869 in eastern Japan and the Hokkaido. The foreign representatives had, on February 18th, issued proclamations of neutrality, and had decided that certain warvessels which had been ordered by the Shogun and some of the *daimyo* should not be delivered until instructions from their home government were received or peace restored. Of these ships the most dangerous was the ironclad ram *Stonewall* which had been purchased by the Shogun's agents in the United States in 1867. This ship had been delivered to the Shogun's representatives, but was manned by an American crew on its voyage to Japan. On its arrival at Yokohama, on April 24, 1868, General Van Valkenburgh refused to deliver it to the Yedo officials, nor would he later allow the imperial representatives to obtain it. At first, Mr. Seward questioned the wisdom of this action, as the ship had already been transferred to the Shogun's flag, but he allowed General Van Valkenburgh discretion in the matter, in view of his knowledge of actual conditions. With the complete success of the campaign in eastern Japan, the Imperial Government requested the foreign representatives to withdraw the proclamation of neutrality. This was done February 9, 1869, and the *Stonewall* was delivered to the imperial agents, in time to take part in the final operations against the rebels at Hakodate.

Upon these stirring events, the fall of the Shogunate and the restoration of imperial power, foreign relations had a most important influence. The Shogunate would certainly have passed away in time. The seeds of decay were already germinating; hostility to its system was rife among many of the powerful feudatories, and loyalty to the Emperor was rapidly increasing. But the crisis created by the new foreign relations hurried the progress of its fall. Its own councils were divided on the question of negotiating the foreign treaties, and its enemies were tremendously strengthened when it was forced to sign the later treaties without imperial approval. Under the pressure of the powers on the one hand, insisting upon the strict observance of the treaties, and of the Court on the other, insisting upon their abrogation, the Shogunate was at its wits' end. And after the imperial approval had been secured and the Shogun was apparently in a strong position, the fact was driven home that in dealing with the strong powers of the West the old dual government, which had functioned so well in the days of seclusion, must give way to a consolidated central power which could adequately protect the rights and interests of Japan. The wise unselfishness of Keiki in surrendering the great powers which had been transmitted to him from his ancestors merits high commendation. And although a more moderate policy on the part of the western lords might have brought about these great changes without the shedding of blood, yet it is easy to understand their desire to carry out promptly and thoroughly the programme on which they had been so long engaged. Americans, who remember how long Northern statesmen controlled the Government of the United States after the Civil War, can understand how it was possible for the clansmen of Choshiu, Satsuma, and to a less extent Tosa, to control the Government of Japan after their success in restoring the Emperor to supreme power in the land.

While the restoration of the Emperor was an event of supreme importance in the history of Japan, it naturally had a great influence on the relations between Japan and the treaty powers. Many of the foreigners saw with some misgivings the passing away of the Government which had so loyally maintained the treaties, and the assumption of power by men who had, in the past, been hostile to foreign intercourse. The British Minister, Sir Harry Parkes, used his great influence to support the imperial administration during the early days of uncertainty. But the course adopted by the new Government was so correct that all doubts were speedily removed. Two events were of great significance. On the 6th of April, the Emperor proceeded to the Nijo Castle, in Kyoto, the former seat of the Shogun's representative there, and in the presence of the higher court nobles and leading feudal lords took the famous oath, which has been the corner-stone of the great changes of New Japan. One of its clauses affirmed that "knowledge shall be sought for all over the world, and thus shall be strengthened the foundations of the Imperial Polity." This was a pledge of enlarged foreign intercourse. And in September, the name of Yedo was changed to Tokyo (Eastern Capital) and it was designated as one of the imperial capitals. There, on November 24th, the Emperor took up his residence in the former castle of the Shogun. The restoration had been completed in form as well as in spirit.

CHAPTER VI

THE RISE OF NEW JAPAN

THE abolition of the Shogunate and the restoration of the Emperor were but the first steps in the remarkable progress which Japan was to make in the next quarter of a century. The immediate effect of these governmental changes was that the Emperor, now ruling in Tokyo, stood forth as the head of the state, imposing his will directly upon the feudal lords without the interposition of the Shogun. The feudal system continued in force, for only a few of the eastern lords had lost their lands as a punishment for their resistance to the imperial commands. And the feudal system meant decentralization, the inability to provide for a national treasury, a national army, or uniform administrative and legal procedure. The first constitution, drawn up to take the place of the Tokugawa régime, had been distinctly conservative, and was based upon the models of the Taiho era, about 700 A.D. In this new Government the positions of influence were held by court nobles and by the lords and *samurai* of the western clans of Satsuma, Choshiu, Tosa, and others. Now the court nobles and the western lords had been, in the past, avowedly anti-foreign, yet the new Government had immediately accepted, without qualification, the obligations incurred by the foreign treaties. The foreign representatives had promptly recognized the new order and had maintained a correct conduct during the civil war, yet it is easy to understand why there was some misgiving as to the real attitude of the new Government. If the opposition to the Shogun had developed largely out of criticism of his foreign policy, would the new administration be strong enough to adopt the very policy which had aroused such resentment? And in one respect, at least, there seemed to be evidence that the Imperial Government was less liberal than that of the Shogun had been.

With the actions of the new Government in domestic affairs the foreign representatives were, of course, not concerned, but in one respect they believed it to be their duty, if not their right, to interfere. This was in regard to the enforcement of old penalties against the practice of the Christian religion. According to the edicts of the early seventeenth century, when the Christian religion was proscribed, the penalty of death was decreed, and these laws were effective at the time of the restoration. The Dutch, in their treaty of October 16, 1857, secured permission to practice "their own or the Christian religion" within their buildings or burial-places, and the Shogunate announced that it had abolished the trampling on religious images (as a test of suspected converts), but it would not permit the introduction of Christian worship or the importation of Christian and other foreign religious books, prints, or images. These provisions, as well as the right to erect suitable buildings of worship, were incorporated in the American treaty of 1858. Townsend Harris, the American Minister, wished to go further than this, and secure a treaty provision for full religious toleration, but his efforts, in March, 1859, were unsuccessful. As a good friend of Japan he desired to see her emerge from the intolerance of past ages to the open-mindedness of the modern world. But the Shogun's officials were surprisingly wise in refusing this request of one whom they respected. In China, the toleration of Christianity was incorporated in the Tientsin treaties of June, 1858. From that time any interference by the Chinese Government with its Christian subjects might be considered a violation of the treaties. This fact, coupled with the abuses of extraterritoriality in China, not only caused constant difficulties for the Government, but also in many ways hampered the sound progress of the faith. The long roll of Christian martyrs in China would have been much reduced if the principle of religious toleration had been allowed to develop in that country as rationally as it did in Japan.

The exclusion laws of Japan had been occasioned by the fears of Christianity as a political agency. So those who opposed the suspension of the old laws were most hostile to any compromise with the Western faith, even to the extent of allowing the foreigners to practice it. With the opening of the treaty ports in July, 1859, some missionaries established themselves at Nagasaki and Yokohama. The Catholic missionaries at the former port soon learned of the existence, near at hand, of communities of Christians, the descendants of the early converts. In spite of the well-known laws prohibiting the Christian faith, and the treaty provisions which restricted the movement of foreigners to certain limits, the missionaries visited the groups, preaching and administering the sacraments in the night. For several years the local officials took no notice of these proceedings, but finally the demand for the enforcement of law became so strong that they were forced to act. In July, 1867, some sixty-five Christians were arrested at Urakami, about four miles from Nagasaki. Shortly afterwards the American Minister, General Van Valkenburgh, happened to visit Nagasaki, and he tried to induce the local officials to release the prisoners, which they refused to do, as the arrests had been made according to law. On his return to Yedo,

THE RISE OF NEW JAPAN

General Van Valkenburgh addressed a letter to the Shogun's ministers of foreign affairs, in which, while assuring them of his desire to refrain from any interference in the internal regulations of Japan, he expressed his regret at the arrest of the Christians at Nagasaki. "The absolute religious freedom of which the United States has set an example to the world, and the entire independence of all religious belief from the interference and control of government," he said, "have in a great measure contributed to the unexampled prosperity and power at which my country has arrived. Intolerance in regard to religious matters would at this moment be regarded in a very serious light by the Christian world, and perhaps be followed to a greater or less extent by the withdrawal of the sympathy of the great Western powers, of which the Government of the Tycoon stands so much in need."

The Shogun's Government held liberal views on this subject, but the pressure of the anti-foreign *daimyo* was so great that it dared not withdraw the Christian prohibitions at once. After the French Minister had promised that French missionaries would not proselyte in the future, or do anything "that could encourage Japanese subjects to infringe or defy the laws of their country," the prisoners were released, without the usual form of recantation. M. Roches urged the French Bishop to have patience, for the day of religious tolerance was at hand.

On learning of the arrest of the Urakami Christians, Mr. Seward, the American Secretary of State, instructed General Van Valkenburgh to confer with his colleagues, and, with their concurrence, appeal to the Japanese Government to abrogate the laws which prohibited Christianity in the empire. "Such a result," he said, "would greatly contribute to the harmony existing between Japan and the Western nations, while it would immediately redound to the welfare and greatness of the Japanese Empire." A copy of this instruction was communicated to each of the other treaty powers in the hope of securing joint action. In reply General Van Valkenburgh expressed the opinion that the present moment would be ill chosen for making such an appeal. And thus the matter rested at the end of the Shogunate.

Soon after the restoration of the Imperial Government, the foreign representatives learned that one of its first acts was the prohibition of "the Christian and other evil religions." Sir Harry Parkes, at Osaka, promptly assured the imperial officials there of the injurious effect such a policy would have upon the treaty powers, and General Van Valkenburgh arranged for a joint protest of all the foreign ministers. Mr. Seward, on learning of it, interpreted the edict literally and as applying to foreigners as well as to Japanese, and he instructed the American Minister that the United States could not acquiesce in or submit to the Mikado's proclamation, and, if necessary, the Japanese Government should be informed that the United States would protect the lives and property of its citizens against any persecution instituted under the proclamation. Of course the edict simply applied to Japanese subjects and was in no way in violation of the treaties, so the foreign representatives believed that nothing more should be done. In June, an edict was issued for the arrest of the Christians at Urakami, and their distribution among some thirty-three of the western *daimyo*, who should take care to induce them to renounce their evil ways. Again the consuls at Nagasaki protested, in the name of humanity, and to point out the bad effect of such a measure upon the reputation of Japan. Mr. Seward now instructed General Van Valkenburgh to delay any formal representation on the subject of the prohibition decree until its effects were more clearly discerned. And in January, 1869, a satisfactory understanding was apparently reached.

But in May, 1869, news came of the arrest of some four hundred Christians in the Goto Islands, and in January, 1870, the remaining Christians near Nagasaki were ordered to be distributed among the clans. Again the foreign representatives protested against these proceedings. At a conference between the four foreign ministers and the leading Japanese officials, the whole matter was discussed, and the deportation was described as a political action and due to the misconduct of the native Christians. Moreover, missionaries were visiting the villages, in violation of the treaties, but, rather than complain to the foreign representatives, the Government thought it would be easier to deal with its own subjects. This led to a memorandum signed by the four foreign ministers promising to do all in their power to restrain the missionaries from preaching outside the foreign settlement, provided that the native Christians be returned from exile.

This renewal of the deportation measures after the assurances given in 1869 was interpreted in certain quarters as a revival of the old anti-foreign hostility. This view was taken by the new American Minister, Mr. C. E. De Long, who had recently arrived in Japan. His inexperience made his opinions untrustworthy, but, on the strength of them, the American Government sought an exchange of views with the other treaty powers, in the belief that the former liberal policy of the Government was in danger and that foreign rights might be in jeopardy. France, as usual, was especially interested in the protection of the native Christians. But the British Government, more accurately informed of the situation through Sir Harry Parkes, believed that in time the prejudice of the Japanese against the Christian religion would be overcome, and that no further steps should be taken. This wise view prevailed. Later in the year the Government returned the Christians to their homes, and no further repressive measures were taken. But the old laws were not repealed. During the visit of Lord Iwakura's mission to the treaty powers, in 1872-73, the desirability of granting religious toleration was repeatedly pointed out by foreign statesmen, with such success that Lord Iwakura advised the withdrawal of the prohibitory proclamations. This was done early in 1873. The laws were not repealed, they simply were not enforced. Religious toleration became law under the constitution of 1889.

For this change in policy much credit must be given to the representatives of the Christian churches, as well as to the representatives of the foreign powers. The Honorable Saburo Shimada, in fact, gives to them the chief credit. "When the country entered upon its new era," he wrote, "the reactionary spirit against Christianity still retained its old prejudice. Fortunately the missionaries and educators, whom the United States sent to Japan about this time, were all men of piety, moderation, and good sense, and their sincerity and kindness produced on the minds of our countrymen a profound impression, such as tended to completely remove the suspicions hitherto entertained towards the Christian religion. . . . The sincerity and patience of these early messengers of the Gospel seldom failed to inspire respect in those who were brought into contact with them. In fact, they were a living testimony, completely dispelling whatever prejudice remained against Christianity in the bosoms of our countrymen, who were naturally led to the conclusion that after all there could be nothing hateful or dreadful in a religion which could produce such men."

The withdrawal of the edicts removed a possible source of friction between Japan and the powers. That the Government had a perfect right to deal with its subjects as it chose was recognized by the foreign nations. No foreign Christians were molested, and the treaty provisions were observed. But religious intolerance was out of harmony with the modern age, while the prohibition of Christianity furnished argument to those who accused the Imperial Government of being at heart anti-foreign. The steps through which Christianity was gradually tolerated in fact, in Japan, long before it was tolerated in law, seem to indicate the superiority of that method over the treaty-made toleration in China.

During these first years of Meiji, changes of all kinds were introduced. Feudalism was abolished by 1871, and national progress under a strong central government was now possible. A national army and navy were commenced to take the place of the feudal levies. Railways were introduced, and telegraph lines erected. Educational reforms were studied, and the great law of 1872, unique in the Orient and in keeping with the best principles of the time, laid the foundations for a system which would offer the opportunities of education to every boy and girl in the empire. No action of the leaders of the early Meiji period was productive of happier results than this.

In 1872 the foreign treaties might be revised at the request of either party. This question of treaty revision became the leading feature of Japan's foreign relations during the next twenty-two years, and for this reason it will be treated in another chapter in some detail. In this place certain other incidents in Japanese-American relations of this period will be mentioned.

If the early attitude of the Government toward the native Christians had created an unfavorable impression in the United States, the action which it took in regard to the coolie ship *Maria Luz*, in 1872, won immediate approval. The United States had been the first power to condemn the Chinese coolie traffic, in its Act of 1862, and long before that time its representatives in China had expressed their disapproval. In August, 1872, the British Chargé, Mr. R. G. Watson, supported by the American Chargé, Mr. C. O. Shepard, called the attention of the Japanese foreign office to the alleged ill-treatment of Chinese coolies on the Peruvian ship *Maria Luz*, then in the port of Yokohama on the way to Peru. As Peru had no treaty with Japan, the captain of the ship was brought into the local court at Yokohama and found guilty as charged, but no penalty was assessed, because of his long detention. All the Chinese passengers, who were in reality coolies or contract laborers, were subpœnaed and brought ashore as witnesses. After the trial, Captain Heriero requested that the Chinese be sent back to the ship, but the Japanese authorities refused to compel them to go. A civil suit was then brought against two of the Chinese to compel the specific performance of the labor contract which they had signed in China or to secure damages. The decision of the judge was in favor of the defendants, and they were not forced to return to the ship. In this way the Japanese dealt a vigorous blow at a traffic which had long been considered disgraceful.

The American Minister, Mr. De Long, had previously been instructed to act in the interests of Peru should any questions arise in Japan. He therefore tried to use his good offices in the matter. For this he was criticized in Japan, and the Secretary of State censured him for taking "any steps which might wear the aspect of giving the support and countenance of the United States to a vessel suspected by the Japanese Government, not without reason, of complicity in a nefarious traffic, of a character particularly odious to the Government and people of the United States." ¡The Government of Peru considered that in the *Maria Luz* affair the flag had been insulted and the honor of the nation affected. It therefore sent a special mission to Japan to settle the dispute. At the request of the Peruvian Minister in Washington, the American Government consented to use its good offices in the matter, on the distinct understanding that in doing so it could not be construed as approving of the coolie trade. Mr. De Long was instructed to act, if the Japanese Government was agreeable to the proposal. His good offices were accepted, and he served as adviser to both parties, persuading the Peruvian to relinquish the demand for a salute to his flag, and urging both sides to accept an arbitration of their differences. This course was decided upon, and the Emperor of Russia selected as arbitrator. Two years later, on May 29, 1875, his decision was handed down in favor of Japan.

In these days the Japanese were eager to learn all that they could of Western methods and ideas. Among their valued teachers and advisers in Japan were many Americans, and to America went many young Japanese in search of Western education. Other countries and their nationals took part in this work of instruction, but in this period the relations between Japan and the United States were more intimate than those with any other power. Among the earliest American friends and teachers of the Japanese should be mentioned the Reverend Guido Verbeck, Dr. S. R. Brown, and Dr. J. C. Hepburn. Under these pioneer missionary-teachers many Japanese studied who later made names for themselves in the service of their state. The Marquis Okuma has acknowledged his indebtedness to Verbeck for instruction in political theory. And after the restoration more and more Americans were employed in the various departments of government. One of these, Dr. W. E. Griffis, who taught in Echizen between 1870 and 1874, later wrote "The Mikado's Empire," which became the popular history of Japan in the West for many years. In 1871, General Horace Capron, recently Commissioner of Agriculture, was appointed adviser to the Colonial Bureau, which had in hand the work of colonizing Hokkaido. There an agricultural college was soon organized at Sapporo by Dr. W. S. Clark, president of the Massachusetts College of Agriculture, where young Japanese came in contact not only with the most effective American methods, but with the best American ideals. Of the many Americans who have contributed to the advancement of Japanese education, the one whose influence was doubtless first in importance was Dr. David Murray, of Rutgers College, who, from June, 1873, until January, 1879, was Superintendent of Educational Affairs and adviser to the Imperial Japanese Minister of Education. He was first called upon to plan for a system of universal education, and the establishment of public schools throughout the empire. He also helped to build up the Imperial University at Tokyo, which had recently been founded, and he laid the foundations for women's education in the establishment of the Tokyo Women's High Normal School. At his instigation the Imperial Academy of Literature and Science was founded, and his " Story of Japan," published in 1894, vied with "The Mikado's Empire" as a popular

history of Japan. In the finance and postal departments
Americans were also employed. And for forty years the
adviser of the Foreign Office was an American. The first
appointee, Mr. E. Peshine Smith, had been a Commissioner of Claims in the State Department. He was
appointed in 1871 and served until 1876. His successor
was Mr. Eli T. Sheppard, who had served as an American
Consul in China from 1868 until 1876. At the time of
Soyeshima's mission to Peking, in 1873, to exchange the
ratified copies of the Sino-Japanese treaty of 1871, and
to discuss the Formosa and Korean questions, Mr. Sheppard had been of great service to the Japanese mission,
especially in its relations with Li Hung-chang. For this
reason, he was offered the post vacated by Mr. Smith,
and the offer was cordially approved by the American
Department of State. Mr. Sheppard served until 1881,
and in that period his advice was sought in the early
efforts for treaty revision. In 1879, he contributed to the
Japan Weekly Mail a series of articles on extraterritoriality in Japan which were of great value in clarifying the
vague notions of the rights and duties of foreigners in
Japan. Mr. Sheppard is now living in California, and his
sympathetic understanding of Japanese affairs is as keen
to-day as it was when he lived in daily association with
the makers of New Japan forty and more years ago. His
successor was Mr. H. W. Denison, whose services for
thirty years were almost invaluable. These, and many
other Americans, had a part in helping the Japanese
bridge the gap between the days of seclusion and the
days of modern international intercourse. Their contributions were always along peaceful and constructive lines.
Unfortunately, Japan was compelled to acquire armaments as well, but for assistance in this field she turned,
naturally, to the great powers of Europe. America, after

the Civil War, was too busy to devote her energies to building up a great army or navy.

The first Japanese mission was sent to the United States. In 1860 came the envoys bearing the ratified copy of the treaty of 1858. The first Japanese Consul was appointed to San Francisco. Mr. Charles Walcott Brooks, who had served as commercial agent there for nine years, was duly commissioned as consul in 1867. Three years later, Arinori Mori was appointed Minister Resident at Washington, where the first Japanese legation was established. And, in 1872, Lord Iwakura's mission was the guest of the American nation as it proceeded around the world to advise the treaty powers that Japan would soon proceed to discuss the revision of the treaties. In this party were several young men who became leaders in the Government, including the late Prince Ito, and the knowledge of America which they gained at this time was of service in later years.

Before the seclusion laws were repealed, several Japanese had visited the United States, usually seafarers who had been picked up by American ships. These were followed by men sent abroad to study, and in the early seventies many young men of rank and fortune were studying in America. Everywhere they were given a cordial welcome, and every opportunity was placed in their way for obtaining the knowledge which they sought. It would make an interesting study to follow the careers of these early travelers and students in America. Many of them returned to their native land with a high opinion of American ways and ideals. Among these may be mentioned Joseph Neesima, the founder of the Doshisha, and Yukichi Fukazawa, who used the columns of the *Jiji Shimpo* to foster good relations with America. Through these observing travelers and eager students, the Japanese

Government soon had in its service many men who knew America, and the European countries as well. Their influence for the development of wise policies based on an understanding of foreign conditions cannot be overestimated. There have been few men, high placed in American public life, who have known Japan intimately. There have been many Japanese in the highest positions who have been familiar, through study or investigation, with American affairs. The constant stream of Japanese students to American schools and universities has been one of the strongest elements in developing and keeping alive the good relations between the two countries which, in spite of temporary misunderstanding in the recent years, still persists. In America the Japanese students were representatives and interpreters of their native land. Few of them were unworthy of their trust, and Americans who came in contact with them learned to appreciate the good qualities of these strangers from the other side of the globe. And on their return they proved even more effective interpreters of America to their own people. Fifty years ago it was natural for this stream to flow from Japan to America and the West. But now it should flow in both directions. American students should visit Japanese universities and technical schools. There is much they could learn there. And it would be a cheap investment if each country would arrange to send as many of their young men as possible to study in the other. Even if the cost should run into the millions, it would be a cheap insurance against the dangers of misunderstanding.

One of the interesting and significant events of this period was the visit to the Orient of General U. S. Grant, formerly commander-in-chief of the American armies, and recently President of the United States. Although a private citizen, without rank or station, he had been received with distinguished honors by the governments and peoples of Europe, but nowhere did he receive greater marks of esteem than in Japan. During his presidency he had shown strong sympathy for the two great nations of eastern Asia. In dealing with China his administration followed the liberal principles of the Burlingame Treaty of 1868, and he had personally welcomed the mission of Lord Iwakura, and expressed the hope that a satisfactory revision of the Japanese treaties might be undertaken. Under his successor the Treaty of Washington, of 1878, was signed, which, so far as the United States could achieve it, restored to Japan the control of her tariff laws. For these reasons, General Grant, because of his own great reputation and because he was an unofficial representative of a power which had been consistently friendly to both China and Japan, was called upon for advice in the settlement of the acute questions which had brought China and Japan to the verge of war. The matters in dispute were the possession of the Ryukyu Islands and the Chinese claim to suzerainty over Korea. By mutual understanding each party agreed to submit its case to General Grant. This was a purely informal and unofficial reference, which in no way compromised the American Government or would give cause for offense if the recommendations of its distinguished private citizen were rejected. At Peking, General Grant held several interviews with Prince Kung and Li Hung-chang, the great Viceroy, and a formal statement of China's case was submitted to him, with the request that he would present the matter to the Japanese Government on his arrival in Tokyo. On the 20th of June, 1879, the General arrived at Nagasaki. An imperial summer palace at Tokyo was placed at his disposal, and his official reception was set, with marked appropriateness, for the Fourth of July.

After a series of receptions and popular demonstrations, up to that time unprecedented, General Grant proceeded to Nikko, accompanied by Prince Ito and a majority of the Privy Council. There the matters in controversy between China and Japan were carefully considered, and his views were set forth in dispatches which were transmitted to the Emperor at Tokyo and to Prince Kung at Peking. On his return to Tokyo, the Emperor paid him the great honor of visiting him at his palace-residence, and of discussing with him some of the troublesome questions which confronted the Imperial Government. In regard to the Ryukyu dispute, General Grant stated that he had advised the Chinese Government to recede from its contention. In the case of Korea, he proposed a joint international control of the political affairs of the kingdom. "This arrangement," he said, "may not be entirely satisfactory to either country, but it will satisfy the conscience of the world and thus shut the door to unfriendly European interference in Oriental affairs, which, above all things else, should be the policy of both China and Japan. Any amicable adjustment of these questions between the two countries is better than war. Your quarrels are their opportunity for unfriendly intervention, and, if war should ensue between the two countries over either of these questions, the powers of Europe will end it in their own way, in their own interests, and to the lasting and incalculable injury of both nations."

Just at this time, Japanese sovereignty was threatened as never before by the extension of the extraterritorial theory in the quarantine case. General Grant had this in mind when he said: "America has great commercial interests in the Far East, but she has no interests, and can have none, that are inconsistent with the complete independence and well-being of all Asiatic nations, especially Japan and China. It seems incredible that rights which Western nations all regard as sacred and inviolable, because absolutely essential to their independence and dignity, should be denied by them to China and Japan."

And this advice was given in closing: "American statesmen have long since perceived the danger of European interference in the political affairs of North and South America. So guard against this danger. And as a measure of self-protection it has become the settled policy of the United States that no European power shall be permitted to enlarge its dominion or extend its influence by any interference in American affairs. It is likewise the policy of America in the Orient, I may say it is the law of our empire in the Pacific, that the integrity and independence of China and Japan should be preserved and maintained."

General Grant's pacific advice in the matter of Chinese relations was accepted. Not only was a peaceful solution of the Ryukyu controversy found, but the Japanese tried to negotiate a treaty of defensive alliance with China, which failed through the inveterate hostility of Li Hung-chang. Peace, however, was preserved for fifteen years, and when the war did ensue three of the European powers proceeded to end it as Grant had predicted — "in their own way, in their own interests, and to the lasting and incalculable injury of both nations." At his farewell audience with the Emperor, on September 1st, he made these parting remarks: "I leave Japan greatly impressed with the possibilities and probabilities of her future. She has a fertile soil, one half of it not yet cultivated to man's use, great undeveloped mineral resources, numerous and fine harbors, an extensive seacoast, abounding in fish of an almost endless variety, and, above all, an industrious, ingenious, contented, and frugal population. With all these, nothing is wanted to insure great progress, except wise discretion by the Government, peace at home and abroad, and non-interference in the internal and domestic affairs of the country by outside nations." These views of the distinguished American seem to have been wise and far-sighted, but they were not so considered in all quarters. Sir Harry Parkes commented at the time: " General Grant is here and is turning the Japanese heads."

Deeds, rather than words, are the real tests of good-will. In this period American good-will was made manifest by the treaties of 1878 and 1886, which will be discussed elsewhere, and by the return of the Shimonoseki indemnity. This was the American share of the indemnity of $3,000,000, payable by the Shogun's Government in lieu of expenses, indemnities, and ransoms, arising from the allied expedition to open the Straits of Shimonoseki, in 1864. The amount was excessive, but was placed at a high figure in order to encourage the Shogun's Government to open more treaty ports instead of paying the full indemnity. But, as we have seen, the Government decided to pay the indemnity rather than open additional ports or even advance the date of opening Hiogo and Osaka. The story of the way in which this indemnity was finally paid is a long and involved one. Under the convention, the sum was to be paid in six installments by November 15, 1866. Three of these payments were made before May 16, 1866, and then the Shogun's Government, practically bankrupt because of the Choshiu expedition, asked for an extension of time. A brief respite ensued, for the powers were pleased with the prompt negotiation of the new tariff in 1866, but the next year the demand for payment was renewed, and the final date was extended to May 15, 1869. Then came the fall of the Shogunate and the civil war. The new Government accepted the obligation to complete the indemnity payment, but begged for a postponement of the installments. This was granted, to May 15, 1872, on condition that the duties on tea and silk should not be raised. In this interval came the reorganization of the Imperial Government and the fall of feudalism. The demands upon the newly created central treasury were great, and a further indulgence was again requested. During Lord Iwakura's mission to the treaty powers he tried to secure their consent to a relinquishment of the $1,500,000 still due, but, although the United States was favorable, Great Britain asked as an equivalent that foreigners be allowed to travel in the interior. Rather than grant this new privilege, at the time when it was desired to curtail the extraterritorial rights of foreigners, the Government determined to complete the payments. Great Britain, France, and the Netherlands received their shares of the fourth installment in February, 1874, and the fifth installment in April. No payment was offered the United States, as that Government had shown a desire to have the outstanding sums remitted, but, in order to maintain the policy of coöperation in Oriental matters, the United States asked that it be placed on an equality with its colleagues. This was done, and the final payment was made on August 1, 1874.

The Convention of 1864 had not stipulated how the indemnity was to be divided among the powers. After an exchange of views, in 1866, it was agreed, on the suggestion of Great Britain, that $420,000 be deducted from the total, in order to compensate for the aggressive acts against the ships of the United States, France, and the

Netherlands by Choshiu in 1863, and that the balance be divided equally among the four powers. This was in place of an earlier proposal that the bulk of the indemnity be divided in proportion to the expenses incurred in the punitive expedition. Under the accepted plan, Great Britain would receive $645,000, and the other three powers $785,000 each.

As the first three payments, in gold, were transferred to the United States, they were invested in government bonds and set aside as a special fund. The premium on the gold, in the days just after the American Civil War, and the discount on the bonds made this a very profitable transaction. Early in 1868, Secretary Seward called the attention of Congress to this indemnity fund, which had been received " without substantial equivalent," and stated that it awaited the disposition of Congress. In 1870 began the efforts to return all or most of this money to Japan. Bill after bill was introduced in Congress, some passing one house and some the other. Repeatedly the Presidents, in their messages, urged that justice be done to Japan, and to China as well, for a large amount of unclaimed indemnity money from that country also lay in the treasury. The delay in securing Congressional action was not due to any question of the justice of the remission, but primarily to the difficulties inherent in the passage of special legislation. By 1883, the Shimonoseki fund was valued at $1,839,533, mostly in bonds. In 1881, the Senate passed a bill which would have returned $1,463,224 to Japan, and the next year the House of Representatives passed a similar measure, which called for $1,516,364. But the point was now made that the Government never paid interest on claims, and this was finally accepted. In 1883, therefore, an act was approved by the President which returned to Japan the exact amount received, $785,000.87 (where the eighty-seven cents came from no one could explain), and cancelled the bonds. By the same act the officers and crews of the two American ships which had taken part in the engagements at Shimonoseki were to be paid $140,000 from the treasury.

The various attempts, between 1870 and 1883, to secure the remission of this fund to Japan had been followed with deep interest by Japanese statesmen, and the actual return of the amount of the original indemnity (although without interest) was welcomed as a " strong manifestation of that spirit of justice and equity which has always animated the United States in their relations with Japan." The money was, after due deliberation, appropriated for the building of the breakwater in the harbor of Yokohama, where it might serve to perpetuate the good-will of the American nation. And the lesson of this kindly act was promptly grasped by the Japanese, for they, in turn, remitted to Korea, that very year, some 400,000 yen of the indemnity of 550,000 payable under the convention of 1882, for the purpose of establishing an educational fund in Korea. It might be added that the United States has also remitted two indemnity funds to China. In 1885, the balance of the award of 1858 was returned, and in 1908 a large portion of the Boxer indemnity, which has been used for the education of Chinese students in the United States.

In the period under discussion, between 1868 and 1894, the relations between the United States and Japan were marked by friendship and mutual esteem. Americans followed with keen interest and admiration the efforts of Japan to master the great contributions of Western thought and science. The American Ministers at Tokyo promptly reported to Washington the innovations and their developments, and frequently the State Department published, for general information, the texts of Japanese laws and regulations, and the reports of the administrative departments. Translations of the early reports of the post-office, education, and finance departments, and the mint, may be found in the American documents, and the penal code of 1880 and the code of criminal procedure were printed there in full. The American Government and people were gratified at the progress of Japan, they were ready at all times to do what lay within their power to contribute to that advancement, for they believed that her enlightened example would be an influence for good upon all the other peoples of the East.

CHAPTER VII

THE REVISION OF THE TREATIES

THE early treaties of commerce were subject to revision after the 1st of July, 1872. The treaties did not expire on that date, but they might be revised, and revision called for the approval of both parties. The effort of Japan to secure this revision proved to be the most important feature of her international relations in the period between 1872 and 1894. Nearer at home, her relations with China and Korea were at times critical, but the questions which arose there were adjusted with relative promptness. The endeavor to revise the treaties, however, was protracted over a score of years and it involved the relations of Japan with all the treaty powers. In these negotiations the United States played a significant if not a dominant rôle.

The principal points at issue between Japan and the treaty powers were concerned with tariff autonomy and extraterritorial jurisdiction. The Japanese Government desired to regain the right to fix its own tariff and to control the conduct of foreigners within the empire. It believed that it had the right to request that these treaty provisions be revised, and it resented the long delay of the powers to grant its legitimate desires. The Japanese thought in terms of abstract right, the right to regain the sovereign authority which had been relinquished. But some of the powers, consulting their own interests, took the position that no concession should be granted without an equivalent. For this reason, the two parties were far apart, and the Japanese nursed a sense of injustice which was little understood or appreciated by most of the foreigners. And this resentment increased as the revision was longer and longer delayed.

The history of the conventional tariff, from its origin in 1857 to the final convention in 1866, has already been given. The specific duties, adjusted on the basis of five per cent, steadily dropped below that figure as the value of the articles increased. The Japanese, very naturally, desired to escape from the limitations imposed on their right to fix their own tariff laws. Some of the great commercial powers, naturally enough, wished to retain the advantage created by the conventional tariff. As might be expected, they were loath to agree to any treaty revision which would restore tariff autonomy to the Japanese. The United States alone was consistently favorable to this desire of Japan.

Although the principle of sovereignty was involved in the conventional tariff, a more serious impairment arose from the extraterritorial rights of foreigners. By this we mean, in brief, the right enjoyed by foreigners, under the treaties, to be tried for offenses in their own courts and according to their own laws. And in civil cases, the court of the defendant was to have jurisdiction. With the origin of these rights in the Middle Ages we are not concerned. The principle had developed through the centuries around the Mediterranean, and it was naturally extended to China in the early treaties. The reason for this was the unwillingness of the Western powers to permit their nationals to be subject to the severe, and at times arbitrary, judicial procedure of China. In 1843, the British secured the right of extraterritoriality in China, and the other treaty powers followed in their steps.

In Japan, as we have seen, the right was not demanded by Commodore Perry, for Dr. S. Wells Williams, the

American interpreter, had been impressed with the difficulties which it had already occasioned in China. But in June, 1854, when additional regulations were signed at Shimoda, a crude form of extraterritoriality was granted, for Americans " found transgressing Japanese laws may be apprehended by the police and taken on board their ships." At the time Dr. Williams told Lieutenant Bent that the Japanese " signed away their sovereignty without knowing it." The next year the Russians gained complete criminal extraterritoriality, and in the 1858 treaties civil extraterritoriality as well was granted. The last, and most complete, statement was found in the treaty with Austria-Hungary, in 1869. Townsend Harris, who had incorporated the system in his treaty of 1858, later said it was against his conscience, and he hoped it would be fully abrogated.

If extraterritoriality was a privilege enjoyed by nationals of the treaty powers, then, like all other privileges, it carried with it duties as well. If foreigners were not subject to Japanese law and procedure for offenses committed in Japan, then the duty reposed upon the foreign powers to see that their nationals were adequately punished for such offenses. This would require the establishment of adequate judicial systems in Japan, with courts for the trial of offenders, with officers to execute the decrees of the courts, and with jails for the detention of criminals. That the privilege was often abused goes without saying. Great Britain made the first adequate provision for performing its duty in the matter, and the United States soon followed, but few of the other countries sent out consuls to Japan who were qualified to preside in their own courts, and few made provisions for the punishment of their guilty nationals.

If, in the days of the Shogunate, the judicial administration of Japan was too uncertain and arbitrary to permit foreign states to entrust their nationals to its authority, then with the development of better courts and codes these extraterritorial rights might well be relinquished. But here a difference of opinion soon arose. Who was to judge as to the efficiency and justice of the new courts? The refusal to abrogate the extraterritorial rights long after the Japanese had compiled a criminal code according to Western models was a serious blow to Japanese pride. As General Grant remarked in 1879: "It seems incredible that rights which Western nations all regard as sacred and inviolable, because absolutely essential to their independence and dignity, should be denied by them to China and Japan." Whether the criticisms of the new Japanese codes and courts were sound or not, we must recognize the perfectly natural desire of the Japanese to regain judicial autonomy, and we must appreciate the resentment which developed during the years in which it was delayed.

During the greater part of the period in which the revision of the treaties was under discussion, the United States was ably represented at Tokyo by the Honorable John A. Bingham, of Ohio. His term of service, from 1873 until 1885, was the longest of any of the American representatives in Japan, and his experience and training gave great weight to his views in Washington. Mr. Bingham had served in the House of Representatives almost constantly since 1855. During the Civil War he had been a judge-advocate of the army, and had served as such in the trial of the conspirators charged with the assassination of President Lincoln. After the war he had taken a prominent part in the work of reconstruction, and in 1868 he had been one of the managers appointed by the House of Representatives to conduct the impeachment trial of President Andrew Johnson. He was thus a man who stood high in the councils of his party, an able lawyer, an eloquent public speaker, and a faithful exponent of the American ideals of his generation.

In the matter of treaty revision Mr. Bingham believed that Japan should promptly regain control of her tariff, and that the extraterritorial privileges of foreigners should cease with the establishment of a reasonably effective judicial system. The latter he believed to be in existence before the end of his residence at Tokyo. In the meantime, he took the position that the treaties only conferred upon foreigners the right to be tried in their own courts, but did not relieve them from the obligation to obey the laws of Japan. And he stoutly opposed any interpretation of the treaties which would serve to weaken the sovereign rights of Japan, with the sole exception of the right of trial and punishment. In this regard, he was constantly at variance with some of his European colleagues, who took the position that their nationals were bound to obey only their national laws, and were not subject to Japanese law. In this contention Mr. Bingham was supported by his Government. The Secretary of State, Hamilton Fish, in commenting upon the hunting regulations proposed by the Japanese Government, said in 1874: " The right of the authorities of Japan to enact and promulgate laws for the government, security, and good order of its own people, cannot, of course, be questioned for a moment, and of the character and sufficiency of these laws, that Government must be the sole judge. Citizens of the United States resident in Japan are expected and required to observe and obey such laws in the same manner and to the same extent that the like obligations rest upon the subjects of that empire. In regard to the enforcement of these laws, and the imposition of penalties for their infraction, citizens of the United States have secured to them, by the provisions of the existing treaties, the right of being tried in the consular courts of their own nation, established in Japan, and according to the mode prescribed by the laws of the United States, and are protected from the infliction of any other penalties than those prescribed or warranted by the laws of their own country."

On numerous occasions Mr. Bingham tried to uphold the right of the Japanese Government to control the conduct of foreigners, subject always to trial in their own courts. In 1871, the Japanese tried to prevent hunting within game preserves, temple groves, and burial-places, as well as within the limits of cities and other inhabited places. Mr. De Long accepted the views of his colleagues that such regulations affecting foreigners could be made only by the foreign powers, but Mr. Bingham later held that they could be made by the Japanese Government and that American citizens were bound by them, and Mr. Fish supported him, as we have seen. In 1876, Mr. Fish instructed Mr. Bingham to issue a notification to American citizens to observe the new press laws. And in 1878, an interesting case arose in which an American citizen boarded a railway train without a ticket and rode from Kobe to Kyoto. Mr. Bingham instructed the consul at Kobe to arrest and try the accused. The consul replied with the query as to where, in American law, he would find authority for the punishment of a citizen of the United States for such an offense; to which Bingham replied that American citizens had been instructed to observe the railway regulations of Japan, and that a civil action for trespass or a criminal one for misdemeanor should be instituted. " As I have before advised you," he added, " our Government intends to respect all its treaty obligations with Japan, and to punish as therein required all offenses committed against Japanese or against Japanese law by Americans in this empire."

Other instances of the attitude of Mr. Bingham might be cited, but the most significant case was that concerning the quarantine regulations in 1878 and 1879. In the summer of 1878, cholera was prevalent in western Japan. The Japanese Government desired to institute a quarantine at Yokohama against vessels arriving from Nagasaki, but the consuls at Yokohama took the position that no ships could be ordered into quarantine without the approval of the consul concerned. This view was combated by Mr. Bingham, "as a substantial denial of the undoubted right of this Government to prevent the importation of pestilence by foreign vessels into the territorial waters of Japan," and he promptly approved of the regulations and instructed the American consuls to advise their nationals of them. The next year cholera spread farther to the east, to Kobe and Osaka, and the Government announced a restoration of the quarantine at Yokohama. Mr. Bingham promptly issued the necessary notification to the Consul-General. But the British Minister, according to his understanding of extraterritoriality, placed the enforcement of the quarantine at the discretion of the local consul. "None of the other European powers represented at this court," wrote Mr. Bingham, "have, so far as I can learn, given public notice of any purpose to observe, in whole or in part, the quarantine regulations of this Government. It remains to be seen how long the Governments of the Western powers will countenance the monstrous pretension that they may each and all lawfully deny to this Government the inalienable right of self-preservation." The German Consul, however, had taken the same position as the

British Minister. On July 11th, the German steamer *Hesperia* arrived at Yokohama from Kobe, and the Japanese officials at once sent it to the quarantine ground for the seven days' detention. The German Consul then sent out his chief staff-surgeon to inspect the vessel, and, on his report that there was no infection on board, the Consul demanded that the vessel be released. This demand was supported by the German Minister at Tokyo and, in the absence of an immediate reply, he gave orders that the ship should proceed to Yokohama, which it did under the escort of the German gunboat *Wolf*. In reply to Foreign Minister Terashima's request for an explanation of this amazing act, Mr. von Eisendecher replied that the quarantine regulations were not binding upon German ships unless sanctioned by the German consular authorities. The affair of the *Hesperia* created intense excitement at the time, and this was heightened after the appearance of cholera in Kanagawa and Tokyo. The Japanese Government could only issue a formal protest, but General Grant, who was in Japan at the time, is said to have remarked that if it had happened in America the German ship of war would have been instantly sunk.

Enough has been said to indicate the dangers involved in the extraterritorial jurisdiction. The privilege was so vaguely defined in the treaties that it was, of course, subject to interpretation. When Japan was weak, this interpretation was made as broad as possible. As Japan grew in power, she would demand a stricter and stricter account, and an acceptance by the powers of the duties which accompanied the privilege. The time would have to come when the peculiar privileges of the foreign residents would have to give way before the rising sense of nationalism of the Japanese.

The steps in this process may be briefly outlined.

The American treaty was revisable after July 4, 1872, one year's previous notice having been given. This notice was given verbally by Mr. De Long on May 5, 1871, and formally by the Japanese Government on June 30th following. Soon afterwards a distinguished mission was dispatched by the Government to inform the powers that Japan desired to proceed to the revision, as well as to study the institutions of the West which might further the progress of Japan. Lord Iwakura, recently Minister of Foreign Affairs, was at the head of the mission, and in his party were Kido, Okubo, Ito, and Yamaguchi, men who played prominent parts in the making of New Japan. Accompanied by the American Minister, the party first visited the United States, and from there proceeded to Europe. Almost two years were spent on this world tour, and the envoys returned on September 13, 1873. No immediate results were obtained during this mission, for Lord Iwakura was not prepared to discuss the Japanese desires. He did learn the views of the powers as to their wishes, and the members of his party gained invaluable information concerning the Western states. Religious toleration, the right of travel in the interior, and the opening of more ports to trade were some of the additional privileges desired by European powers.

Early in 1873, acting on the advice of Mr. Smith, its American adviser, the Japanese Government negotiated a treaty with the Italian Minister which would open the country to Italian travelers, who would be subject to Japanese jurisdiction. The United States, believing that it was not yet safe to surrender the rights of extraterritoriality in Japan, joined the European powers in urging the Italian Government not to ratify this convention. It was the policy of the administration to coöperate with the treaty powers.

THE REVISION OF THE TREATIES

At this time the foreign representatives, through joint action, were trying to secure the right of travel in the interior outside the treaty port limits. On September 27, 1873, they submitted a draft of regulations for the issuance of such passports, based upon a plan proposed by the German Minister. The Minister of Foreign Affairs replied, on December 20th, that it would be difficult to deal with this matter so long as foreigners enjoyed extraterritorial rights. Mr. Bingham believed that the Government would be satisfied if foreigners were made subject to Japanese laws and regulations, enforced by their own consular courts. He was instructed in this, as in other matters, to act in harmony with his colleagues so far as possible. The Japanese now realized that they had something to bargain with. The desire of the powers for greater facilities of travel and trade might lead them to accept some modification of the irksome treaties.

Realizing the deficiencies in their judicial administration, the Japanese now sought revision of the tariff regulations pending the time when, with the introduction of new courts and codes, they might justly ask that consular jurisdiction be relinquished. In this period Mr. Bingham repeatedly supported the Japanese claim for tariff control. Mr. Evarts, the new Secretary of State, accepted Mr. Bingham's views as to a separate treaty, rather than those of his predecessor, which preferred joint action. He, therefore, negotiated and signed at Washington, on July 25, 1878, a convention revising certain portions of the existing commercial treaties. This treaty annulled the existing tariff, harbor, and trade regulations, forbade discriminatory duties on imports and exports from and to either country, removed the export duty on goods shipped to the United States, and recognized the sole right of Japan to control its coasting trade.

The Japanese Government, in turn, agreed to open Shimonoseki and one other port to citizens and vessels of the United States. But the tenth article, in view of the conduct of the other powers, rendered the treaty nugatory. " The present convention shall take effect," it read, " when Japan shall have concluded such conventions or revisions of existing treaties with all the other treaty powers holding relations with Japan as shall be similar in effect to the present convention, and such new conventions or revisions shall also go into effect." Unfortunately no other maritime power would sign a similar treaty. In fact the United States was denounced on all sides, and its motives were subjected to grotesque misinterpretation. It was true that the United States would have suffered less than any other country if Japan were permitted to levy its own import duties. But there was no valid reason why all the powers should not have consented to this appeal of Japan for the right to establish its own fiscal system. The treaty of 1878 failed, but through no fault of the United States. It was a splendid gesture, which was denounced by those who should have imitated it. The time might not have been ripe for the relinquishment of the extraterritorial privileges, but there was no excuse, save the maintenance of a selfish advantage, for retaining the conventional tariff.

In order to remove the occasion for the extraterritorial rights of foreigners, the Government had been engaged in the compilation of a penal code based upon the best European precedents. Additions to the old penal code had been made in 1873, and about the same time a committee was appointed to compile a penal code, a code of criminal procedure, and a civil code. The first two were drafted largely with the advice of M. Boissonade, a French legal expert. They were promulgated in July,

1880, and were to come into effect on January 1, 1882. With the introduction of this Western system of criminal law the Japanese believed that they had made ample provision for the protection of the personal rights of foreign residents. So, in 1880, Count Inouye, the new Minister of Foreign Affairs, tried to secure the approval by all the foreign representatives in Tokyo of a plan which would restore judicial autonomy after the introduction of the new codes, and would raise the conventional tariff rates. A premature publication of this proposal created such opposition in Japan that the scheme was dropped for the time.

In 1882, a diplomatic conference was convened in Tokyo, over which Count Inouye again presided. The first subject to be discussed was the revision of the tariff, but on June 1st the minister presented a proposal for the eventual abolition of extraterritoriality. During a transition period of five years foreign judges were to sit in the Japanese courts to deal with criminal and civil cases involving foreigners, with some minor qualifications, and at the end of that period extraterritorial jurisdiction was to cease. Although this proposal received the endorsement of the American Minister, it failed of approval by his colleagues, and from the discussion it was evident that revision might be long delayed, until the Japanese codes and courts had been completely revised and their operation tested by time. The tariff proposal was met by a counter-proposition, which was worked out by a joint committee. It would have increased the duties to approximately ten or eleven per cent ad valorem. Nothing tangible was accomplished at this preliminary conference, but an exchange of views had taken place and the various points then considered were embodied in a memorandum of August, 1884, which became the basis of the more important conference of 1886.

After the failure of the 1882 conference, Mr. Bingham recommended that the United States make a separate treaty along the lines proposed by Japan, but, as the treaty of 1878 remained inoperative, the Washington administration realized that no good would be achieved by separate action. It did not fail, however, to express its sympathy with the desire of Japan to regain tariff autonomy and to secure treaties similar in terms and in duration to those of Western states. Although some doubt remained in the mind of the Secretary of State as to the wisdom of relinquishing extraterritoriality without an intermediate period of mixed jurisdiction, yet he believed it was possible for Japan to offer such positive and effective guarantees of impartial judicial administration as to overcome that difficulty. Japan now proposed to call a second conference at Tokyo. Mr. Richard B. Hubbard, the successor of Mr. Bingham, was instructed to attend it, and, while supporting Japan's claim for separate terminable treaties dealing with both the tariff and the judicial administration, he was told to accept any acceptable compromise which might bring about a solution of the existing *impasse*. "The chief object of the United States," wrote Mr. Bayard, the Secretary of State, "is to secure to Japan, as far as practicable, complete autonomy. The speediest and most effectual way of accomplishing this end appears to be by coöperating with the other treaty powers, at the same time taking care not to depart from our settled policy of avoiding entangling alliances." If, again, the work of revision should fail, then the United States would consider whether the desired result might be reached by independent negotiation. Mr. Hubbard entertained views very similar to Mr. Bingham's as to the justice of Japan's cause, and he was her stanch advocate in the protracted discussions which followed.

THE REVISION OF THE TREATIES

In the interval between these two diplomatic conferences, the United States had taken another step in
order to support Japan "in her efforts toward judicial
autonomy and complete sovereignty." This was in the
negotiation of an extradition treaty. Japan had, as an
act of comity, arrested and surrendered an American
fugitive from California. The American Government
recognized that this was an executive proceeding which
was in no way affected by extraterritorial jurisdiction,
and that a mutual understanding as to future cases,
incorporated in a treaty, was desirable. On the other
hand, one of the great powers maintained that it had the
right, under the extraterritorial grant, to follow and seize
her fugitive subjects within the Japanese borders. The
treaty, as proposed by the United States, was promptly
negotiated and signed on April 29, 1886, the ratifications
being exchanged at Tokyo on September 27th, while the
second diplomatic conference was in session.

In May, 1886, Count Inouye opened the deliberations,
which were attended by the ministers of the United
States and twelve of the European treaty powers. As
a basis for discussion the memorandum of 1884 was
presented. The tariff schedule drawn up in 1882 was
accepted by the Japanese Government, which meant
that a conventional tariff would continue in force, though
with higher rates than at present. But the chief discussion
turned on the question of extraterritoriality. The plan
proposed by the Japanese Minister was set aside in favor
of one drawn up by the British and German representatives. This called for a majority of foreign judges in
courts dealing with foreigners; for a majority of foreigners
on juries summoned in such cases; and for foreign public
prosecutors. Within two years, Japan was to organize
her law courts according to Western models and to carry

into effect the codification of her criminal, civil, and commercial law and procedure. At the end of three years, the consular jurisdiction was to cease, except in questions of personal status. And in return for this relinquishment of extraterritoriality, Japan was to open the whole empire within two years to foreign travel, trade, and residence, with the right to acquire and hold real and personal property. After many conferences, which were carried over into 1887, a jurisdictional convention containing some modifications of the above plan was drafted. News of its terms leaked out and aroused bitter criticism among Japanese who had hoped for a restoration of all the sovereign powers impaired by the old treaties. And the Cabinet itself was unwilling to accept such half-way measures, so, on July 29th, the conference was adjourned *sine die*. The draft convention had intimated that the new codes would have to be submitted to the approval of the foreign powers. The Cabinet preferred to complete the codes in the first instance, and then, at a later conference, submit them "as the best evidence of the sincere intention which continues to animate the Government for the assimilation of its administration and laws with the West."

Count Inouye soon afterward retired from the post of Minister of Foreign Affairs after an unequaled term of service of eight years. His successor was Count Okuma, leader of the Progressive Party. The latter's policy included a strict interpretation of the treaty rights of foreigners, on the one hand, and separate negotiations for treaty revision, on the other. He was willing to open the country to foreign trade and residence, but with fewer concessions than his predecessor had agreed to. First he turned to Mexico, a state which had little trade with Japan and no residents there. The negotiations took place in Washington, and a reciprocal and terminable treaty was signed on November 30, 1888. Mexican subjects were granted the right of travel, trade, and residence in the empire, but not the right to own land, and they were to be subject to Japanese law and jurisdiction. No tariff rates were fixed, and no tariff discriminations would be made. The "most favored nation" clause was qualified, so that neither power might claim conditional privileges accorded to a third power without making reciprocal concessions.

The United States had already expressed its readiness to negotiate separately in case the joint discussions should prove ineffective, so it now made the formal offer. On February 20, 1889, a new treaty of amity and commerce was signed by Mr. Hubbard, in Tokyo, with the full approval of the President and Secretary of State. By its terms, Japan was opened to the travel and residence of American citizens, but land might not be owned until consular jurisdiction had ceased. In the interior, American citizens were to be under Japanese jurisdiction, but the consular courts would function at the treaty ports for five years. The tariff would still be partly conventional. By a separate declaration it was agreed that foreign judges would be appointed to the supreme court, so that a majority of the court would be foreigners in cases involving American citizens. Before this treaty reached Washington, the administration had changed, and Mr. Blaine, the new Secretary of State, reserved the convention for further consideration. In the meantime similar negotiations had been inaugurated with some of the other powers. Germany signed a treaty in June, and Russia also agreed to the proposal. The publication in the London *Times*, of March 11, 1889, of an outline of the proposed British treaty, furnished the Japanese people their first information as to the nature of the new terms.

Once more public indignation was aroused at the concessions offered by Count Okuma. Within the Cabinet sharp differences of opinion arose. Finally, in October, a fanatic hurled a bomb at the Foreign Minister, with serious, though, happily, not fatal results. In the face of such popular opposition, the Cabinet resigned and the new treaties were withdrawn, with the exception of that with Mexico, which had been ratified and exchanged.

In February, 1889, the constitution was promulgated, and the next year the new law for the organization of the courts was decreed. About the same time, part of the new civil code, the code of civil procedure, and the commercial code were published. These were all subjected to further revision before they finally went into effect in 1898 and 1899. In 1890, the Imperial Diet was summoned for the first time, and its members advocated a resolute demand for the restoration of complete judicial and fiscal autonomy.

Finally, in 1893, Count Mutsu, Minister of Foreign Affairs, determined to turn in the first instance to Great Britain. That power had greater interest in the conventional tariff than any other, for it led in exports to Japan, and it also had more nationals resident there, whose position would be affected by the loss of extraterritoriality. The negotiations, also, were conducted in London, where less influence could be exerted by the merchants and residents in Japan. Under these conditions a separate treaty was negotiated in less than a year, and the signatures were affixed on July 16, 1894. This master treaty, which brought about the revision of all the old conventions, was reciprocal and terminable. The former treaties had been unilateral, in which Japan had granted concessions with few reciprocal grants. Consular jurisdiction would cease in five years, in 1899, and a conventional tariff, with duties ranging from five to fifteen per cent ad valorem, was established for certain articles, all others to be governed by a statutory tariff enacted by Japan. The coasting trade was still to be open to British ships, but foreigners were not granted the right to own land.

With Great Britain leading the way, the other treaty powers promptly followed. The second treaty was signed with the United States, on November 22, 1894, and, according to its established policy, no tariff concessions were exacted. This treaty, however, would last for at least thirteen years after 1899, instead of twelve as in the other cases. Germany and France demanded and received tariff concessions, but all the treaty powers enjoyed the privileges of the conventional tariffs under the " most favored nation " clause. The negotiation of the new treaties continued throughout four years after 1894. The success of Japan in the war with China has frequently been cited as the reason for the successful revision of the treaties at this time. This overlooks the sequence of events. The revision was effected primarily because Great Britain was at last ready to meet the desires of the Japanese. The negotiations had been successfully carried through, and the treaty had actually been signed before the war between Japan and China broke out. The amazing success of Japan in that war doubtless convinced some of the powers of the wisdom of recognizing the full status of Japan, but as a matter of fact the revision would have rapidly proceeded if there had been no war. The negotiation of the British treaty was the crucial test.

With the abolition of consular jurisdiction in 1899, Japan regained the judicial autonomy which she had lost under the old treaties. But she did not gain tariff autonomy, because she was compelled to make certain concessions to the great European commercial states. On the one hand, European nationals in Japan denounced their governments for abandoning them to the mercy of the Japanese courts, while Japanese editors berated their diplomats for yielding anything at all. But without a compromise on the tariff, judicial autonomy could not have been gained.

The effects upon Japan of this long struggle for treaty revision have never been adequately appraised. One effect was to stimulate the adoption of Western methods in order to assimilate the Government and especially the judicial administration to those of the West. But it could hardly have been an unmixed advantage to compel a people to organize its whole judicial system along foreign lines in order that the rights of a handful of alien residents might be safeguarded. Another effect was to inculcate a strong sense of the injustice and selfishness of the treaty powers. The retention of extraterritoriality by the powers struck at the pride of the Japanese, but the maintenance of the old tariffs was felt to be absolutely unjust. So, with the repeated failure of the revision negotiations, a wave of anti-foreign feeling swept over the land. And with it went the willingness to sacrifice, if need be, to make Japan strong enough in armaments to demand the restoration of rights which had been lost in days of weakness. Mr. Swift, the American Minister, who attended the army maneuvers in April, 1890, reported to his Government: "That the splendid showing of military and naval strength and discipline manifested on this occasion will tend to render His Imperial Japanese Majesty's Government firmer in their overtures for modifications of existing treaties upon points with which they have long been dissatisfied seems to me not improbable." If some Japanese developed a cynical attitude toward foreign relations in these days, there was some excuse for it. Certain of the Western powers had shown them how to make the most of every advantage, no matter how acquired. And the young men of [the late eighties and early nineties who passed through these years of bitterness became the men who in later years and to-day have had great influence on their nation's policies. It would have been better if some of the powers had thought a little more of the feelings of a whole people than of the privileges of their own merchants and residents.

Throughout this period the attitude of the United States toward Japan was [consistently friendly and sympathetic. The United States sought no special privileges in Japan and was ready at any time to relinquish those which it enjoyed under the old treaties. There is not a fairer page in the whole history of America's foreign relations than that which records its efforts to further the just claims of Japan. If all international intercourse were conducted with equal sympathy and good understanding, there would be little need of armaments. In the diplomatic conferences the American Ministers, Bingham and Hubbard, constantly advocated the "golden rule," and the treaty of 1878 and the draft of 1889 were positive evidence of their Government's views. But, unfortunately, in those days the United States had small influence in foreign affairs. Its expressions of good-will were cynically received in many quarters and misinterpreted in others. The Japanese statesmen, however, never for a moment doubted the honorable intentions and the genuine good-will of the American Government.

CHAPTER VIII

JAPAN AND HER NEIGHBORS

THE Government of the United States has always tried to maintain the most friendly relations with the peoples of eastern Asia. It has never sought for special advantages, nor has it at any time threatened the political or territorial integrity of their states. It has, furthermore, tried to act as the good friend of Eastern nations when they were involved in difficulties with other powers. In 1858, commercial treaties were negotiated almost simultaneously with both China and Japan. In the Japanese treaty, Townsend Harris inserted this clause: "The President of the United States, at the request of the Japanese Government, will act as a friendly mediator in such matters of difference as may arise between the Government of Japan and any European power." And in the treaty of Tientsin, William B. Reed wrote a similar assurance: "If any other nation should act unjustly or oppressively, the United States will exert their good offices, on being informed of the case, to bring about an amicable arrangement of the question, thus showing their friendly feelings." These statements in themselves would have meant little if the Eastern statesmen had not become convinced of the non-aggressive policy of the United States and of its desire to further the best interests of their nations. The proof of this was soon forthcoming. But, when the relations between China and Japan became strained, then the United States had to pursue a policy of scrupulous fairness lest it weaken the confidence which both powers had in its good-will. In this chapter we will consider the part played by Americans and their Government during the period of friction which led up to the war between Japan and China in 1894.

The first offer of mediation, strangely enough, came from Japan, at a time when Korea had given the United States cause for offense. In August, 1866, the American merchant ship, *General Sherman*, on a trading voyage to the west coast of Korea, was destroyed and her people were killed under circumstances which are still shrouded in mystery. Two months later, a French expedition with seven ships and four hundred soldiers tried to force their way to Seoul, to secure reparation for the execution of French missionaries, but they were repulsed. In January, 1867, an American ship of war visited Korea to ascertain the fate of the crew of the *General Sherman*, but without success. Learning of these events in the neighbor kingdom, the Grand Council of the Shogun addressed General Van Valkenburgh on May 10, 1867, as follows: "Corea being the neighbor of Japan, with which friendly relations have been maintained so long, the Tycoon feels much grieved at learning, in view of the sincere friendship subsisting between Japan and the United States, that a wrong has been perpetrated upon American citizens, and he will not fail therefore to tender friendly advice to Corea and to endeavor to induce that country, with due regard to the friendship which should govern the intercourse between neighbors, to mend its course in future." A mission would be sent to Korea for this purpose. "And if, on reflection of the wrong that has been committed and through our influence, he should sue for peace, we hope that the flag of the United States will return; that retaliation will be abandoned, and the means for friendly intercourse be found. ... We have only to add, that it is of course uncertain whether the Coreans will be dissuaded from persisting in their course. Yet it is the wish of the Tycoon that no effort should be left untried, with the object of promoting peace in this part of the world, and we further request your excellency to use your best endeavor in the same direction." Mr. Seward, in due time, instructed General Van Valkenburgh to express the thanks of the American Government for this friendly offer, and to assure the Shogun that, if no satisfactory explanation or apology were furnished by Korea, it would be necessary to consider how proper reparation might be obtained and honor satisfied.

The Japanese mission was not received by Korea, nor was a second one sent over by the Imperial Government in 1868. And again, in 1869 and 1871, the Koreans refused to have any diplomatic intercourse with Japan. This conduct aroused the anger of the military men of Japan, who believed that Korea should be punished for her haughty attitude. The King of Korea, who had ascended the throne in 1863, was a boy, under the influence of his unscrupulous father, the Tai Wen Kun. The latter was bitterly hostile to foreigners, and he looked down upon the Japanese with contempt, as traitors to the spirit of the East through their acceptance of Western ways. In 1867, another boy ascended the imperial throne of Japan. But the latter saw his empire rise from feudal impotence to strength and power, while the Korean monarch witnessed the steady decline of his kingdom until its very independence was lost.

The United States tried again, in 1868, to secure some explanation from the Koreans, and in 1871 a strong squadron was sent over, bearing Mr. F. F. Low, the American Minister to China, for the purpose of securing a treaty. During this visit, an American surveying expedition was fired upon by a Korean fort, and in retaliation five forts were destroyed. But no treaty negotiations could be undertaken, so the expedition sailed away.

In this year, the Japanese sent over a mission to negotiate a treaty with China. The mission was successful, and on July 29, 1871, a treaty was signed at Peking by Muneki Date and Li Hung-chang. This treaty is of interest, in view of later developments, because its terms were absolutely reciprocal. If either party were aggrieved by a third party the other would render assistance or exercise its good offices. The extraterritorial provision was made reciprocal, the nationals being under the joint jurisdiction of their consul and the local official at the treaty ports, and of the local authorities in the interior. And the "most favored nation" clause was not inserted. Neither power was ready to give the other the large privileges which had been exacted by the Western countries.

This treaty had scarcely been signed when two occasions for controversy arose, one over the Chinese claim to suzerainty in Korea, and the other over the possession of the Ryukyu (Loochoo) Islands. The latter dispute came to a head first.

The Ryukyu Islands, which lie between Japan and Formosa, had accepted political obligations to both Japan and China. In the twelfth century the *daimyo* of Satsuma was made lord of the twelve islands of the South Seas, but his control was lost and not regained until the early seventeenth century. From that time the islands were considered a dependency of the Satsuma fief. But in 1373, the Chinese Emperor had conferred investiture on the King of Ryukyu and annual tribute was sent up to Peking. In July, 1854, Commodore Perry had negotiated a treaty between the kingdom and the United States, and France and the Netherlands had promptly followed. With the unification of Japan, after the fall of the Shogunate and the abolition of feudalism, it was determined to bring the Ryukyu Islands within the jurisdiction of the empire. The first steps were taken in 1872, when the new King was ordered to send a member of his family to Tokyo to announce his accession and to congratulate the Emperor upon the restoration. The King was then proclaimed a noble of the realm and given a residence in Tokyo, where all the former *daimyo* resided. The American Minister, on October 20, asked if the Japanese Government would observe the terms of the compact between Ryukyu and the United States, to which an affirmative reply was given. Thus the United States did not question this positive action of Japan. But China had not been consulted in the matter, and the issue was soon raised.

In December, 1871, sixty-six natives of Ryukyu were wrecked on the southern coast of Formosa, and fifty-four of them murdered by the savages. This was reported to the Governor of Satsuma in June following, and led to the administrative measures already mentioned. In addition, the Cabinet considered the possibility of sending an expedition to punish the savages, and asked Mr. De Long for information about Formosa and about the expedition of Admiral Bell there in 1867, to investigate the massacre of the crew of the ship *Rover*. General Le Gendre, the American Consul at Amoy, had accompanied this expedition, and made two other visits to Formosa, and it happened that he was in Japan on his way home when the Japanese were considering a similar mission. On the recommendation of Mr. De Long, he was engaged by the Japanese as an adviser. This brought upon Mr. De Long the censure of his Government, for, according to the Act of August 18, 1858, diplomatic officers were prohibited from recommending any person for employment in the country in which they resided. Mr. De Long had advised the Japanese Government to use peaceful means in dealing with China, but the employment of General Le Gendre as an adviser in military operations was held by the Department of State to be inconsistent with the peaceful policy he had recommended.

Before taking any action, the Japanese decided to discuss the matter with China and ascertain exactly what responsibility China assumed for the acts of the Formosans and the Koreans. A mission under Lord Soyeshima was dispatched to Peking, presumably to exchange the ratifications of the treaty of 1871. General Le Gendre accompanied the mission as an adviser. The ratifications were promptly exchanged at Tientsin, and at Peking Lord Soyeshima took part in the final discussions of the audience question, and was the first foreign representative to be received by the Emperor of China, in the nineteenth century, without performing the objectionable kowtow. In discussion with the Chinese Foreign Ministers, the Tsung-li Yamen, he was told that in regard to Korea the internal administration and questions of peace and war were left to the local government, while the admission was made that the Formosan aborigines were beyond the reach of Chinese government and culture. The Ryukyuans, they said, were Chinese subjects, which the Japanese promptly denied.

The reply of the Chinese Ministers seemed to indicate that Japan would have a free hand to deal with Korea, so the idea of a punitive expedition was considered and agreed upon by the leaders of the Government, including Lord Sanjo, the Prime Minister, and General Takamori Saigo, the Minister of War. But the mission of Lord Iwakura was expected to return shortly from its visit to the Western powers, and so momentous a decision should not be taken without consideration of the views which he might present. In the discussions which followed his return, in September, Lord Iwakura, and Okubo, Kido, Ito, and others who had accompanied him, strongly opposed the project. They argued that Japan had many things to do before she could afford to engage in such a venture. The new Government must be firmly established, public works of many kinds introduced, commerce and industry developed, and the relations with the treaty powers improved, before a war, which would retard all these enterprises, was undertaken. The final discussion was held in the presence of the Emperor, and he decided in favor of peace rather than war. The advocates of a strong policy retired from the Government and the peace party was left in control. It was a momentous decision, and a wise one, even though it alienated some of the stoutest supporters of the restoration and brought about, eventually, the *samurai* revolt in Satsuma, in which General Saigo lost his life. But at the time bitter criticism of this weak-kneed policy arose. To quiet this, by showing that the Government was not unmindful of the honor of Japan, and to give employment to some of the more adventurous souls, the expedition to Formosa was decided upon.

Public notice of the intentions of the Government were given in a proclamation of Lord Sanjo, the Prime Minister, on April 17, 1874. It recited the murder of the fifty-four people of Ryukyu in 1871, and the looting of the property of four Japanese in March, 1873. It repeated the verbal statement of the Chinese Ministers to Lord Soyeshima, and announced: "As this island of Formosa is near to Japan, and such wrecks as described may occur again, it seems necessary for the protection of our commerce that the people inhabiting these parts of Formosa should be restrained from committing such acts in the future. And in pursuance of this determination Saigo, as chief, with a number of subordinates, has been dispatched thither, with instructions to investigate the preceding matters, and to institute such proceedings as shall guarantee safe conduct for our people in the future. As it may be possible that these people may not pay proper regard to his mission, and create a disturbance, a sufficient guard has been dispatched with him."

As thus described, the expedition was not unlike that of Commodore Perry to Japan, which, in the first instance, sought to secure good treatment of shipwrecked American seamen. But in the case of Formosa there entered at once the question of Chinese sovereignty. Would China tolerate this invasion of a part of her domain, even though she might have admitted her inability to control its savage inhabitants? Although the Japanese Government offered assurances that it had no intention of committing a hostile act against China or the Chinese subjects in Formosa, yet, if China should take steps to prevent the expedition, a clash might easily follow. For this reason, Mr. Bingham, the American Minister at Tokyo, was alarmed to learn that three American citizens had been employed to serve with the expedition and an American ship had been chartered. The Americans were General Le Gendre, who was associated with Shigenobu Okuma, the President of the Formosan Commission; Lieutenant Commander Douglas Cassel, U.S.N., who had received a leave of absence from the navy and held a temporary commission as Commodore in the Japanese service; and Lieutenant James R. Wasson, formerly of the United States Engineers, but recently in the employ of the Hokkaido colonization department, who was appointed Colonel of Engineers. Mr. Bingham at once protested against the employment of any American citizens or vessels in any expedition hostile to the Government of China, as such employment was expressly forbidden by the laws of the United States. The reply of Minister Terashima not being satisfactory, Bingham again protested, "until the written consent of China be first obtained in approval of the proposed expedition to that island"; and he requested that the steamer and the three citizens be detained until this consent was obtained. Mr. Terashima promptly replied that orders had been given to detach the steamer and the American citizens, and that Bingham's letters to the latter had been transmitted. The *New York* was held at Nagasaki, as promised, but Lieutenant Commander Cassel and Lieutenant Wasson refused to obey the instructions of Mr. Bingham, and they proceeded to Formosa with the first transport, arriving there on May 7th. General Le Gendre, whose personal acquaintance with the Formosan savages would have made his services especially valuable in the field, returned to Tokyo to take part in the diplomatic discussions there.

In acting as he did, Mr. Bingham was actuated by no ill-will for Japan. He had already won the confidence of the Japanese Foreign Office through his sympathetic support of Japan's claim to legislative autonomy. But he was also mindful of his country's duty to China, and he did not wish to appear to endorse a measure which might lead to war between the two Eastern nations. As soon as the news of the expedition reached Peking, Prince Kung promptly advised Dr. S. Wells Williams, the American Chargé, of the report that the United States had loaned one of its men-of-war to convey troops for Japan, that two of the Japanese commanders were American citizens, that General Le Gendre accompanied the expedition, and that an American steamer had been chartered to convey troops. He cited the treaty promise that the United States would use its good offices if any nation used China unjustly or oppressively, and he asked Williams to inquire into the matter, and, if the reports were correct, to see that the officers and ships were recalled. The American Consuls in China were instructed by Consul-General Seward to discourage, or, within the provisions of the law, to prevent, Americans from taking part in the expedition, and Rear-Admiral Pennock instructed the American commander at Amoy to command all American citizens to withdraw from all enterprises unfriendly to the Chinese Government, and to avoid all acts inconsistent with treaty obligations, on pain of forfeiting all claim to American protection. That war was believed imminent was clear from the steps taken by the foreign consuls at Shanghai to secure the neutralization of the settlements there. Mr. Bingham's proceedings were approved by his Government as soon as the serious possibilities of the expedition were realized.

General Yorimichi Saigo, with the main body of troops, which finally numbered 3600 men, landed in Formosa on May 22d. Several engagements with the savages took place, and the operations were conducted with great difficulty because of the wild nature of the country. Informal negotiations took place with Chinese representatives sent over from Amoy, but, as they demanded that the Japanese withdraw and offered no satisfactory guarantees, no agreement could be reached. In July, General Le Gendre was sent on a mission to Amoy to discuss the matter with the Viceroy. He was arrested there, by the American Consul, and sent to Shanghai, where he was released, as he could not be successfully prosecuted under the American Act of 1860. Lieutenant Commander Cassel's leave of absence was now revoked, but by the time the order reached him, the expedition was over. General Le Gendre promptly started north and joined Mr. Okubo, who had been sent over to negotiate with China.

The negotiations lasted from September 14th until October 30th. Twice the British Minister, Mr. Wade, used his good offices to bring about an agreement. Okubo proposed that an indemnity of 3,000,000 yen be paid before the Japanese evacuated the island. This the Chinese refused to do, although they were willing to pay an unspecified amount as a gift to the families of the murdered seamen. The negotiations were on the point of breaking up, which would have meant war, when the Chinese finally agreed to admit that the Japanese were justified in sending over the punitive expedition, and to pay 100,000 taels for the families of the injured people, and 400,000 taels for the roads and buildings constructed by the Japanese in Formosa. Such a treaty was signed on October 31, 1874, and it provided also that all the documents exchanged should be returned and destroyed, so as to leave no ground for contention in the future, while China agreed to control the Formosan savages henceforth.

Although this convention recognized the status of the Ryukyuans as Japanese subjects, the Chinese Government did not accept all its implications. The Japanese proceeded to incorporate the islands more completely in the realm, sending down a garrison in 1875 and ordering the King to cease the payment of tribute to China. The next year a court was established there, in spite of the protests of the Ryukyu officials. In 1878, two commissioners from Ryukyu asked the ministers of the United States and other treaty powers at Tokyo to request their countries to exhort Japan to allow Ryukyu "to remain in every respect as before." And the first legation estab-

JAPAN AND HER NEIGHBORS

lished by China in Tokyo sent a similar memorial to Mr.
Bingham, the same year, based upon the promise of the
United States to use its good offices. The United States
Government assured both powers of its readiness to
extend its good offices for the maintenance of peace, if
they should deem it desirable. But, as we have already
seen, by mutual consent the matter was left to the
consideration of ex-President Grant, who visited China
and Japan in 1879. His unofficial and personal advice
was that China accept the Japanese contention in the
matter, and he suggested that high commissioners be
appointed to adjust the difficulties by treaty. Mr.
Shishido, the Japanese Minister at Peking, was appointed
a high commissioner to negotiate such a treaty in the
summer of 1880, and after three months' effort a draft
was agreed upon. But the signature was delayed, and
finally the matter was again referred to the Chinese
Superintendents of Trade for consideration and report.
After waiting three months after the completion of the
treaty, Mr. Shishido decided to retire from Peking, and
this attempt to settle the matter came to an end. Later,
in 1881, China sent a minister to Japan to discuss the
subject, and the next year both governments desired
the good offices of the United States, but nothing was
accomplished, and the pressure of other foreign complications caused China to recognize tacitly the *status quo*.

Between 1874 and 1882, the relations between Japan
and China were involved through the Ryukyu controversy and the Formosan expedition which grew out of it.
In these years, also, a more serious dispute began to
develop concerning Korea, which finally brought the two
countries to blows. The cabinet crisis of 1873 over the
Korean problem has already been mentioned. In 1875,
a party of Japanese seamen, engaged in surveying the

coast, were fired upon, and in retaliation the fort was bombarded and its armament destroyed. This revived the old demand for war upon Korea. But the advocates of a policy of peace were still in control in Tokyo, and they decided to dispatch a high commission to negotiate, if possible, a treaty of peace and amity. Two foreign precedents were followed by the Japanese. One was that of the Perry mission to Japan, for General Kuroda, the High Commissioner, was accompanied by two men-of-war and four transports bearing several thousand men. The other was that of the French treaty with Annam, in 1874. Annam, like Korea, was a vassal state of China, recognizing this fact by the acceptance of investiture of the sovereign from the Chinese Emperor, and by the payment of tribute every four years. By the treaty of 1874, France recognized the entire independence of Annam and granted the King protection against foreign aggression and internal disorder. In accepting this treaty, Annam seemed to dissolve her old relations with China, although she had no intention of doing so. The Japanese, therefore, inserted such a clause in their treaty: "Korea, being an independent state, enjoys the same sovereign rights as Japan." The Koreans, however, had no desire to accept the full implication of this declaration. And China refused to consider either treaty as breaking the old bonds of dependency on the part of the two neighbor states.

The Korean treaty of 1876 was modeled on the commercial treaties which Japan had negotiated with the Western powers. The Japanese in Korea were to enjoy extraterritoriality in criminal matters, but this right was not granted Koreans in Japan. During the course of these negotiations, Mr. Mori informed Li Hung-chang, at Tientsin, that Japan was not sending a punitive expedition to Korea, but one designed to open the country to foreign intercourse and to secure a commercial treaty. Although Li maintained that Korea was a tributary state of China, he made no objection to a mission with such pacific objects. So the agitation for the conquest of Korea, which had disturbed Japanese politics for the past three years, ended in the peaceful opening of the country, exactly as the United States had opened Japan twenty-four years before. But there were many *samurai* who felt keenly that the Government had acted weakly in the matter.

The negotiation of a commercial treaty by Japan revived American interest in Korea. In 1878, Commodore Robert W. Shufeldt, who had commanded the vessel sent over to investigate in 1867, was instructed to visit Korea to reopen by peaceful measures negotiations with that Government. The State Department directed Mr. Bingham to apply to the Japanese Minister for Foreign Affairs for letters to the Korean authorities which would facilitate Shufeldt's mission. Count Inouye was unwilling to give such letters, "on the ground that it might produce complications in the execution of the Japanese treaty, and that it appeared that the Koreans were still disinclined to open their country to Occidental nations." He did give Commodore Shufeldt a letter of introduction to the Japanese Consul at Fusan. But when the Commodore visited that port in May, 1880, the Korean Governor refused to forward a letter to the King, stating that the Japanese were the only foreigners with whom he could hold intercourse. Returning to Japan, he persuaded Inouye to forward the letter under cover of a dispatch of his own, but this was again rejected by the Koreans, partly because of an error in form, and, furthermore, because Korea had never had intercourse with other foreign nations.

JAPAN AND THE UNITED STATES

While Shufeldt was trying to deal with Korea through the good offices of Japan, Li Hung-chang learned of his mission and invited him to visit Tientsin. Here an interview took place on August 26th, in which Li promised to use his influence with the Government of Korea to accede to the request of the United States for a friendly treaty. As the relations between China and Russia were on the breaking point, over the Kuldja affair, it is possible, of course, that Li was anxious to win the goodwill of the United States in this crisis. Commodore Shufeldt now returned to the United States, as the term allotted for his cruise had expired. But the next year he was sent to China again on a secret mission, and he was granted permission to aid in the reorganizing of the Chinese navy if requested.

His first interview with Li was held on July 1, 1881, but now the Viceroy was less interested in the Korean treaty, perhaps, as Shufeldt thought, because China had settled her dispute with Russia. Li said that he had addressed the Korean Government on the subject, but no reply had been received, so the Commodore waited for months to hear from Korea. Finally, in December, when he was on the point of leaving China in disgust, a representative of Li informed him that Korea was now ready to negotiate with the United States. In the meantime Commodore Shufeldt had been appointed a special envoy to negotiate such a treaty. For some months the discussion with Li was delayed, but finally it began in Tientsin on March 25th. The treaty between the United States and Korea was to be negotiated in China, and the Koreans would accept whatever China advised. The only difference of opinion between Li and Shufeldt arose over the first clause of the treaty. Li desired to insert the statement: "Korea, being a dependent state of the Chinese Empire, has nevertheless heretofore exercised her own sovereignty in all matters of internal administration and foreign relations." Such a statement Commodore Shufeldt could not accept, and finally the American envoy carried his point. In May, Commodore Shufeldt proceeded to Chemulpo in an American ship-of-war, accompanied by three Chinese naval vessels and a representative of the Chinese Government. No negotiations were necessary in Korea, and, after the usual formalities, the treaty as agreed upon at Tientsin was, with a single modification, signed on May 22, 1882. The United States was, therefore, the first Western power to secure a treaty of friendship and commerce with Korea. The Japanese Minister at Seoul, Mr. Hanabusa, was prepared to use his good offices, but the rapid completion of the negotiations rendered them unnecessary. After the signature of the treaty, the King forwarded a letter to President Arthur which stated that "Korea is a dependency of China, but the management of her governmental affairs, home and foreign, has always been vested in the sovereign." This was an anomalous position which could not be accepted in international intercourse.

In this treaty Commodore Shufeldt inserted a clause very similar to that found in the American treaties with China and Japan. "If other powers deal unjustly or oppressively with either government, the other will exert their good offices, on being informed of the case, to bring about an amicable arrangement, thus showing their friendly feeling." In later years the Koreans attached great importance to this promise of American good-will.

Within a few months of the signing of the American treaty came the first attack upon the Japanese in Korea, on July 23, 1882, resulting in the expulsion of the legation and the loss of several Japanese lives. Again the question

149

of peace or war had to be decided, and again the Emperor decided in favor of peace. Hanabusa was sent back to Japan, with strong support, to secure reparation. Chinese ships and men were also sent over, and, just as negotiations were on the point of breaking, the Koreans decided to sign a convention, promising to punish the guilty men, to pay 550,000 yen as an indemnity, and to make additional commercial concessions.

In May, 1883, General Lucius Foote exchanged the ratified American treaty, and took up his residence as Minister at Seoul. This prompt inauguration of American official intercourse was considered by Japan as an act of friendship not only to Korea, but to Japan.

The following year came the second attack upon the Japanese legation, and this time Chinese troops were involved. This brought to a head the question of China's right to interfere in Korea. At this time, China was involved with France over the Annam controversy, and there was a possibility that war with both France and Japan might ensue, in which case Japan could furnish the troops and France the ships. But the Japanese Government had no such intention. The Chinese Minister at Tokyo had promptly asked Mr. Bingham to use his good offices to "smooth over" the difficulty with Japan, and the American Minister promptly acted. Count Inouye assured him that Japan would endeavor to settle all the questions with China in an amicable and friendly spirit. Inouye was sent to negotiate with Korea, and Ito went over to Tientsin in February, 1885, to deal with Li Hung-chang. On the day before he sailed, he called upon Mr. Bingham, and the latter urged that war should be avoided and that a peaceful settlement might be reached if both China and Japan would agree to withdraw their military forces from Korea and to recognize the rightful and exclusive autonomy of Korea within its territorial limits. "Mr. Ito, it gives me pleasure to say, concurred in the views thus expressed by me, and indicated a purpose to seek a settlement with China on that basis."

And such was the ultimate arrangement. China expressed regret for the conduct of her troops in Seoul, both countries agreed to withdraw their forces, and not to send others in to preserve order without notifying the other nation. Although China would not recognize the independence of Korea (despite the fact that she had just been compelled to recognize the French protectorate over Annam), she was compelled to admit that Japan stood on an equal footing with her in that country. In these discussions Ito pointed out that Japan could not see Korea remain under foreign influence. "Why should China," he argued, "with an immense territory covet a far distant country such as Korea at the danger of disturbing the friendship between the brother empires of the Far East?" But the interference continued until war resulted, and, just ten years after Ito reasoned with Li at Tientsin, the great Viceroy, humbled by defeat, had to acknowledge what he had refused to admit in the day of his power.

Between 1885 and 1894, China continued to assert her superior position in Seoul, where Yuan Shih-kai resided as Chinese Commissioner. The events which followed may be rapidly summarized. In March, 1894, a rebellion of members of the Tong Hak sect broke out. They were anti-government, and to some extent anti-foreign. The impotent Korean Government seemed unable to suppress this rebellion. Yuan Shih-kai urged Li Hung-chang to send over Chinese troops, but the latter did so only after a direct appeal from the Korean King was received in June, and on doing so he promptly notified Japan. The

Japanese Government, in turn, had prepared to send over troops as well. When the Chinese notification was presented at Tokyo, the statement was used that the troops were being sent "in order to restore the peace of our tributary state." That was an assertion which could not be acquiesced in by Japan, and on it hinged all the subsequent controversy. Before either body of troops arrived, the rebellion had been suppressed by Korean soldiers, and the government was now even more alarmed at the presence of both Chinese and Japanese troops on its soil. The King first asked the Chinese to leave, but they refused to go until the Japanese did so. By the middle of June, the situation was most tense. Japan took the position that the rebellion had been due to official corruption and oppression, and she decided to ask China to join her in inaugurating radical reforms which would guarantee peace in the future. The Chinese Minister in Tokyo replied that even China would not interfere in the internal affairs of Korea, and surely Japan, who had recognized the independence of Korea, could hardly assert such a right. Japan now decided to bring about the needed reforms without the coöperation of China.

The representatives of the United States, in Seoul, Tokyo, and Peking, were keenly interested in these developments, as were, of course, all the foreign diplomatic agents. On June 22d, Mr. Sill, at Seoul, was instructed to use his good offices to preserve peace. Two days later the Korean Minister of Foreign Affairs appealed to the diplomatic corps begging them to use their good offices, especially in securing the withdrawal of the Japanese troops. They promptly signed a joint note addressed to both the Chinese and Japanese representatives. The latter referred the matter to his Government, and no definite reply seems to have been given. The former was instructed to reply that as Japan refused to withdraw her troops, the Chinese forces would remain. The Korean King now asked for protection in the American legation if it should prove necessary, and this was offered the royal family and certain high officials. Early in July, the Chinese asked the good offices of England and Russia, and, on the 7th, Viceroy Li asked the United States to take the lead in urging Japan to withdraw her troops. On July 5th, the Korean Minister in Washington requested the President to use his good offices. He was told that the United States would not intervene forcibly. Mr. Gresham, the Secretary of State, discussed the situation with the Japanese Minister and said that it would be very gratifying to the United States "if Japan would deal kindly and fairly with her feeble neighbor, whose helplessness enlisted our sympathy." He was assured that Japan did not covet any Korean territory and that her demands were in the interest of peace. Mr. Dun, at Tokyo, had been instructed to inquire the reason for sending Japanese troops to Korea and what demands were expected to be enforced thereby, and the Japanese reply indicated that the question at issue was that of instituting needed reforms. On July 8th, the British Ambassador requested the United States to join with Great Britain in a friendly intervention to avert war, but the American Government could not join another power even in such a cause. In the meantime further dispatches from Tokyo had given assurance to Washington, so when the Chinese Minister, on the 13th, asked that the American Minister at Tokyo join his colleagues in an effort to induce Japan to abandon her hostile purpose, he was told that the United States had already made a strong but friendly representation to Japan, and that it could not unite with other powers in any kind of intervention. The course was open to China to offer to settle the controversy by friendly arbitration.

It is interesting to note how the views of the three American representatives were influenced by their environment. Mr. Denby, Chargé at Peking, reported, on June 26th, that "the action of Japan is criticized here as hasty and unduly bellicose." Mr. Sill wrote, on the 29th, from Seoul: "I may add that Japan seems to be very kindly disposed toward Korea. She seems only to desire, once for all, to throw off the yoke of Chinese suzerainty, and then to assist her weak neighbor in strengthening her position as an independent state, by aiding her in such reforms as shall bring peace, prosperity, and enlightenment to her people, a motive which pleases many Korean officials of the more intelligent sort, and one which I imagine may not meet with disapproval in America." And Mr. Dun, at Tokyo, accepted the sincerity of Japan's motives.

After the *coup d'état*, on July 23d, when Japanese troops took possession of the palace, the King summoned the foreign representatives and described his situation. All that they could do was to attempt to cable the facts to their governments. Events now moved rapidly. Under Japanese pressure, Korea abrogated her treaty with China and requested the Japanese troops to expel the Chinese forces. And, on July 25th, a naval engagement occurred, and the Chinese transport *Kowshing* was sunk. China declared war on July 31st and Japan on August 1st.

Then occurred an incident which testified as nothing else had done to the regard in which the United States was held by both the great empires of eastern Asia. Both China and Japan requested that the representatives of the United States take charge of the archives and protect the interests of their nationals in the enemy country.

"This service entailed a considerable amount of labor of a delicate and sometimes embarrassing character, but it was discharged cheerfully, gratuitously, and to the satisfaction of the two interested countries."

The success of the Japanese arms was entirely unexpected by many of the Europeans in the Far East. They had overestimated the strength of China and failed to appreciate the progress which Japan had made. By the middle of September, the Chinese troops had been expelled from Korea, and their fleet defeated at the Yalu. In October, the British Government asked the United States to join with it, Germany, France, and Russia, in intervening between China and Japan, on the understanding that the independence of Korea should be guaranteed by the powers and that Japan should receive an indemnity for the expense of the war. This the President refused to do. The British Government then made it clear that only diplomatic action was contemplated. England alone then approached Japan, and, on October 25th, Japan rejected the offer. On November 2d, the Tsung-li Yamen made a special request to the President to intervene, basing the action upon the promise in the treaty of 1858. And, on the 3d, they asked the ministers of the United States, England, France, Germany, and Russia to request their Governments to act, offering to recognize the independence of Korea and to pay an indemnity, to be decided jointly by the foreign powers. Before these dispatches arrived, the President had assured both belligerents that he was ready to tender his good offices if they would be acceptable. And he would act jointly with other powers in determining the amount of the indemnity if Japan consented. This offer by the President of his sole mediation proved embarrassing to the Tsung-li Yamen, for, after requesting it, they had turned to the European powers, including Italy. However, they were relieved from their difficulty, for, on November 17th, Japan declined to accept the President's offer, preferring to have China approach her directly on the subject of peace. The American Minister at Peking was designated as the medium through whom the Chinese advances might be made.

Then followed the visit to Japan of Mr. Detring, Commissioner of Customs at Tientsin, on November 26th, as a special commissioner from Li Hung-chang. As he was not properly accredited, he was not received. The second attempt, in February, failed also because the Chinese commissioners did not possess full powers. Finally, in March, Li Hung-chang took upon himself the bitter task of suing for peace. On the 17th of April, 1895, the Treaty of Shimonoseki was signed, in the negotiation of which each commission employed an American as an adviser, Mr. John W. Foster being attached to the Chinese, and Mr. H. W. Denison to the Japanese mission.

After the conclusion of peace, the Emperor addressed a personal letter to the President of the United States. It might well be quoted here:

"GREAT AND GOOD FRIEND: During the war between our Empire and that of China, which has now happily been brought to an end by the conclusion of a treaty of peace, the diplomatic and consular officers of the United States in China, with Your Excellency's gracious permission and acting under Your Excellency's wise direction, extended their friendly offices to our subjects in China and on many occasions afforded them succor and assistance.

"Again, as the war was nearing its final stage, the representatives of the United States at Tokyo and

Peking, by Your Excellency's authorization, provided the way whereby China was able to approach directly our Government, and it was through the facilities afforded by those two representatives by direct reciprocal communication between the Governments of Japan and China that all the preliminaries looking to the opening of negotiations for the definite termination of hostilities were adjusted. The manner in which those delicate services in the interest of peace were performed left nothing to be desired.

"And we take this opportunity to express to Your Excellency our high appreciation of those acts on the part of Your Excellency as well as on the part of Your Excellency's officers, acting under Your Excellency's wise directions, which not only tended to mitigate the severities and hardships of the war and finally to promote the successful issue of the negotiations for peace, but served to draw still closer the bonds of friendship and good neighborhood which happily unite our two countries."

CHAPTER IX

THE OPEN DOOR IN CHINA

In the war with China, the Japanese forces had been uniformly successful on sea and land. China had not only been defeated; she had been humbled, and not by a Western power, as in the past, but by an Eastern power upon whom she had been accustomed to look down in contempt. The incompetence and corruption shown during the war destroyed the last vestige of respect for the Manchu Government which either Europeans or Japanese might have had. It was true that Japan came into contact only with a fringe of the empire, that only a few of the northern coast provinces took any part in the operations; but it was also true that China was unable to make use of her great resources of men and materials. Her inefficiency and lack of national pride rendered her powerless in the presence of a highly organized people like the Japanese.

So at Shimonoseki, Marquis Ito and Count Mutsu practically dictated the terms of peace to Li Hung-chang, although the attempt to assassinate Li, by a Japanese fanatic, caused some mitigation in the terms. The treaty called for the recognition by China of the independence of Korea, the cession of the Liaotung Peninsula, Formosa, and the Pescadores Islands, the payment of an indemnity of 200,000,000 taels, and the negotiation later of a satisfactory treaty of commerce. The compact was signed on April 17th, but before that day Russia had taken steps to bring about a three-power intervention to rob Japan of one of the fruits of victory. Germany and France joined with her, and on April 23d, their ministers at Tokyo presented identic notes advising Japan to restore the Liaotung Peninsula, as "the Japanese occupation of that territory not only endangered the existence of the Chinese capital and of Korean independence, but would upset the peace of the Orient." Count Witte, the Russian Minister of Finance, had assumed responsibility for this intervention, in order that the presence of Japan might not interfere with his plans for the Russian penetration of Manchuria. For ten days the Cabinet considered this unexpected situation, while the diplomats tried to ascertain if Russia really meant to fight, and, if so, if Great Britain might be relied upon for any support. Then, when the hopelessness of opposing the three powers was evident, for Russia had greatly strengthened her naval forces in the Pacific, Japan agreed to give up Liaotung, on May 3d. In November, by a separate agreement, China agreed to pay an additional indemnity of 30,000,000 taels. Sixteen years before, General Grant had warned the Emperor of Japan that if war occurred over Korea the European powers would end it "in their own way, in their own interests, and to the lasting and incalculable injury of both nations," and the events had confirmed his prediction.

In spite of the bitterness caused by the three-power intervention, Japan emerged from the war with enhanced prestige and with a large indemnity. The successful revision of the foreign treaties, which had been going on since 1894, meant that in 1899 she would regain the judicial autonomy which she had yielded up in 1858. Japan had been admitted to the family of nations, but her experience in the past had convinced her that "eternal vigilance was the price of peace." In the world as she knew it, right and justice seemed to be measured in terms of battleships and army corps.

As has been so often the case, the war between China and Japan settled one problem, but gave birth to others far more serious. China had been compelled to recognize the independence of Korea, but in her place a far more aggressive power appeared to challenge Japan's influence in the peninsula. Between 1895 and 1904, Russia became increasingly powerful in Korea, until Japan was compelled to fight a second war to prevent that strategic territory passing under hostile control. Korea continued to be a storm center of Japanese diplomacy, as it had been ever since 1869.

And, on the other hand, it was bad enough for China to be defeated by the neighbor people whom she liked to call "dwarfs," to have to cede territory and accept a burden of debt, but in addition she had given the three European allies what was practically a signed note with the amount unspecified. Nobody imagined, for a moment, that Russia, Germany, and France had incurred the ill-will of Japan because of an altruistic interest in the welfare of China. The old Middle Kingdom would have to pay, and pay liberally, for the European intervention in 1895. Up to that time, Great Britain had been the dominant influence in Peking, but now Russia, supported by her allies, took the lead.

This was evident when Russia and France forced China to borrow money for the first indemnity payments from them instead of from British bankers. The first loan, of 400,000,000 francs, was borrowed from a group of Russian and French banks and guaranteed by the Russian Government. Two later loans, however, were made through British and German banks, amounting to £32,000,000. Russia was also interested in securing the right to build her Trans-Siberian Railway across Manchuria to Vladivostock. This concession was apparently

THE OPEN DOOR IN CHINA

gained by November, 1895. About this time, Li Hung-chang, whose policy was now one of dependence upon Russia, negotiated a convention with Count Cassini, at Peking, which covered the railway rights in detail, and when he was in St. Petersburg, in July, he signed a convention of alliance with Prince Lobanoff, which, among other articles, provided for the lease to Russia of the harbor of Kiaochow, for a term of fifteen years. Russia's influence was supreme, and Witte's plans for the peaceful penetration of Manchuria seemed to be accepted by both countries.

Germany, however, had no intention of standing by with empty hands. She knew exactly what she wanted, and she set about to obtain it. Ever since the intervention, in 1895, she had been considering which port along the coast would best serve her purposes as a naval base and trade center. Her warships had surveyed the coast from Fukien to Shantung, where Kiaochow had been described by Baron von Richthofen as the finest port in North China. Count Witte tells us that in 1896 the Kaiser had personally secured the promise of the Czar not to oppose the German occupation of this harbor. If this was the case, then the Czar had yielded, in ignorance, what Lobanoff had secured for Russia herself. It is probable that Germany could have secured this concession directly, for China was in no position to oppose her, especially if Germany were supported by Russia. But instead Germany preferred to take advantage of a missionary outrage to support her demand. For this act she will ever be denounced. On the 1st of November, 1897, two German missionaries were murdered in a little village in the Tsaochow prefecture in Shantung. There is no agreement among authorities as to the exact nature of the crime or the reason for it, and the local officials seem to have acted promptly in investigating the matter. The crime occurred in the southwestern part of the province, far away from the coast, but soon after news reached the German representatives, a small fleet entered the Bay of Kiaochow, landed an armed party to occupy the Chinese forts, and held the port pending a diplomatic settlement of the dispute. The German demands were presented on November 22d. They contained items which were usually associated with missionary reparation — an imperial tablet to be erected to the memory of the murdered priests; an indemnity; the punishment of the Governor; and repayment of the expenses incurred at Kiaochow. But, in addition, Germany demanded a lease of the harbor, and the sole right to construct railways and open coal-mines in Shantung Province. For a time China tried to refuse the last three demands, but Germany stood firm, and dispatched reënforcements under Prince Henry of Prussia. No European power would come to the aid of China in this crisis, and America failed to realize the issue involved. So China gradually yielded. To save her face, the reparation for the missionary murders was first provided for, and this convention has never been published. Then, on March 6, 1898, a second convention dealt with the lease-hold and the railway and mining rights. This states that "the Imperial Chinese Government consider it advisable to give a special proof of their grateful appreciation of the friendship shown to them by Germany," and the two Governments, therefore, "inspired by the equal and mutual wish to strengthen the bonds of friendship which unite the two countries, and to develop the economic and commercial relations between the subjects of the two states, have concluded the following separate convention." Germany was given a lease of both sides of the entrance of the Bay of Kiaochow for ninety-nine years, and a neutral zone, fifty kilometers wide, was created around its shores. She was given the right to construct two railways and to develop mining properties within thirty *li* from each side of them, and German manufacturers and merchants were to be first approached whenever China desired foreign assistance, in persons, capital, or materials, for any purpose whatever in the Province of Shantung.

This was the beginning of the vicious circle of demands upon China. The Russian fleet had entered Port Arthur soon after the Germans occupied Kiaochow, and on March 3d a request was made for the lease of Port Arthur, Dalny, and the lower part of the Liaotung Peninsula. Such a lease, for twenty-five years, was signed on March 27th. The effect of this proceeding upon Japan can easily be imagined. Within three years after Russia had taken the lead in forcing her to give up a fortress which her troops had taken in war, on the ground that her occupation of it would endanger Peking and the independence of Korea, Russia herself had moved in. The Japanese Government had no illusions. The Russian peril must be met, and six years of feverish preparation followed.

During these weeks China, ever trying to play off one power against another, had offered to lease Weihaiwei to Great Britain. At first the British Government was not disposed to consider this favorably, but after Russia leased Port Arthur it instructed its minister at Peking to obtain a lease on the terms on which Russia held Port Arthur. China agreed to this on April 2d. But at this time Weihaiwei, which had been captured during the late war, was occupied by the Japanese pending the payment of the indemnity. Japan approved of the proposed lease. The final payment was made on May 9th, and the Japanese promptly evacuated the city. On the 24th, the British flag was raised, although the convention was not signed until July 1st.

France, naturally, had watched the proceedings of her allies with deep interest. She, in turn, demanded the Bay of Kwangchow, in Kwangtung Province, and a lease for ninety-nine years was signed on April 10th, but not ratified by China until January 5, 1900. This cession caused Great Britain to demand compensation, which took the form of a ninety-nine-year lease of Kowloon Peninsula, opposite the British island of Hongkong, which was signed on June 9th. China had been powerless to resist the great European powers; she did feel strong enough, however, to refuse a demand by Italy of Sanmen Bay, in Chekiang.

In addition to securing these leaseholds, the powers had marked out for themselves certain spheres of interest or influence in China. France led the way, and secured the promise, on March 15, 1897, that China would not alienate or cede the island of Hainan to any other foreign power, either as a final or a temporary cession. Great Britain followed, while the German demand for Kiaochow was being pressed, and on February 11, 1898, was assured that China would never alienate any territory adjoining the Yangtze River to any other power. On April 10th, France secured a similar promise as to the provinces bordering Tongking, namely, Kwangtung, Kwangsi, and Yunnan. And on April 26th, China assured Japan that she would never alienate any part of Fukien to any power. So far these assurances had been of a negative nature. China had agreed not to cede territory, but she had not promised to grant any special privileges to the power requesting the assurance. But the promises were interpreted by Western publicists to mean that the various powers had created spheres of influence in the regions specified. Germany, of course, already had Shantung as her sphere, and Russia was left in control of the region beyond the Great Wall. This understanding was supported by agreements between the interested powers. In September, 1898, Great Britain and Germany agreed not to encroach upon each other's sphere in railway building, and a similar agreement was entered upon by Great Britain and Russia on April 28, 1899. These were the days when the "break-up of China" was considered as a matter of course, and the Great Powers had ear-marked the regions which they expected to claim when the partition occurred. Japan, whose military successes had brought about the collapse of Chinese resistance, took little part in these aggressive moves. Next to China herself, she had more at stake than any other power in this threatened European control of her ancient neighbor. But she took no part in the scramble for concessions, except to protect herself from European control of Fukien Province, opposite Formosa. And the United States also stood aloof. A few Americans realized what was going on in China, but the interests of both government and people were centered in another part of the world.

The year which witnessed the European aggressions upon China and the threatened dissolution of the empire saw an even more amazing phenomenon — the United States, without premeditation or warning, suddenly became an Asiatic power. The cause of this surprising development arose in Cuba, where a rebellion against Spain had been in progress since 1895. The harsh measures of reprisal adopted by the Spanish administration had aroused American sympathy for the cause of the insurgents, and this was stimulated by the unfortunate destruction of the battleship *Maine* in the harbor of Havana on February 15, 1898. Finally, on the 20th of April, the American Congress resolved "that the people of Cuba are and of right ought to be free and independent," and that it was the duty of the United States to demand the withdrawal of Spain from the island. Before an ultimatum could be presented, the Spaniards had broken off diplomatic relations and war was declared.

Up to this point, the United States had been solely interested in Cuba, but in the Far East the Spaniards possessed a rich colonial empire in the Philippine Islands. There an insurrection had been carried on between 1896 and 1898, and, when the United States seemed about to take up arms in defense of the Cubans, the Filipino leaders hoped that the American Republic would realize their aspirations also. Commodore Dewey, with the Asiatic squadron, was at Hongkong. He received orders to proceed at once to the Philippine Islands and capture or destroy the Spanish fleet. On the 1st of May, he entered the harbor of Manila and accomplished his purpose thoroughly. This raised the question — Should Dewey be recalled or should he be supported, and an expeditionary force sent out to take the city of Manila and expel the Spaniards? This was a momentous decision in its results. Soon a force was assembled at San Francisco, and the first soldiers entered the harbor on June 30th. In the meantime Admiral Dewey had been placed in a difficult situation by Admiral Dietrichs, who had brought down a formidable German squadron from Kiaochow.

With the coöperation of the Filipino insurgents, under General Aguinaldo, Manila was soon completely invested, and, on August 13th, the city surrendered to the American commander. The day before (but actually on the morning of the same day) a protocol had been signed in Washington under which the city and harbor of Manila were to be surrendered pending the conclusion of a treaty of peace. The commissioners met at Paris in October, and on the 10th of December the treaty was signed. Under its terms the Philippine Islands were ceded to the United States and $20,000,000 were to be paid to Spain, nominally for the debt incurred for pacific improvements in the islands. This brief summary of events does not adequately indicate the uncertainty which prevailed in the United States as to its proper course in dealing with the archipelago. In May, perhaps not one person in a thousand had ever heard of the islands, and certainly few dreamed of extending American rule far overseas. In the protocol, of August, the disposition of the archipelago was left to future discussion. In September, the instructions given the American peace commissioners called for the cession of Luzon, but the commissioners themselves were not in agreement, and they cabled for additional instructions. On October 26th, President McKinley instructed them to demand the whole archipelago, and he indicated that he had come to this conclusion because of the interests of the Filipino people, "for whose welfare we cannot escape responsibility." This was the reason which appealed most strongly to the American people. Many believed in the commercial advantages which would follow the occupation of these rich islands off the coast of Asia, but the average citizen looked upon the annexation as the acceptance of a responsibility which would eventually cease when the Filipino peoples were prepared to look after their own interests.

The uncertainty which prevailed in Washington, between the 1st of May and the ratification of the treaty on the 6th of February following, had a serious effect in the islands. For a time it looked as if the treaty would fail in the Senate, and a change of two votes would have defeated it. So the commander of the American forces was unable to follow a well-defined policy in dealing with the insurgents, who, naturally enough, believed that the United States would confer upon them the freedom which it had won for the Cubans. Thus, the Filipino leaders were able to organize a revolutionary government, preparatory to taking over the administration of the islands. When it was evident that the United States had determined to take possession of the territory, friction increased between the Filipinos and the Americans, and open warfare broke out on February 5th. The United States acquired the islands from Spain, but it also took over a serious insurrection, which, started against Spain, was now turned against the American conquerors.

During the Spanish-American War, most of the European powers were more friendly to Spain than to the United States. Great Britain was the striking exception, and in the Far East Japan was also friendly. Ever since 1894, certain of the Filipino leaders had been trying to secure Japanese support or recognition in their struggle against Spain, so some of the Japanese officials, including Marquis Ito, were familiar with conditions in the islands. But Japanese interests were small, and only a few hundred resided there. Although at the present time Japan would probably resent the appearance of a strong foreign power so near her shores, in 1898 she had no distrust of the United States. And when the first Philippine Commission passed through Japan in February, 1899, Marquis Ito offered to go to the islands, in a private capacity, and use his influence to remove the misunderstandings which had arisen between the Americans and the Filipinos. "He said that Americans did not understand Asiatics, but he was an Asiatic himself and did understand the Filipinos, and thought that he could settle the whole affair." This offer was not accepted, for a distinguished commission had been sent to the islands to investigate conditions and report to the President.

The annexation of the Philippines gave the United States a stake in Asiatic affairs. It awakened an interest in the Far East which had been slight before. America took a new and broader interest in foreign affairs, and her success in the late war won for her the respectful attention of the European powers. This was promptly manifested in a constructive policy which she proposed in China.

During the war the Hawaiian Islands were annexed to the United States by joint resolution of Congress of July 7, 1898. This was preceded by a treaty between the Republic of Hawaii and the United States of June 16, 1897. The Japanese Government protested against the treaty of annexation primarily because it would tend to endanger the rights of Japanese subjects in Hawaii, for they made up by far the largest national group there. Assurances were given that Japanese treaty rights and pending claims would not be affected by the annexation, and the protest was not pressed. The annexation by joint resolution followed, as there was some doubt as to the ratification of the treaty by two thirds of the Senate.

The United States had taken no part in the scramble for concessions in China in 1898. Her interests were occupied in the Cuban insurrection and in the Spanish War which followed. But the creation of foreign lease-holds and spheres of influence — with all that they might imply — was at variance with American policy in the Far East, which had always stood for equality of opportunity. In 1899, John Hay, the Secretary of State, discussed the matter with Mr. W. W. Rockhill, a distinguished American diplomat, and the latter presented his views in a memorandum on August 28th. He pointed out that the commercial interests of all the powers favored the "Open Door" or equality of treatment and opportunity for all comers. But the political interests and geographical relations of Great Britain, Russia, and France had forced them to divide China up into spheres of interest, in which they enjoyed special rights and privileges. These spheres of interest, he believed, must be accepted as existing facts. He then outlined the policy which, promptly accepted by Mr. Hay, became the famous "Open-Door policy" in China. Mr. Rockhill believed that the initiative for these negotiations should be taken by the United States. "Such a policy cannot be construed as favorable to any power in particular, but is eminently useful and desirable for the commerce of all nations. It furthermore has the advantage of securing to the United States the appreciation of the Chinese Government, who would see in it a strong desire to arrest the disintegration of the empire, and would greatly add to our prestige and influence in Peking." This policy, he believed, would meet with the hearty approval of the Japanese Government, because it was "so clearly advantageous to Japan and so much in line with its own policy in China."

On September 6th, Mr. Hay sent instructions to the American Ambassadors at Berlin, London, and St. Petersburg to inform the Government to which each was accredited of the desire of the United States that it would give formal assurance that it, within its respective sphere of whatever influence:

"First: Will in no way interfere with any treaty port or any vested interest within any so-called 'sphere of interest' or leased territory it may have in China.

THE OPEN DOOR IN CHINA

"Second. That the Chinese treaty tariff of the time being shall apply to all merchandise landed or shipped to all such ports as are within said 'sphere of interest' (unless they be 'free ports'), no matter to what nationality it may belong, and that duties so leviable shall be collected by the Chinese Government.

"Third. That it will levy no higher harbor dues on vessels of another nationality frequenting any port in such 'spheres' than shall be levied on vessels of its own nationality, and no higher railroad charges over lines built, controlled, or operated within its 'sphere' on merchandise belonging to citizens or subjects of other nationalities transported through such 'spheres,' than shall be levied on similar merchandise belonging to its own nationals transported over equal distances."

Similar instructions were sent to the minister in Japan on November 13th, to Italy on the 17th, and to France on the 21st. To this request Italy alone gave an unconditional assent, but, as the other powers replied that each would acquiesce if the others would, Mr. Hay, on March 20, 1900, instructed the American representatives to notify the respective Governments that, as all the powers had accepted the proposals of the United States, "this Government will therefore consider the assent given by it by —— as final and definitive."

In thus securing the assent of the interested powers to the Open-Door policy, Mr. Hay had been following the long-established precedents of American diplomacy in the Far East. The policy which he proposed would be, he was confident, approved by the Governments and people of Great Britain and Japan. The open door in China was advocated in those countries long before the phrase was familiar in the United States. But the force of this understanding has been frequently misapprehended. Its sanction was moral rather than physical. The United States had secured an open approval of this policy of equal opportunity from each of the interested powers. If any one offended in the future, it would be a violation of its plighted word. But no treaty obligations were incurred. The United States assumed no responsibility to compel one or all the other powers to keep the faith. The United States Senate, at that time, would hardly have ratified a treaty which would have imposed such heavy obligations upon its Government. In later years most of the powers accepted the Open-Door policy as a part of their treaty obligations, but the United States never did so. Its contribution toward this desirable end was in securing the promise of all the powers to respect this policy, and in its own undeviating fidelity to the cause which it had espoused.

While the foreign chancelleries were considering the Open-Door policy as proposed by the United States, an organization was being perfected in North China whose purpose was the expulsion of the troublesome aliens. In the summer of 1898, the Emperor of China, grieving over the humiliation of the old Middle Kingdom by both the Japanese and the Europeans, had accepted the advice of some liberal officials and of Kang Yu-wei, a Cantonese scholar who had studied Western history and politics, and many wide-reaching reform decrees were issued. For a hundred days the reformers were in control, and then reaction, represented by the Empress Dowager and her trusted supporters, seized the upper-hand — the Emperor was deposed, and the reformers were driven out. This change at the Court was reflected in the provinces, especially in Shantung, where the Governor no longer tried to suppress a secret society known as the "Fists of Public Harmony," but whose members were later spoken of as "Boxers." This society at first had been anti-Manchu, but in some way it was turned into an anti-foreign organization, and its purpose was to drive out the foreigners and all Chinese who affiliated with them, especially the Christians. By May, 1900, the movement had assumed a serious aspect, and the Chinese Government seemed unable or unwilling to suppress it. At the end of that month, a small force of marines arrived to guard the legations in Peking, but when a larger force tried to reach the city, in June, it was driven back by the combined imperial and Boxer forces. The Taku forts had been taken by the allied warships, without the help of the Americans, while the expedition was on its march toward Peking. China now considered herself at war with all the powers.

On the 20th of June, the siege of the legations in Peking began. Within the weak defenses were gathered the official representatives of eleven nations, and subjects of three others (including three thousand Chinese Christians). The military forces numbered four hundred and fifty officers and men representing six European countries, the United States, and Japan, while practically all able-bodied civilians took some part in the defense. "Among the military," wrote Mr. H. B. Morse, the distinguished American historian, "the Japanese Colonel Shiba was, by general consent, the most distinguished. . . . He was reckless in courage, unceasing in his vigilance, and fertile in plans; and he was highly esteemed by men of Western nations, by whom, hitherto, the Asiatic had been regarded as of an inferior mould." On the one hand, the besieged had to defend their lives, and on the other, their nations made hurried preparations to relieve them.

Prompt action was necessary if the legations were to be rescued in time. Japan, of all the powers, could spare the required troops and could land them at Tientsin within a few days. Russia would need most of her troops to police Manchuria; Great Britain was engaged in the Boer War; the United States could spare a couple of thousand from the Philippines, where the insurrection was still in progress; while Germany, France, and Italy had few at hand. Great Britain appealed to Japan, on June 22d, to send additional forces, but Japan was afraid to move without the approval of the other powers. Lord Salisbury then asked the Russian, French, and German Governments if they would approve the immediate dispatch of a force of 20,000 or 30,000 Japanese. The replies, couched in diplomatic language, indicated that they were unwilling to have Japan take the lead in this humane enterprise, so when Great Britain again urged Japan to move, the latter asked assurance that she would be protected from complications and indemnified for her outlay. Great Britain promptly guaranteed the financial obligation. Thus two valuable weeks had been lost because of the jealousy of certain of the powers. Japan then hurried over reënforcements to Tientsin, and contributed the largest body of troops to the relief expedition.

The foreign concessions at Tientsin were relieved on June 24th, but it was not until July 14th that the adjacent native city was taken by assault. Then three weeks were lost while more troops assembled. The Russian commander believed that the field force should number 80,000 men, and it was finally decided to wait until at least 60,000 were available for the expedition and for holding the line of communications. Great Britain had steadily urged a rapid advance, even with fewer troops. On July 20th, a cipher message was received from Mr. Conger, the American Minister, which stated that the legations were still under fire and that prompt relief only could prevent a general massacre. This caused the American Government to advocate a forward movement. The view of the British and American commanders prevailed, and, on August 4th, the relieving force left Tientsin, with only 18,800 men instead of the 40,000 formerly deemed necessary. Of this number 8000 were Japanese commanded by Marshal Yamaguchi, and 2500 were Americans under Brigadier-General Chaffee. Great Britain furnished 3000, Russia 4500, and France 800 men.

This was in many ways a most remarkable expedition. Never before had the armed forces of Europe, Asia, and America coöperated in so humane a cause. For the first time Japanese soldiers stood side by side with their Western brothers in arms. And they were eager to win the good opinion of their European and American comrades. That they succeeded is evident from the record. H. C. Thomson, an English journalist, wrote: " It is impossible to express the universal admiration excited all through this campaign by the conduct of the Japanese — by their extraordinary self-restraint as well as by their courage and military capacity. The women and children have been perfectly safe in their hands, and after the heat of battle has been over they have spared even the Chinese soldiers, merely making them work as coolies, and paying them forty cents a day, like the rest of the Chinese coolies in Japanese employment."

While the expeditionary force was assembling at Tientsin, the American Government made a statement of its policy in a circular note to the powers on July 3d. This was "to seek a solution which may bring about permanent safety and peace to China, preserve Chinese territorial and administrative entity, protect all rights guaranteed to friendly powers by treaty and international law, and safeguard for the world the principle of equal and impartial trade with all parts of the Chinese Empire." This policy received the general concurrence of all the powers, and from this time it became the custom to link the "open door" and the "territorial integrity" of China as two accepted doctrines.

After ten days of stiff fighting, the eighty miles were traversed, and Peking was entered on August 14th. Two days later, the Japanese led the forces which relieved the heroic missionaries and their Chinese converts in the Pehtang Cathedral. With the events which followed, the thorough looting of the city, and the punitive expeditions, in which no Americans took part and few Japanese, and that reluctantly, we are not concerned. After the relief of the legations and the suppression of the disorders, the next step was the restoration of friendly relations with China. In the negotiations which followed, and which were carried on until the final protocol was signed September 7, 1901, the United States, Great Britain, and generally Japan worked in harmony. They were opposed to the severe penalties proposed by the Germans, and they advocated a moderate indemnity, but on the latter point they were outvoted by the Continental powers. The indemnity was finally fixed at 450,000,000 taels, of which Russia, Germany, and France received far more than Great Britain, Japan, or the United States, far more, in fact, than could have been justly claimed.

During the relief operations, the six powers worked together in general harmony. At times differences arose between the three European powers and Great Britain, the United States, and Japan. But after the occupation of Peking, Russia's conduct gave occasion for alarm. She had advocated the prompt evacuation of the city, but the associated powers had failed to concur. And then, while protesting that she had no designs of territorial acquisition in China, she suddenly turned and overran Manchuria, capturing the capital, Mukden, October 2d. This led to the Anglo-German agreement of October, which was an enunciation of the principles of the open door and integrity of China. The United States, France, Italy, Austria, and Japan accepted the principles there recorded.'

During these days Russian diplomacy was closely following the successful precedent laid down in 1858 and 1860. In the former year, a Russian Minister negotiated with the Chinese at Tientsin, in apparent harmony with his colleagues of Great Britain, France, and the United States, while, unknown to the latter, Count Muravieff at Aigun was forcing the Chinese to cede to Russia the left bank of the Amur. Again, in 1860, the Russian Minister at Peking gained the whole seacoast of Manchuria, secretly, after the British and French had negotiated their second conventions. So in 1900, while M. de Giers was taking part in the discussions at Peking in company with his colleagues, Admiral Alexieff, at Port Arthur, negotiated a convention with Tseng Chi, the Tartar General, which would have made Manchuria a Russian protectorate. The first news of this agreement was published in London on January 3, 1901, and, although both Russia and China denied its authenticity, Japan, the United States, Great Britain, and Germany warned China of the danger of negotiating with one power while she was trying to restore friendly relations with all. Russia pressed for a ratification of the convention. On February 28th, the Chinese Government appealed to the United States, Japan, Great Britain, and Germany to join in a mediation between her and Russia. Russia then modified her demands somewhat and demanded that the convention be signed by March 26th. China again appealed to the powers to influence Russia to extend the time for negotiation, and the United States again warned China and Russia not to engage in separate negotiations. Germany, Great Britain, and Japan suggested that the convention be placed before the diplomatic conference at Peking, which Russia refused to do. The time was extended to April 1st, and, finally, in view of the moral support afforded China, Russia temporarily withdrew the agreement on April 6th. The final protocol of the Boxer settlement was not signed, as we have seen, until September 7th. Russia had failed in 1901 because of the publicity which was lacking in 1858.

During the Chinese crisis, from 1898 until 1901, the United States, Great Britain, and Japan had worked in harmony. Each believed in the wisdom of the Open Door and the territorial integrity of China. And certainly no power had more at stake than Japan. But China was unable to defend herself against the thinly veiled aggressions of Russia, and Russia could count upon the support of France, and often of Germany. Japan had most at stake, for the southward march of Russia to ice-free ports meant the eventual occupation of Korea and South Manchuria, and this would be intolerable. But Japan, alone, could hardly face the old triple entente which had humiliated her in 1895. She must have some support. The United States had enunciated principles in which Japan heartily agreed, but the United States could not be counted upon to maintain them by force. The United States had uniformly refused to enter into alliances for any purpose, and few could imagine an American army engaged against Russia in defense of Chinese integrity. Great Britain, on the other hand, had long feared the Russian advance, first toward India and now toward Korea and China, where British commercial interests would be jeopardized. She was, therefore, well disposed

to an alliance which would strengthen her against Russia
in the Far East. A difference of opinion arose in the highest circles in Japan as to whether an alliance should be
made with Great Britain, which would probably lead to a
clash with Russia, or whether an attempt should be made
to settle the conflicting interests with the latter country.
In view of what we now know were the influences which
prevailed at the Czar's Court, it is evident that no stable
arrangement could have been arrived at. Russia would
not have tolerated Japanese interference in her scheme
of state. So, on the 30th of January, 1902, the Anglo-
Japanese Alliance was signed in London. In it the two
high contracting parties recognized the independence of
China and Korea and declared that they held no aggressive tendencies in either country. The special interests
of Britain were in China, while, in addition to those which
she possessed in China, Japan was held to have political,
commercial, and industrial interests in Korea. If either
party, in defense of these interests, should become involved in war with another power, the other party
would observe a strict neutrality, but, if other powers
should join in hostilities against one of the allies, the other
would come to its support, conduct the war in common,
and make peace in mutual agreement with it. The agreement was to remain in effect for five years.

This agreement meant, in short, that, should Japan
come to blows with Russia, Great Britain would hold the
ring and prevent Russia's associates from overwhelming
the smaller nation. Russia and France replied, on March
19th, to the effect that they had many times affirmed the
principles laid down in the Anglo-Japanese agreement,
but if the aggressive action of third powers or new
trouble in China should threaten the integrity of that
country or its free development, which would endanger

their own interests, they reserved the right to discuss the means of assuring their safety. This may be said to have extended the Franco-Russian Alliance to the Far East.

The resolute actions of Japan and Great Britain caused Russia to appear to withdraw from her Manchurian adventure. On the 8th of April, she signed a convention with China in which she agreed to evacuate Manchuria within eighteen months, a definite zone to be relinquished each three months. But Russia had no intention of keeping this pledge.

In Korea, since 1895, Russian influence had steadily increased, while that of Japan suffered a severe blow in connection with the assassination of the Queen in October. Japan had watched this tightening of Russian control with great alarm. So when Russia failed to keep her agreement with China, and at the close of the first year had not only not removed her troops from the second zone, but tried to secure additional privileges, it was decided, at a conference before the throne, on June 26, 1993, that Japan would approach Russia directly and endeavor to secure from her an unequivocal assurance of her intention to respect the independence and territorial integrity of China and Korea.

The negotiations, which continued between the 12th of August and the 6th of February, following, cannot be discussed here. Russia refused to respect the integrity of China. As the Russians were massing troops on the Korean border and strengthening their naval forces in the Far East, Japan decided to break off negotiations. This was done on February 8, 1904, and hostilities began on the night of the 9th at Port Arthur.

The United States promptly urged both Japan and Russia to respect the neutrality of China and to limit the area of hostilities as much as possible. Both powers agreed to this, although Russia insisted that all Manchuria should be included in the war zone. When during the progress of the war it was rumored that some of the neutral powers might lay claim to Chinese territory, the United States again gave expression to its well-known policy of the Open Door and the territorial integrity of China, and received new adhesions to it from the European powers. And early in 1905, Russia complained to the United States of alleged breaches of neutrality by China, which both China and Japan denied.

It must be remembered that this war was fought on Chinese territory, presumably in order to prevent the acquisition of Korea and Manchuria by Russia. But Japan never would have made such sacrifices if her own national interests had not been at stake. Japan was, therefore, fighting for herself, in self-defense. But it was the weakness of Korea and China which had compelled her to enter the arena. For this reason there was, naturally, much indignation in Japan because China would not raise a hand in her own defense. The weakness and the supineness of China had involved Japan in this dangerous enterprise. This fact colored the attitude of many Japanese toward China in the coming years.

During the war public opinion in the United States was strongly favorable to Japan. She was believed to be engaged in a war of self-defense, and her audacity in challenging the Russian Colossus aroused great admiration. The uniform success of her forces on land and sea, her excellent hospital and sanitary arrangements, her humane treatment of prisoners-of-war, all redounded to her credit, while the stories of Russian incapacity and corruption confirmed the views long held of that country's bureaucracy.

After the destruction of the Russian fleet in the Sea of

JAPAN AND THE UNITED STATES

Japan, on May 27th and 28th, 1905, it was evident that a continuation of the war would be disastrous. President Roosevelt, who had watched the struggle with deep interest, believed the time had come when peace would be to the interests of both parties. Having assured himself that each side wished him to act, he sent an identic note to the two powers urging them to appoint plenipotentiaries to consider terms of peace. The suggestion was promptly accepted. On the 9th of August, the commissioners met at Portsmouth, New Hampshire, as guests of the American nation. During the progress of the negotiations, President Roosevelt used his great influence to prevent their failure. The chief dispute arose over the indemnity, which Japan demanded and Russia stoutly refused to yield. Mr. Roosevelt, in conference with Japanese and Russian representatives in Washington, and acting through the American Ambassador at St. Petersburg, and with the support of the Kaiser, constantly worked for a compromise. On the 5th of September, the treaty was signed. Japan secured the recognition of her paramount political, military, and economic interests in Korea, and forced Russia out of South Manchuria, but took for herself the leasehold and railway rights which Russia had held there.

The effects of the war upon Japan were wide-reaching. Her achievements won for her a place among the great military powers of the world, but the place had been dearly bought in blood and treasure. Japan was now the recognized leader of Asia, and there was scarcely a place in the vast continent where her success was not acclaimed and her example held up for imitation. And the peace gave her great interests and responsibilities on the mainland. The war left in its wake many problems of domestic and foreign affairs, some of which remain unsolved even to this day.

CHAPTER X

AFTER THE RUSSO-JAPANESE WAR

For fifty years the relations between the United States and Japan had been uniformly friendly. And this was true not merely of the Governments, but of the people as well. In the decades which marked the rise of New Japan there were many occasions when the United States could manifest its good-will for Japan and its desire to see her stand forth as a great independent and progressive power. And it may be said that the American people, so far as they were informed concerning Far Eastern affairs, were interested in and well disposed toward Japan. No uncertain demonstration of this sympathy was given during the Russian war.

And yet the year 1905, which saw the triumph of Japan on Manchurian battle-fields and Eastern seas, witnessed the first signs of a change in public opinion on both sides of the Pacific. In Japan, it flared up without warning in the anger of many of the people at the peace terms, and in the belief that the United States, under Mr. Roosevelt's leadership, had been responsible for the loss of an indemnity. And in the United States, there appeared the beginnings of a Japanese immigration problem as well as the voicing of suspicions regarding the foreign policies of Japan. The immigration question in California rapidly came to a head, and will be discussed in some detail in another chapter. The criticism of Japanese policy developed more slowly, but its constant reiteration could not fail to influence public opinion.

During the war both Japan and Russia made effective use of propaganda to present their cause before the neutral world. In the United States, Baron Kaneko, a Harvard graduate and a personal friend of President Roosevelt, performed a very useful service, and Baron Suyemitsu was an able expounder of the Japanese point of view in Great Britain. The American press was almost uniformly friendly to Japan during the war, but at its close a distinct change might be noticed. It has frequently been remarked in the United States that this was due in large part to the personal popularity of Count Witte, at the peace conference, and to his success in securing publicity for the Russian point of view. But in the recently published memoirs of the Count we find that he deliberately set about to accomplish this end. "By my course of action," he wrote, "I gradually won the press over to my side, and consequently also to the side of the cause which the will of my monarch had entrusted to my charge, so that when I left the trans-Atlantic Republic practically the whole press was on our side. The press, in its turn, was instrumental in bringing about a complete change in the public opinion of the country — in favor of my person and of the cause I upheld."

From this time most absurd articles were printed and accepted by a people too little informed to distinguish between fact and fancy. This is, of course, a fundamental difficulty in maintaining good relations between peoples widely separated in race and culture. So few people in either country really know much about the other — for to understand is to pardon — and it is so easy to suspect the motives of a stranger. Among the tales which passed into circulation was one to the effect that Japan, which had just defeated the greatest military power of the West, would now attack the others in turn until Europe was driven out of Asia and even the Americas were overrun.

AFTER THE RUSSO-JAPANESE WAR

Americans were warned that Japan could easily wrest the Philippines from them, and then Hawaii, and finally the whole Pacific Coast. Canadians were told that British Columbia really was the Japanese objective. The Australians were alarmed lest their sparsely peopled northern territory might invite invasion, which, it was asserted, would surely come when the Anglo-Japanese Alliance expired in 1911. In French reviews I have read that Japan would soon conquer French Indo-China, and the Dutch were alarmed lest their rich tropical empire tempt the new war lords of the East. Even British India was not too remote for their intrigue. And Mexico and the west coast of South America were also mentioned as probable scenes of Japanese aggression. These statements are by no means fanciful. They may be found in many serious articles published soon after 1905. They seem absurd, of course, when they are brought together in a single paragraph, and we find that, according to these publicists, the Japanese were about to launch offensives in every direction and become embroiled with the United States, the British Empire, France, the Netherlands, and the South American Republics. China, of course, was to be promptly overrun, commencing with South Manchuria. And a very alarming prediction was one in which Japan would organize the wealth and man-power of China to provide and equip the armies which would revive the days of Ghengis Khan and create a real "Yellow Peril."

There was no truth in any of these alarming statements. Some individual Japanese, inspired by the success of the imperial forces in the late war, might have dreamed of a great expansion of the empire, but the leaders of the state realized the price which Japan had been compelled to pay for victory, and knew that many years of peace were needed to bind up the wounds of war. Yet it must be remembered that such stories were current throughout the West, and that they are at the bottom of most of the suspicion which to-day exists of Japanese policies. In the United States, for example, certain journalists, for one reason or another, prophesied an immediate Japanese invasion. This might come at any time, and without warning, but surely before the Panama Canal was constructed. And then, when the canal was opened, and hostilities had not been proclaimed, it was just as easy to predict that the canal could easily be destroyed by airships and then the invasion would begin. It did little good to demonstrate that the invasion of California was a military operation of the utmost difficulty, if not impossible of achievement. Many Americans, fed upon such startling statements, looked with alarm to the time when war would break. It is interesting, of course, to note that in all these stories the offensive was to be taken by Japan. No American dreamed of invading Japan, except as a phase of a war which might be forced upon his country. But these constant alarms had the expected reaction in Japan, and newsmen there warned their people to prepare for an American invasion. Thus, out of the fertile imagination of ignorant or thoughtless writers on both sides of the Pacific, arose the specter of war between two countries which had for half a century enjoyed the most friendly of relations. Before 1905, a newsman who predicted a war between Japan and the United States would have been greeted with derision in both countries. After that year, the possibility of such a conflict was viewed with alarm by many people in both lands.

Thoughtful Americans paid little attention to the war-scares. They had learned to discount the utterances of a certain type of journalist. But the conduct of Japan in China and Korea seemed to indicate that an imperialistic policy had been adopted. This fact, and the well-known influence of the military leaders in Japan, served to weaken their confidence. The American people love peace and they believe instinctively in fair play. Their warm sympathy for Japan had arisen, in large part, because they believed Japan had been badly used by the European powers. And if they believed, in turn, that Japan had adopted a similar policy toward her weaker neighbors, this sympathy would be diverted to the peoples who seemed entitled to it. After the Russian War, Japan followed closely the precedents set by Europe in its dealings with China. Before that time Japanese diplomacy had been largely modeled on British and American precedents. The trusted adviser of the Foreign Office from 1881 until 1913 was an American, Henry W. Denison. When Japan, therefore, took over the Russian lease of Port Arthur and the Russian railway, and when she sought to strengthen her economic and political interests in Manchuria, it was natural that Americans, who had criticized the conduct of the European powers in 1898, should apply the same standard of criticism to Japan. There were some who criticized Japan alone, but they were manifestly unfair. A single standard should be applied to all the powers who sought or held special privileges in China.

If the military successes of Japan alarmed many of the uninformed Americans, the increasing influence of the military party gave food for thought to others. The United States was so fortunately located that it could develop with little fear of foreign aggression. Thus the people were peace-loving and until recent years paid but little attention to their army and navy. Throughout its history the military forces have always been under the control of the civil officials. But conditions were otherwise in Japan. When Japan first came in contact with the West, she was hopelessly weak in army and navy, and she was practically at the mercy of the Great Powers. It was not until the Shogunate was abolished and feudalism had passed away that a national army and navy could be created. Under wise leadership and with great sacrifices these forces, based upon conscription, were developed. In the war with China, they acquitted themselves well, and their leaders became national heroes. In the Russian War even greater triumphs were won and the whole world admired their achievements. Moreover, they were the saviors of Japan, for if they had failed the nation would have been crushed by the Russian giant. No wonder the people acclaimed Oyama, Kuroki, Nogi, and Togo. Japan had been forced to fight her way to safety. She had been compelled to rely upon her armed forces as the United States had not. And she naturally held in high esteem the forces which had made her safe and had won for her a high position in the councils of the world. These military and naval leaders were also men of great personal capacity. They had been drawn from the pick of the young men of Japan, and their influence was great. Before the Russian War the civilian leaders had generally been able to win the Emperor's support for their policies. But after the war the military leaders, confident in the wisdom of their plans, had great influence. As these facts became known in the United States, they occasioned more and more comment. This was not because Japan had built up an effective army and navy, but because there was some doubt as to which part of the Government would direct its activities — the civilian Cabinet, who would normally think in terms of peace, or the professional soldiers, whose training led them to rely upon force.

In Japan, a similar change in public opinion toward

America might have been noted in the years after 1905. This was due to the California question, the widely current war talk, and suspicion of America's conduct in Manchuria. In some quarters the Japanese press printed quite as absurd stories as did the American journals. Misunderstandings were frequent, and explanations never seemed to remove all the doubts.

So far we have discussed the change in public opinion, but this is as it should be. The policies of states are to-day largely directed by what the people believe. Their opinions may be based upon error or misinformation, but if they believe them sincerely they will act upon them. This is especially true in a democracy like the United States, and with the development of popular participation in government in Japan, the time will come when public opinion will make and unmake ministries. It is not enough to consider the official relations between states. It is now imperatively necessary to understand what the people are thinking about their neighbors. And it is the duty of those who are in possession of information to make it available so as to combat error in every quarter. In the nine years between the Russian War and the Great War, while doubts and fears began to trouble many of the people on both sides of the Pacific, the relations between their Governments were always friendly and correct. A good understanding and the traditional friendship prevailed.

In Manchuria the actions of Japan seemed to be at variance with the policy of the Open Door and the integrity of China, to which, at the suggestion of the United States, she had given adhesion in 1899 and 1900. In addition, she had confirmed these principles in various treaties, including her alliance with Great Britain and the Portsmouth Treaty. Before discussing some of the incidents which occurred in this period in Manchuria, a few general statements may be useful.

Japan emerged from the Russian War burdened with an enormous debt of over a billion dollars. In return she had received the South Manchurian Railway, half the island of Saghalien, and a nominal sum in payment of the expenses of the Russian prisoners in Japan. It is evident that at first the Government had no idea of using the acquired railway to develop Japanese special interests in South Manchuria. In October, 1905, Count Katsura, the Premier, signed a memorandum with Mr. E. H. Harriman, the American railway manager, for the transfer of the South Manchurian Railway to a syndicate, to be formed by Mr. Harriman, which would operate under Japanese law. Mr. Harriman proposed to buy up the Chinese Eastern Railway (the Russian railway in Manchuria), and secure transportation rights over the Trans-Siberian, thus forming a round-the-world transportation system financed by American capital. If this scheme could have been carried out, the political dangers involved in foreign railway ownership in Manchuria would have been largely removed. But Baron Komura, who returned from Portsmouth soon after Mr. Harriman left Japan, was opposed to the scheme. He argued that China would first have to agree to the transfer of the Russian rights to Japan before Japan could sell them to the syndicate. And he was opposed to the plan on principle, for he believed that, as the railway was the only valuable asset which Japan had won in the war, the people would resent bitterly the transfer of this productive enterprise to foreigners. On this point he was doubtless right, for great indignation had already been manifested because of the slight gains from a war which had seemed to be so entirely successful. In the Treaty of Peking, in December, China agreed to the transfer from Russia to Japan and insisted that the road be worked by a company composed of Chinese and Japanese shareholders. This nullified the memorandum signed by Count Katsura. It is evident, I believe, that the Government had been convinced by Baron Komura, and had decided to use the railway to further the interests of Japan. Mr. Harriman never abandoned his great scheme, and to the day of his death he was engaged in trying to work out some way of organizing the round-the-world system which had so appealed to his imagination.

The decision to exploit Manchuria seems, therefore, to have been reached after the war, rather than long before it, as some publicists have alleged. At this point we must note a fundamental difference of opinion between the Chinese and the Japanese statesmen. The Chinese took the position that Japan had gallantly plunged into war in order to free Manchuria from the Russian menace, and to safeguard the integrity of China. For all that Japan had done they professed much gratitude, but, in addition, they expected that Japan also would withdraw and thus demonstrate the unselfishness of her deeds. The Japanese, in the course of the war, had arrived at very different conclusions. They had been compelled to fight Russia because of the weakness of China. They had sacrificed much in blood and treasure, and they were entitled to compensation. All that they asked was no more than China had freely given Russia — the Port Arthur leasehold, the railway and the mining rights. And there were some who believed, and did not hesitate to say, that Japan was entitled to all of South Manchuria, for Russia would surely have taken it if Japan had not intervened.

This sharp difference of opinion between the two countries explains much that followed. China tried to limit

JAPAN AND THE UNITED STATES

Japanese activities in South Manchuria, and when she was too weak to do so, she then tried to enlist Great Britain and the United States by means of concessions granted to their nationals. Japan, on the other hand, tried to secure the full measure of the rights surrendered to her by Russia, and such additional rights as she could persuade or force China to grant. It goes without saying that in this period the relations between the two neighbors were badly strained, and in 1909 an ultimatum was delivered before China would consent to the rebuilding of the Antung-Mukden Railway.

In the meantime the United States was interested in these developments because of its championship of the Open Door and because of the commercial interests of its nationals in Manchuria. Immediately after the war, frequent charges were made that the Open Door was violated in Manchuria, and that Japan had taken advantage of her politica lsupremacy to foster the commercial interests of her subjects. There is no doubt that Japanese merchants carried on a thriving trade before the evacuation of the country and before foreign merchants were allowed to enter. Other charges were advanced, of failure to pay the Chinese customs duties, of rebates on the Japanese railway, and of interference with the local tax collections. For some of these charges there may have been a basis of fact. The Japanese Government protested, time and again, that it was observing scrupulously its Open-Door pledge. Some questionable proceedings may have been the acts of minor officials, and others may have been committed by private Japanese. After the disturbed conditions caused by the war were adjusted, these complaints generally ceased. An English publicist, Mr. Angier, who visited Manchuria in 1908, reported: "The charge made against Japan that she was not playing the game has not been brought home. It has produced the Scotch verdict of not proven." And he pointed out that the Japanese were wise enough to see that the more South Manchuria was developed by foreign capital, the greater would be Japan's share in the trade. No country should be more interested in the Open Door in China than Japan, because of her geographical propinquity.

In addition, the situation in Manchuria was complicated by a struggle for railway concessions. China, fearing lest Japan use her railway for political as well as economic purposes, tried to enlist British and then American capital in rival enterprises. Japan, resolved to make the most of her Manchurian concessions, naturally opposed all competition. In November, 1907, China gave a concession to British capitalists to build a short line from Hsinmintun to Fakumen, with the ultimate right to extend it to Tsitsihar, four hundred miles north on the Trans-Siberian. Japan promptly opposed this concession as a violation of one of the secret protocols of the Peking Treaty of 1905, in which China agreed not to construct any main line in the neighborhood of and parallel to the South Manchurian Railway, or any branch line which might be prejudicial to its interests. Her ally, Great Britain, supported her, and the concession was not carried through. At the very time that this concession was under discussion, the Viceroy of Manchuria, Hsu Shi-chang (now President of China), and the Governor of Mukden, Mr. Tang Shao-yi, had negotiated with Mr. Willard Straight, American Consul-General, an outline of agreement for an American loan of $20,000,000, with the right to establish a Manchurian bank which would be the financial agent of the Government in mining, timber, and agricultural development and in the construction of railways, notably one from Tsitsihar to Aigun on the Amur River. This agreement could not be carried out because of the panic of 1907 and the impossibility of raising the funds in the United States.

The next year, Mr. Tang Shao-yi proceeded to the United States, nominally to thank that country for the remission of the Boxer indemnity, but also to complete the arrangements for the Manchurian loan. But while he was *en route*, the Emperor and the Empress Dowager died, in Peking, and Yuan Shih-kai, his patron, was in disfavor with the Prince Regent. Under these circumstances Mr. Tang did not proceed with his financial mission.

At this time, in order to answer the various criticisms which had been directed against Japanese policy in Manchuria, the Ambassador at Washington, Baron Takahira, and the Secretary of State, Mr. Root, exchanged notes on November 30, 1908. These notes contained a frank avowal of the aim, policy, and intention of each Government. It was the wish of each to encourage the free and peaceful development of their commerce on the Pacific. Their policy was to maintain the *status quo* in that region and to defend the principle of equal opportunity for commerce and industry in China. They would reciprocally respect the territorial possessions belonging to each other, and they would support, by all pacific means at their disposal, the independence and integrity of China and the Open Door. "Should any event occur threatening the *status quo* as above described or the principle of equal opportunity as above defined, it remains for the two Governments to communicate with each other in order to arrive at an understanding as to what measures they may consider it useful to take."

This exchange of notes has sometimes been described

as a treaty. Such was not the case. A treaty, to bind the United States, must be ratified by two thirds of the Senate. These notes represented the views of the Executive Departments of Japan and the United States. They contained nothing new. But at a time when the Open Door and the integrity of China seemed endangered, Japan and the United States affirmed their support of those principles. Japan had recently entered into similar agreements with France, and with Russia in 1907. In some quarters in China these notes were entirely misinterpreted, and were considered to be an endorsement of strong measures by Japan. On the other hand, their sole purpose was to restate the previous pledges of both Japan and the United States.

After a study of many of the alarming statements which have been written about American-Japanese relations since 1905, a very comforting conclusion can be reached — and that is that few of the gloomy predictions have been justified by the march of events. And this was never demonstrated more clearly than in the summer of 1908. From a journalistic point of view the relations between the two countries were tense. The California school case of 1906 had left much bitterness in Japan, occasioned the more by surprise that such a demonstration against her should appear in America, a country which had been so uniformly friendly in the past. On both sides of the Pacific there had been much loose talk and the possibility of war was lightly discussed. At this juncture President Roosevelt gave orders for the battleship fleet to proceed into the Pacific on its way around the world. The reason for this was to give the American people, and other peoples as well, a demonstration that the Pacific was as much a field for naval maneuvers as the Atlantic, where up to this time the major portion of

JAPAN AND THE UNITED STATES

the fleet was always concentrated, and, as President Roosevelt later wrote, "that its presence in one ocean was no more to be accepted as a mark of hostility to any Asiatic power than its presence in the Atlantic was to be accepted as a mark of hostility to any European power." At this time it was not believed possible to take a fleet of great battleships around the world, and the President desired to ascertain if it could be done. When the plans were announced, many people promptly misinterpreted the purpose of the cruise, and others predicted a disastrous conclusion. By some it was considered to be a threat to Japan, while others, including high naval authorities in certain European nations, were convinced that the Japanese fleet would certainly take the offensive. In certain quarters the wish was father to the thought, for the German Kaiser rarely missed an opportunity to warn Americans of the impending conflict with Japan. Nothing would have served his purpose better than to have the United States and Japan, one a friend and the other an ally of Great Britain, cripple themselves in a needless conflict.

The world cruise of the battleship fleet was carried out as President Roosevelt had planned. Australasia, the Philippines, China, and Japan were visited, and a striking demonstration of seamanship and efficiency was given. But, in President Roosevelt's opinion, "the most noteworthy incident of the cruise was the reception given to our fleet in Japan. In courtesy and good-breeding, the Japanese can certainly teach much to the nations of the Western world. I had been very sure that the people of Japan would understand aright what the cruise meant, and would accept the visit of our fleet as the signal honor which it was meant to be, a proof of the high regard and friendship I felt, and which I was certain the American

196

people felt, for the great Island Empire. The event even surpassed my expectations. I cannot too strongly express my appreciation of the generous courtesy the Japanese showed the officers and crews of our fleet; and I may add that every man of them came back a friend and admirer of the Japanese."

At this time Manchuria was considered to be one of the danger spots of the world. China was alarmed at the presence of Russia in North Manchuria and Japan in South Manchuria. Each power used the railroad as a powerful agency in developing its commercial and political interests. In spite of predictions that Russia would soon strike back at Japan to regain the sphere of influence which it had lost, the two countries had rapidly reached the decision that coöperation was better than strife, as the agreement of 1907 testified. All of which occasioned more alarm in China. Mr. Harriman had not abandoned his scheme for securing a round-the-world transportation system. Late in 1908, Russia seemed willing to sell her North Manchurian system, if Japan would sell the southern part, but Japan again refused. Tang Shao-yi then suggested that an international syndicate be formed to buy up both the Japanese and the Russian lines, in which China would gladly coöperate.

The next year, Mr. Harriman tried to deal with Russia for the North Manchurian line (the Chinese Eastern Railway), while Mr. Straight, in coöperation with a British firm, secured from China a concession for a railway from Chinchow, on the Gulf of Pechili, to Aigun, on the Amur. But on the 9th of September, 1909, Mr. Harriman died, and there was no one in America able or willing to undertake his colossal scheme. The Chinchow-Aigun concession was ratified by an imperial edict in January, but the project was never carried out.

JAPAN AND THE UNITED STATES

At this point the United States took the initiative in trying to reconcile the conflicting interests in Manchuria. It consisted of a proposal, by Mr. Knox, the Secretary of State, to Great Britain, Russia, France, Germany, Japan, and China, that [the six powers coöperate to advance funds to enable China to repurchase the lines held by Russia and Japan before 1937, when this right might be exercised. The lines would then be administered by a joint international commission during the term of the loan. An alternative proposition was for the powers to coöperate in building the Chinchow-Aigun Railway. This proposal, which was advanced with the best of motives, the desire to eliminate the rivalries in Manchuria and to quiet the assertion that the Open Door and the integrity of China were endangered, was supported by China alone. Both Japan and Russia disapproved of the scheme, and Great Britain and France supported their allies.

In its reply, Japan asserted that there was nothing so exceptional in the present condition of things in Manchuria as to make it necessary or desirable to set up there an exceptional system not required in other parts of China. The political rights of China were undisturbed and the Open Door was respected. Moreover, an international railway administration, as proposed, would, in its opinion, sacrifice economy and efficiency to political exigencies, while divided responsibility would lead to serious disadvantages. Furthermore, many Japanese industrial and commercial undertakings had grown up alongside the railway, which could be protected against pillage and attack because Japan possessed that line of communication, and the Government could not surrender the means by which such protection and defense were made possible.

Bearing in mind the price, in blood and treasure, which Japan had paid for that strip of steel, it is doubtful if any

198

other country, similarly placed, would have replied save as it did. It was quite possible, and the announced intention, to use the railway to develop her industrial and commercial interests without violating either the Open Door or the integrity of China. And she believed herself entitled to every legitimate advantage which her sacrifices had won. And, on the other hand, the sincerity of Mr. Knox's motives cannot be questioned. He was seeking no selfish advantage for America, but equal opportunities for all peoples. Perhaps his proposal might have been more favorably received if the matter had been handled more cautiously, and all the powers consulted before the scheme was made public. But that seems very doubtful. A very prompt result of the incident was the signing of the Russo-Japanese Treaty of July 4, 1910, for the maintenance of the *status quo* in Manchuria.

The war with Russia had been caused, in large part, by Russia's threatening position in Korea. Japan had fought China to prevent foreign control of the peninsula, and after that war Russia had stepped into the place vacated by the Middle Kingdom. Japan did not intend to have that happen again. Within two weeks after the declaration of war, Japan signed a treaty with Korea which guaranteed the independence and territorial integrity of the Korean Empire and the safety of the Imperial House. In August, 1904, Korea agreed to accept Japanese financial and diplomatic advisers. The former was Mr. Megata, a Harvard graduate, and the latter was Mr. Durham White Stevens, an American citizen. In November of the following year, a Japanese protectorate was established. The United States and the other treaty powers recognized the logic of events and withdrew their legations from Seoul. The Emperor, in a personal letter to President Roosevelt, had begged him to use his good offices with Japan, but Mr. Roosevelt realized that Korea "had shown herself utterly impotent either for self-government or self-defense," and he refused to intervene. During the next three years, under Marquis Ito, as Resident General, many striking improvements were made, which won the admiration of foreigners who were familiar with conditions in the old days. So long as he lived, the independence of Korea was respected, but unhappily that great statesman lost his life at the hands of a Korean fanatic in Manchuria on October 26, 1909. In destroying one of the best friends the Koreans had, the assassin hurried the destruction of his country's independence. On the 22d of August, 1910, a treaty was signed by which the Emperor of Korea ceded his rights of sovereignty to the Emperor of Japan.

The annexation of Korea, in spite of repeated promises to preserve its integrity, has occasioned the most circumstantial criticism of the indirectness of Japanese foreign policies. Although every step in the process was "correct" diplomatically, and the final annexation was consumated through a treaty and not by proclamation, yet, taken by itself, the result was in direct opposition to the pledges. But in a world where precedents count for much, be they good or ill, the Japanese could defend their conduct by many examples. The British occupation of Egypt was in violation of a pledge to retire. The Austrian annexation of Bosnia and Herzegovina tore up a solemn treaty. Korea was not the only weak Asiatic country which had passed under foreign control. And measured by national interests the Japanese had a better claim to Korea than the British to their Indian possessions, the French to Indo-China, the Dutch to the East Indies, or the Americans to the Philippines. In Korea, the Japanese could say, with an American statesman, that "a condition and not a theory" confronted them. Or, as Mr. McKinley said, in justifying the annexation of the Philippines, "the march of events rules and over-rules human action." Japan should be judged not by the way in which she acquired Korea, but by the use which she made of her great responsibilities toward the Korean peoples.

In 1911, two treaties were negotiated which testified to the strong desire of the Governments of the United States and Japan to maintain the traditional friendship. The first was the new commercial treaty to take the place of that of 1894. The treaties negotiated by Japan in 1894 and the succeeding years, at the close of the long struggle for treaty revision, would expire in 1911. But by an amendment to the American treaty, its life was prolonged until 1912. Japan desired to proceed to the negotiation of new treaties in order to remove the conventional tariffs which were found in some of the European compacts and thus to put in force her own statutory tariff in 1911. She turned first of all to the United States, and the American Government was quite willing to waive the additional year to which it was entitled. As the American treaty contained no conventional tariff, the only change which Japan desired was the elimination of a statement, in the 1894 treaty, to the effect that the treaty rights of trade and residence should not affect the laws, ordinances, and regulations with regard to trade, the immigration of la-borers, police, and public security which were in force or might thereafter be enacted in either country. In 1894, there had been no problem of Japanese immigration to America, but the treaty made it possible for the American Government to control immigration by domestic law. In 1907, the Japanese and American Governments had agreed upon a passport system to regulate the immigration of laborers. Japan desired the elimination of the old treaty provision in order that the new system, based upon mutual agreement and good faith, should not be replaced by an exclusion law, which would offend the pride of the Japanese people. The Washington administration was willing to grant this desire, and the clause was omitted. In official correspondence which was attached to the treaty, the Japanese Government promised to maintain with equal effectiveness the limitation and control of laborers which it had exercised since 1908. This change in the treaty weakened the ability of the United States to deal promptly with Japanese immigration if at any time the "gentlemen's agreement" seemed to work unsatisfactorily. But the administration was willing to trust Japan, and the trust has not been misplaced.

Japan was unable to eliminate all the conventional tariffs. Several of the European states insisted upon treaty stipulations, but the rates were raised, and in certain cases Japan secured reciprocal concessions. The new treaties would remain in force until 1923, and at that time Japan should be able to secure complete tariff autonomy.

The other treaty was the renewal of the Anglo-Japanese Alliance, on July 13, 1911. The origin of this agreement, in 1902, has been considered. During the course of the Russo-Japanese War, on August 12, 1905, it was renewed for ten years, and its scope extended to include British interests in India. By this agreement either ally would at once come to the aid of the other, "if, by reason of unprovoked attack or aggressive action, wherever arising, on the part of any power or powers, either contracting party should be involved in war in defense of its territorial rights or special interests mentioned in the preamble." The important change in the 1911 agreement was the insertion of a new clause: "Should either high contracting party conclude a treaty of general arbitration with a third power, it is agreed that nothing in this agreement shall entail upon such contracting party an obligation to go to war with the power with whom such treaty of arbitration is in force." The purpose of this clause was to prevent Great Britain being involved with the United States, with whom a convention of general arbitration had been negotiated. In consenting to it, Japan testified to her confidence that the good relations between herself and the United States would not be disturbed. Unhappily, the general arbitration treaty failed in the United States Senate. But in September, 1914, a "peace commission" treaty was signed by Great Britain and the United States, and this was accepted, by Japan and Great Britain, as equivalent to a treaty of general arbitration.

The Anglo-Japanese Alliance has been used by ignorant and designing people all over the world to arouse antagonism against the two signatories. Its purpose and its obligations have been grossly misinterpreted. In 1902 and in 1905, it was directed against Russia, whose policies were aggressive. Its effect was weakened when, in 1907, the Anglo-Russian and the Russo-Japanese ententes were consummated. It was never directed against the United States, for it would strain the imagination to conceive of the United States directing an "unprovoked attack or aggressive action" against either of the allies. And it has only once been put into operation, and that was against Germany. Yet many publicists in many lands have solemnly assured their readers that Great Britain would join Japan in forcing America to change its immigration policy. The alliance would continue until 1921, and until one year after it was denounced.

JAPAN AND THE UNITED STATES

In 1912, Japanese and American banking interests joined the six-power consortium for making general loans to China. This grew out of the four-power consortium of 1911, organized to provide funds for reforming China's currency. In the latter group were banks of the United States, Great Britain, France, and Germany. Japanese and Russian groups joined these to form the six-power group. Much was expected of this international banking coöperation, but in 1913, the new American administration withdrew its support from the American group, on the ground that the conditions of the loan seemed to affect the administrative independence of China. With the commencement of the Great War, the German group was forced to withdraw and the European allies had no funds available for investment in China. During the war China was financed largely by Japanese capital. But just at its close a new four-power consortium was projected, which will be considered later.

The Chinese Revolution, breaking unexpectedly in October, 1911, and resulting in the overthrow of the Manchu dynasty and the establishment of a republic early in the next year, profoundly affected the situation in the Far East. The American people naturally rejoiced in the overthrow of an alien despotism and the establishment of democratic institutions among so vast a population. Knowing little of conditions in China, they interpreted a Chinese republic in terms of their own experience, and they have been very sympathetic with the efforts of the Chinese people to govern themselves. But, as a matter of fact, China has suffered all the trials incident to such a change in government among a people largely illiterate and with little political experience. Political strife and civil wars have disrupted the country and retarded its progress. Japan, with great industria and commercial interests in China, and with better knowledge of conditions there, has tried not only to protect, but to expand, these interests. No matter what she did, her conduct was bound to occasion criticism. At no time could the Peking Government be considered really representative of China, so negotiations with it were certain to arouse the antagonism of the anti-Peking forces. Great wisdom and patience were needed in dealing with China during those days of disorganization, and it can hardly be said that the Japanese always manifested either of these requisites. And these Sino-Japanese relations affected public opinion in America for certain very simple reasons — because Americans believed in the principles of the Open Door and the integrity of China, because they admired the attempt to establish a republic, and because they would instinctively sympathize with any people who seemed to be harshly used by a more powerful neighbor. It was not easy to get the facts in the United States, and many false and exaggerated statements were published, but it may be accepted as a matter of course that, under the general conditions which prevailed, public opinion in America would instinctively sympathize with China whenever she was involved in a dispute with any foreign power.

CHAPTER XI

JAPAN, AMERICA, AND THE WORLD WAR

On the 5th of August, 1914, Great Britain declared war upon Germany, and thus the great British Empire, with its peoples and lands and interests in every continent, was engulfed in a world war. Japan was bound to Britain by an alliance, first signed in 1902, renewed in 1905, and again in 1911. She also had entered into agreements with France and Russia for the maintenance of peace in the Far East. With Germany or Austria she had no such understandings. The Anglo-Japanese Alliance had permitted Britain to withdraw most of her naval strength from the Pacific, to concentrate it in the North Sea. So when she called upon Japan to come to her aid, under the terms of the alliance, Japan accepted the responsibility. The interests of Great Britain were endangered by the German ships of war operating from their base at Tsingtao, and Japan was ready to assume the major burden of removing this menace.

The Anglo-Japanese Alliance was the reason which brought Japan promptly into the war. Much as she may have desired to eliminate the German naval base, or to settle a score which had rankled since Germany's interference, with France and Russia, in 1895, it is unreasonable to believe that Japan would have declared war so promptly on such pretexts. On the 15th of August, she advised Germany to surrender Tsingtao, for eventual restoration to China, and, when the ultimatum expired on the 23d, without any response from Germany, war was declared.

JAPAN, AMERICA, AND THE WORLD WAR

The operations against Tsingtao were conducted by a force of some 20,000 Japanese, and 925 British and 300 Sikh troops. The operations proceeded cautiously, in order to avoid needless loss of life, and, on November 7th, the city was surrendered. In the meantime, the Japanese navy had been engaged in policing the Pacific and Indian Oceans, in convoying Australian troop-ships to Egypt, in capturing the German islands north of the equator, and in driving Von Spee's squadron down the Chilean coast until the British fell upon it and destroyed every vessel off the Falkland Islands. Premier Lloyd George, in opening the Imperial Conference in London, on June 20, 1921, said: "We have found Japan a faithful Ally who rendered us valuable assistance in an hour of serious and very critical need. The British Empire will not easily forget that Japanese men-of-war escorted the transports which brought the Australian and New Zealand forces to Europe at a time when German cruisers were still at large in the Indian and Pacific Oceans."

In addition to these military and naval services, Japan rendered great assistance to the Allies through the supplies of all description which she furnished to Russia, and which did much to maintain the strength of the eastern front.

Japan gave her adhesion, in October, 1915, to the Declaration of London, signed by Great Britain, France, and Russia, to make war and peace as one, and she was one of the signatories to the new five-power declaration of November 30, 1915, after Italy entered the war. Japan was, therefore, from the early days of the war, one of the Allies. No attack upon Japan has been more malicious than that she, at any time, proposed to desert her allies and join the Central Powers. Such treason would have been unthinkable. Even if the Japanese Government had been lacking in all sense of duty and integrity, it would have been suicidal to break with the great maritime powers, and especially with her old ally, Great Britain. On the other hand, it is interesting to speculate on what might have happened if, in 1914, Japan had been bound to Germany by an alliance, and had thrown her army and navy against Russia, cut off supplies from that country, and attacked the British and French dependencies in Asia and around the Pacific.

In conducting her operations against Tsingtao, Japan followed the precedents of the Russo-Japanese War. The conditions were fundamentally the same. Russia and Germany held fortified leaseholds on Chinese soil. To attack them, military operations had to be conducted within Chinese territory. In both cases China declared her neutrality, and, in 1904, Japan and Russia agreed to limit the war zone to South Manchuria. In 1914, Japan proposed to land troops at Lungkow, in Shantung, and advance across the peninsula, attacking Tsingtao from the rear. She advised China of this decision, and asserted that China gave her assent. The landing took place on September 2d, and the next day China proclaimed a war zone, including the port of Lungkow.

It has frequently been asserted that, in advancing across Chinese territory, the Japanese acted exactly as the Germans did in invading Belgium. But certain differences at once appear. Germany had solemnly promised not only to respect but to protect the neutrality of Belgium. When she demanded that Belgium grant her a right of way, Belgium refused, and to her undying credit risked all she possessed to maintain her neutrality. China, on the other hand, promptly protected herself from later German reprisals by proclaiming a war zone. It was unfortunate that her neutrality should be disre-

garded, but it was a price she had to pay for having tolerated the presence of a fortified foreign leasehold on her
shores. The precedents of 1904, which had created no
discussion at the time, were used against her. There is no
convincing reason for believing that Yuan Shih-kai seriously proposed to join the Japanese and British in driving the Germans out of Tsingtao.

After the military operations were over, friction between China and Japan increased. The Chinese demanded the withdrawal of the Japanese from the German
railway, between Tsingtao and Tsinan, the capital of
Shantung. The Japanese, again following the Manchurian precedent, refused to leave until the war was over
and the disposition of the German rights settled by treaty.
The Japanese also insisted that the Chinese customs
service be placed under the control of Japanese, in place
of the late German officials, and after long discussion an
agreement was reached. On January 7, 1915, China proclaimed the revocation of the war zone. This occasioned
a sharp reply from Japan, that she would not recognize
this action; it also aroused much popular ill-will in Japan,
and is the reason usually given for the presentation to
China, on January 18th, of the famous Twenty-One
Demands.

The purpose of these demands, according to the instructions given Mr. Hioki, the Japanese Minister at
Peking, was "to provide for the readjustment of affairs
consequent on the Japan-German War and for the
purpose of ensuring a lasting peace in the Far East by
strengthening the position of the Empire." Thus, they
would provide for China's acquiescence in any arrangement which Japan and Germany might agree to concerning the German rights in Shantung; they would
strengthen and enlarge Japanese interests in South Man-

churia and Eastern Inner Mongolia; and they would give Japan a dominant position in China as a whole.

These matters had doubtless been under consideration in Japan for some time, especially the Manchurian and Mongolian articles. The instructions to Mr. Hioki were dated December 3, 1914. The adoption of this strong policy toward China has been ascribed to Baron Kato, Minister of Foreign Affairs, and head of the Doshikai Party. The Okuma Ministry lacked support in the Lower House of the Diet. It was thought that a successful Chinese policy would win popular support. It is of interest to note that, on December 25th, the Lower House was dissolved, and in the election on March 25, 1915, the Okuma Ministry was successful. After this date, the Japanese demands were moderated, and the final treaties were much less objectionable than the original demands. There is no question that domestic politics entered into the question, nor that the opponents of Marquis Okuma and Baron Kato bitterly attacked their Chinese policy.

The international situation also was favorable for a move of this kind. Ever since China had been forced to deal with the Western powers, she had tried to offset her own weakness by playing one power against another. After Japan became dominant in South Manchuria, China had tried to enlist British and American interest. In 1915, the European powers were too occupied to rally to China's support, and no material aid could be counted upon from America. But China had learned of a new weapon which she has been able to use effectively, and which has had increasing value in recent years, the weapon of publicity.

The immediate occasion for presenting the demands was, apparently, the revocation of the war zone decreed by China.

JAPAN, AMERICA, AND THE WORLD WAR

The Twenty-One Demands were divided into five groups. The first dealt with Shantung. China was called upon to give full assent to all matters which the Japanese and German Governments might agree to concerning the disposition of German rights in Shantung; to engage to cede no territory or island to a third power within the territory or along its coast; to permit the Japanese to build a railway connecting Chefoo or Lungkow with the Kiaochow-Tsinan line; and to open certain cities and towns in the province for the residence and commerce of foreigners.

The second group dealt with South Manchuria and Eastern Inner Mongolia. The lease of Port Arthur and the term of the Japanese railways in South Manchuria were to be extended to ninety-nine years; Japanese subjects in the two regions were to be permitted to lease or own land for buildings, commercial or industrial uses, or for farming; they were to have liberty to enter, travel, reside, and carry on business in both regions; they were to have the right of mining; the consent of Japan was to be necessary whenever China proposed to grant to other nationals the right of constructing a railway or of supplying funds for the same, or for making a loan under the security of the taxes of both regions; Japan was to be first consulted whenever China needed political, financial, or military instructors there; and the control of the Kirin-Changchun railway was to be given Japan for ninety-nine years.

The third group was concerned with the great Hanyehping Coal and Iron Company operating on the Yangtze. This company, at an opportune time, was to be made a joint concern, and the Chinese were not to permit the company to dispose of any rights of property without the consent of the Japanese Government. And, furthermore, no mines in the neighborhood should be permitted to be worked without the consent of the company, or any other measures taken which might affect its interests.

The fifth group, miscellaneous in nature, contained the most objectionable features. China was to agree to engage influential Japanese as political, financial, and military advisers; she was to grant Japanese hospitals, temples, and schools in the interior the right to own lands; in certain localities she was to place the police under joint Japanese and Chinese administration or employ Japanese in these police offices; she was to obtain arms from Japan or establish an arsenal in China under joint Japanese and Chinese management, supplied with materials and experts from Japan; she was to grant Japan the right to construct railways connecting Wuchang with the Kiukiang-Nanchang line, Nanchang with Hangchow, and Nanchang with Chaochow; Japan was to be first consulted whenever China needed foreign capital in connection with the railways, mines, harbor works, and dockyards in Fukien Province; and China was to grant to Japanese subjects the right of preaching in China.

These demands contained many very valuable concessions which China was asked to yield to Japan. For them no *quid pro quo* of any kind was offered. In this, and in many other respects, Japanese diplomacy was following the sinister precedents of European diplomacy in China in the past. What equivalents had been given China for the great concessions extorted by the powers since treaty-making began in 1842? For most of the Japanese demands a precedent, in the record of Russia or other European powers, might be found. But Japan relied too much upon these precedents. They were bad in themselves, and they should never have been imitated. The Chinese, an Asiatic people, naturally resented bitterly this imitation, on a large scale, by Japan of the worst of European examples. And whereas in the old days few Chinese knew or cared about the concessions forced from China at Nanking or Tientsin or Peking, in the twentieth century the spread of modern education, and the rapid development of a Chinese press, caused the evil tidings to be diffused from one border of the land to the other. The Chinese were aroused by the Japanese demands as they had never been in the past.

In many of these articles Japan showed an appalling lack of sympathy with China. The Chinese opposed strenuously the throwing open of South Manchuria and Eastern Inner Mongolia to Japanese travel and residence, with the right to own land and carry on business, because, as long as extraterritoriality prevailed, intolerable conditions would arise. The Japanese, scattered over the country, would be removed from Chinese control and subject only to their own consuls and their own laws. And, as a matter of fact, in 1916 and 1917, Japan demanded the right to establish police boxes throughout that region, to protect and to control the conduct of her subjects. Now, Japan had suffered greatly from the abuse of extraterritoriality by Europeans, but never as grievously as China had. In order to force the powers to relinquish this right, Japan had interpreted her treaties strictly, and had refused to open her country to travel and residence until the aliens would consent to place themselves under Japanese jurisdiction. She should have been the last of the powers to have forced a great extension of the extraterritoriality problem upon China.

The articles requiring China to accept Japanese advisers were needlessly irritating. To be sure, China had accepted European and some Japanese advisers in various capacities. But advice which is forcibly accepted is rarely very effective. The presence of such advisers would be a constant provocation to the Chinese, and, if their advice were not taken, then Japan would have accomplished nothing or she would be compelled to take the next step and force China to act on the advice her nationals had given.

The demand that Japan be given a veto on railway and other development in South Manchuria, Eastern Inner Mongolia, and Fukien was a denial of the principle of the Open Door as understood by America and Great Britain, as was the control of new mining operations in the Yangtze Valley.

The Shantung demands were based upon Japan's experience after the Russian War. Russia had ceded her interests in South Manchuria to Japan, but China had to give her assent to the transfer, which required several months of negotiations at Peking. This time Japan decided to secure China's consent before the peace treaty, lest at the close of the war China should refuse to sanction the transfer.

In presenting the demands directly to President Yuan, instead of through the Minister of Foreign Affairs, an unusual procedure was adopted. The request that secrecy be observed was not unusual, for even to-day open covenants are not openly arrived at. The publication by Japan, on February 14th, of a summary of the demands, omitting the fifth group and certain other details, while lacking in frankness, was not exceptional. It was far more than Russia divulged when she was trying to establish her protectorate over Manchuria in 1900.

The conduct of the negotiations can only be summarized here. The first conference was held on February 2d. China agreed in the course of the discussions to fifteen of the original demands, some in principle and six in detail.

On February 12th, China submitted a counter-project, some of whose terms were accepted by Japan. Twenty-four conferences were held up to April 17th, and on the 26th, the Japanese Minister presented a revised list of twenty-four demands, covering the points already agreed upon and moderating others. By this time some of the more objectionable of the fifth group had been withdrawn, and now Japan offered, in case China would accept the amended proposals, to restore the German leased territory, should she receive it at the close of the war, on four conditions. Most American accounts of these transactions have been based on "China's Official History of the Recent Sino-Japanese Treaties." It should, therefore, be noted that its copy of the revised demands omits this important offer. The Chinese replied in an amended project on May 1st. This was considered unsatisfactory, and an ultimatum was presented at three o'clock on the afternoon of May 7th, advising the Chinese to accept without amendment all the items in Groups I, II, III, and IV, and the Fukien item in Group V, of the revised demands, before six o'clock P.M. on the 9th. The offer to restore Kiaochow would still hold good. China accepted the revised proposals, and the treaties were signed and notes exchanged on May 25th.

The terms of the treaties were far more moderate than the original demands. The first treaty was in respect to the Province of Shantung. It was practically the first group, with the important modification that, instead of allowing Japan to build a railway from Chefoo or Lungkow, China agreed to use Japanese capital should she decide to build it herself. The other treaty dealt with South Manchuria and Eastern Inner Mongolia. In this the demands of the second group were modified considerably. Suitable cities and towns in Eastern Inner Mongolia were to be opened for the residence and trade of foreigners, and Japanese might engage in joint undertakings there with Chinese citizens. The right to own land in South Manchuria was not granted. Japan also promised that, "in the future, when the judicial system in the said regions shall have been completely reformed, all civil and criminal suits involving Japanese subjects shall be wholly tried and decided by the law courts of China." And, instead of turning over the Kirin-Changchun railway to Japanese control, the loan agreement was to be modified on the basis of other agreements with foreign capitalists.

Notes were exchanged covering a number of points. China agreed never to lease or alienate any territory or island in Shantung; the cities to be opened to trade in that province would be decided upon after consultation with the Japanese Minister; the lease of Port Arthur would expire in 1997, the South Manchurian railway concession would be extended to 2002 — the right of purchase by China before that time being canceled — and the Antung-Mukden concession would last till 2007; the cities and towns to be opened in Eastern Inner Mongolia would be decided upon after consultation with the Japanese Minister; nine mining districts in Manchuria would be open to Japanese enterprise; Japanese capitalists would be first called upon to supply foreign loans for railway-building in South Manchuria and Eastern Inner Mongolia, and, should China propose to raise foreign loans on the taxes of these regions, Japanese capitalists would first be consulted; if China should desire to employ advisers and instructors on political, financial, military, and police matters in South Manchuria, preference would be given to Japanese; land leases in South Man-

churia were to run up to thirty years and be uncondi-
tionally renewable; the police laws and regulations and
taxation in South Manchuria would be discussed with
the Japanese consular officer before enforcement; a postponement of three months of most of the articles of the
second treaty was agreed to; the Chinese Government
engaged to agree to any arrangement concluded between
the Hanyehping Company and the Japanese capitalists,
and promised not to confiscate or nationalize it without
the consent of the Japanese capitalists, or to permit it to
contract any foreign loan other than Japanese; and,
finally, China declared that it had given no permission
to foreign nations to construct any dockyards or naval
bases or other military establishments on the coast of
Fukien Province, nor did it intend to borrow any foreign
capital for such purposes.

In return for these concessions, Japan promised to restore the leased territory of Kiaochow Bay, on condition:
that it be opened as a commercial port; that an exclusive
Japanese concession be established at a place designated
by the Japanese Government; that an international concession be established if the foreign powers desired it; and
that the disposal of the German properties be arranged
by mutual agreement between China and Japan before
the restoration.

These negotiations of 1915 have been discussed in some
detail because of their great significance in any study of
the Far Eastern situation at the present moment. Their
effect was to isolate Japan, to bring down upon her the
bitter enmity of all thoughtful Chinese, and to confirm
the suspicions which had arisen in Europe and America
of the aggressive policies of Japan in China. No advantage which the concessions could bring her could recom-
pense Japan for the hostility aroused from one end of

JAPAN AND THE UNITED STATES

China to the other. The boycott was a prompt demonstration of Chinese enmity. And since those days of
humiliation China and her friends — and she has many —
have never ceased to denounce Japan at the bar of public
opinion. In Europe, among the allies of Japan, much
criticism was voiced. There was a touch of insincerity in
much of this, because Japan had learned these methods
from European diplomats who had been acclaimed for
their astuteness. If every foreign right in China which
had been founded upon force was set aside, China would
be freed from most of her embarrassing treaty obligations. But the fact remains, that Japan lost many good
friends in Europe because of these events.

In the United States the criticism was more outspoken.
Not only were some of the treaty provisions believed
to be contrary to the Open-Door policy, but the whole
course of the negotiations was repugnant to American
ideas of twentieth-century diplomacy. Little justification was found for the Japanese demands, and great
sympathy for China was expressed. In conformity
with its well-established policy, the American Government, on May 11th, advised both China and Japan that
it could not recognize any agreement entered into between
the two countries "impairing the treaty rights of the
United States and its citizens in China, the political or
territorial integrity of the Republic of China, or the international policy relative to China commonly known as
the Open-Door policy."

Finally, it is gratifying to note that in Japan much outspoken criticism of this drastic policy was voiced. At first
raised by publicists well informed in Chinese affairs, who
realized the heavy price Japan was paying in the loss of
Chinese friendship, it gradually gained in strength. The
fall of the Okuma Ministry in the following year has been

generally ascribed to dissatisfaction with its Chinese policy. Certainly the two following ministries have tried to make amends for the events of 1915. In entering the new consortium in 1920, Japan waived the right of monopoly of loans for railways in South Manchuria and Eastern Inner Mongolia, and no doubt other concessions will be made in the future in order to establish better relations between the two neighbors.

After the war with Russia, Japan had succeeded, without question, to the Russian interests and concessions in South Manchuria. She expected a similar surrender of the German rights in Shantung, and her promise to return the leasehold to China was considered gratuitous, but unnecessary. At no time had she offered to return the German economic concessions. Her treaty with China in 1915 guaranteed, on its face, that China would agree to the future disposition of the German rights, interests, and concessions. Her next step was to make sure that her allies would support her claims at the Peace Conference. In 1915, Great Britain, France, Russia, and Italy had agreed upon certain dispositions of German, Turkish, and Austrian territory, notably that Russia was to have Constantinople. It was only natural that Japan should also stipulate, in advance, that certain of her desires should be granted. These understandings were arrived at early in 1917, before the United States entered the war, and they were kept secret for two years. Great Britain, through its ambassador at Tokyo, assured Japan on February 16, 1917, that it would support Japan's claims in regard to German rights in Shantung and possessions in the islands north of the Equator, if Japan would treat in the same spirit Great Britain's claims to the islands south of the Equator. The latter assurance Japan promptly gave. Japan then made a similar request of France and Russia, on February 19th. France replied, on March 3d, that it would support the Japanese claims, on condition that Japan "give its support to obtain from China the breaking of its diplomatic relations with Germany, and that it give this act desirable significance." Russia had also urged Japan to support a movement to induce China to break with Germany, but seems to have agreed to support the Japanese claims without any conditions. Japan had been unwilling to have China enter the war unless her claims to the German rights were guaranteed by her allies. A little later, Italy gave her verbal assent to the Japanese request, at Rome. In these ways Japan felt assured that the German rights in Shantung would pass into her hands; she had won the approval of China and the support of her allies in advance.

Just at this time the United States entered the war. The development of public opinion in the United States affords an interesting subject of analysis. At the very outbreak of the Great War a few Americans realized the vital issues at stake in this struggle between a militaristic empire seeking domination and the free nations of Europe, but they were few, indeed, for most of their fellow citizens were too little informed of European conditions to understand the situation, and their traditional dislike for European entanglements caused them to view the catastrophe as a European rather than as a world problem. The presence of great numbers of residents of European stocks, sympathizing with one or the other of the belligerents, rendered the development of a united attitude toward the war slow and difficult. But public opinion swung more and more away from the Central Powers when facts became available as to their responsibility for the war and as to their ruthless conduct of its operations.

JAPAN, AMERICA, AND THE WORLD WAR

When, after repeated promises to the contrary, Germany proposed to renew ruthless and unrestricted submarine warfare, in February, 1917, there could be no doubt as to the part America must play. Relations were broken off on February 3d, on the 2d of April President Wilson asked Congress to declare a state of war with Germany, which was promptly done, and on the 6th the formal resolution was signed by the President. America had entered the war. She must now speedily draw upon her great resources of men and treasure and materials to turn the balance. As Lloyd George solemnly declared: "It was a race between Hindenburg and Wilson."

The entrance of the United States into the war soon produced a profound impression in Japan. It quite altered the nature of the struggle. The idealistic utterances of President Wilson were eagerly read in Japan, and the issues of the war were defined as never before. In the preceding years, the war had seemed a thing apart from Japanese life and interests, a European struggle, in which Japan had little at stake. These views vanished when Japan found herself allied with all the great liberal powers of the world in a struggle to preserve the best ideals of civilization. The liberal element in Japan found much encouragement in the state papers of the American President. And the remarkable demonstration of American energy in preparing for the struggle opened the eyes of others who had believed that democracy was but another name for inefficiency.

A few months later, China entered the war. The way in which this was brought about is of significance in this story. In 1915, Japan had refused to support a proposal of Great Britain, France, and Russia to have China enter the war. President Yuan had made such a proposal, but Japan considered it was designed to secure support for his imperial designs. She also realized how insignificant would be China's contribution, as civil war had already broken out because of Yuan's attempt to restore the monarchy. But in 1917, as we have seen, she had agreed to support the proposal. The United States had called upon all the neutral powers to join her in dissolving relations with Germany because of the latter's submarine outrages. American influence in Peking was strong, and, in spite of some opposition in official circles, China severed relations with Germany on March 14th. After the United States entered the war, it was expected that China would promptly follow. All factions favored the move, the military party because it would mean supplies and money which would strengthen its hands, the Parliament because it would win for China a place at the Peace Conference. But Parliament refused to pass the resolution as long as the Cabinet of General Tuan was in office. This occasioned a bitter political strife during which Parliament was illegally dissolved. Then came the dramatic attempt to restore the Manchu dynasty, and the restoration of the Republic by the old military leaders. A majority of the Parliament retired to Canton and set up a government there, in opposition to Peking. During this confusion, the United States advised China that entrance into the war or continued relations with Germany were matters of secondary importance to the continuance of her political union and the maintenance of national development. And she expressed the very sincere hope "that China, in her own interest, and in that of the world, will immediately set aside her factional political disputes, and that all parties and persons will work for the reëstablishment of a coördinate government and the assumption of that place among the Powers of the world to which China is so justly entitled, but the full attainment of which is impossible in the midst of internal discord." From this it may be inferred that the United States certainly offered no inducements to have China enter the war.

With the elimination of the hostile Parliament, the premier, General Tuan, proceeded to consider the declaration of war. The representatives of the powers in Peking were approached, and certain concessions were demanded. Some of these were rejected, but they did agree to remit the installments of the Boxer indemnity for five years and to permit the Chinese tariff to be raised to an actual five per cent. Then, on August 14th, war was proclaimed by presidential mandate, rather than by an act of Parliament as required by the constitution. China certainly entered the war because of the example of the United States. But the United States could hardly be held responsible for the methods which she used or for the internal dissensions which the question produced. Nor did the United States ever promise to support China's claims at the Peace Conference.

During the early part of the war, German propaganda in the United States had played upon the existing fear of Japanese aggression to divert American sympathy from the Allies. The fact that Japan was associated with the Allies was used to frighten ill-informed people. And the usual alarming misrepresentations of the Anglo-Japanese Alliance were repeatedly voiced. Just before the United States entered the war, the American secret service secured possession of a note from Dr. Zimmermann, German Secretary of State for Foreign Affairs, to the German Minister to Mexico, proposing an alliance with Mexico, for which Mexico would receive the lost territory in New Mexico, Texas, and Arizona. Mexico, in turn, was to suggest that Japan join in this scheme, and at the same time offer to mediate between Germany and Japan. These instructions were to be acted upon as soon as war between Germany and the United States broke out. The whole scheme, so far as Japan was concerned, was an absurd one, and the publication of the note did much to arouse American opinion against Germany.

Shortly after the United States entered the war, the Japanese Government sent a special mission, under Viscount Ishii, formerly Minister for Foreign Affairs, to congratulate the United States on its decision and to arrange for the coöperation of the two countries. The mission was received with warm hospitality throughout the United States, and the brilliant addresses of its chief did much to inform the American people of the part which his Government had played in the war and of its association with the cause for which the Allied and Associated Powers were fighting. The most interesting event of his visit was the exchange of notes with Secretary Lansing, on November 2, 1917. The purpose of these notes was: "In order to silence mischievous reports that have from time to time been circulated, it is believed by us that a public announcement once more of the desires and intentions shared by our two Governments with regard to China is advisable." Then followed the significant portion of the notes: "The Governments of the United States and Japan recognize that territorial propinquity creates special relations between countries, and, consequently, the Government of the United States recognizes that Japan has special interests in China, particularly in the part to which her possessions are contiguous." For the rest, the two powers pledged their support to the principles of the independence and territorial integrity of China and the Open Door.

In recognizing the fact that "territorial propinquity

creates special relations between countries," the note simply testified to a geographical truism. The special interests of Japan in Korea and China had been recognized by Britain long before. The United States, in turn, has special interests in the American continent. Taken in connection with the pledge to support the integrity of China and the Open Door, the recognition of Japan's special interests created no new status. Yet China took alarm, and declared, on November 12th, that she would not allow herself to be bound by any agreement entered into by other nations. The Lansing-Ishii notes stand on the same plane as the Root-Takihira notes of 1908. They are not the equivalent of a treaty; they have no binding force on either country; they were simply the declaration of a policy, which might be changed by either Government at any time. But, after these repeated affirmations, the policy possesses a moral sanction as effective, if not as legal, as a formal treaty.

After the unfortunate results of the 1915 negotiations, Japan adopted a more moderate policy toward China. During the Ministry of Count Terauchi, 1916–18, large sums were loaned to the Central and Provincial Governments of China by Japanese bankers, with support, and at times at the request, of the Japanese Government. In this way Japanese interests were greatly extended on the mainland. On the surface these measures were reasonable enough. China was hopelessly in need of funds, and the old banking organizations could no longer supply the demands, because of the war. Japan, for the first time, had the money available and could make whatever arrangements its bankers desired without European competition. Before 1914, China had been financed largely by British, with some German, French, and American capital. The profits on these transactions had been great, and Japan was anxious to secure some of them, as well as to become, if possible, the dominant creditor nation in China. But the internal situation in China made this a dangerous proceeding. With China divided between the north and the south, any loans to the Northern Government would arouse the resentment of the Constitutionalists, for they believed, and with good reason, that the money was being used to maintain the military party in power in Peking. But the Peking Government was the only one recognized by the powers, and the Japanese bankers felt confident that their advances would be safe. After the collapse of the Russian Government and the signature of the Brest-Litovsk Treaty, Japan and China signed a military and a naval agreement in May, 1918, for coöperation against the common enemy, and an advance of 20,000,000 yen was made for the purchase of arms. But the most significant of the many loan agreements was one concluded on September 24, 1918. At the request of China, the Japanese Government agreed to induce its bankers to advance money for the construction of two railways in Shantung Province, from Tsinan to Shunteh and from Kaomi to Hsuchow. A preliminary advance of 20,000,000 yen was paid. These loan options had previously been granted to Germany on December 31, 1913. On the same day Baron Goto, Minister of Foreign Affairs, notified the Chinese Minister that Japan would withdraw the troops stationed along the Kiaochow-Tsinan railway, except for a detachment at Tsinan; that the latter railway would be worked as a joint Japanese and Chinese enterprise as soon as its status should have been established; and that the civil administration established by the Japanese in Shantung would be abolished. The Minister replied that "the Chinese Government are pleased to agree to the above-mentioned articles proposed by the

Japanese Government." Although a summary of these arrangements was given out at the time, their significance was not properly understood until China sought the restoration of the German rights in Shantung at Paris. Then the "secret compacts" of 1918 served to weaken greatly her legal case.

America's great contribution to the Allied cause was the raising, training, equipping, and transportation to France of some 2,000,000 soldiers. Their presence turned the tide, and the despair of March, 1918, was turned into the triumph of Armistice Day in November. Japan, for reasons which were valid, sent no troops to Europe. Japanese destroyers took part in the struggle against submarines in the Mediterranean, and there they coöperated with American forces. But after the Treaty of Brest-Litovsk, something had to be done to prevent the Germans from overrunning Russia. This was primarily a Japanese problem, but she promptly consulted with her allies as to the best course to pursue. After several months of consideration, a proposal formulated by the United States was adopted by Japan, on August 3d, and by the other powers. It called for sending a joint expedition to Siberia to rescue the Czecho-Slovak troops who were fighting their way across Siberia to secure transport to the western front. This military assistance, it was hoped, would "steady any efforts at self-government or self-defense in which the Russians themselves may be willing to accept assistance." In adopting this plan, the Japanese Government announced: "They reaffirm their avowed policy of respecting the territorial integrity of Russia, and of abstaining from all interference in her internal politics. They further declare that, upon the realization of the objects above indicated, they will immediately withdraw all Japanese troops from Russian territory, and will leave wholly unimpaired the sovereignty of Russia in all its phases, whether political or military."

Vladivostok had been occupied in April by Japanese, British, and American sailors. American, Japanese, British, and some French and Italian troops took part in the expeditionary force. The Trans-Siberian Railway was opened for its entire length, the former German and Austrian prisoners were retaken and disarmed, and the Czecho-Slovak troops were rescued. The announced object of the expedition was achieved. Then the question arose as to whether the intervention should continue against the Bolsheviki, and in some quarters an effort was made to secure adequate support for Admiral Kolchak and the Omsk Government. When that movement collapsed, there was no Russian force which might be supported, and American public opinion did not approve of open war upon Russia. Early in 1920, the American troops were withdrawn, and Japan promptly took control of Vladivostok.

The whole Russian problem had bristled with difficulties. It goes without saying that there were many conflicting views as to what should be done in Siberia. Americans might have an academic interest in what went on there, for Bolsheviki control would not endanger any American territory. But for the Japanese it was a very vital problem, and the presence of a Red Government at Vladivostok, so near to Korea where discontent was rife, could not be considered without alarm. For these reasons, Japan sent in more troops than had been anticipated, and massed large forces in Korea and North Manchuria. Accurate information is not available as to many of the things which took place in Siberia between 1918 and 1921. We can only note the problem created there by the collapse of the constituted government and the alarm occasioned by Bolsheviki pronouncements against all organized authority. Until the situation is cleared up, we must rely upon Japan to keep the pledge which she freely gave in 1918, and we must sympathize with her for being like the man in the Chinese proverb who tried to ride a tiger — it was easy to get on, but extremely difficult to get off. At present Japan holds the northern part of the island of Saghalien, pending reparation for the massacre of Japanese soldiers and civilians at Nikolaevsk in March, 1920. This island, it must be remembered, was formerly claimed by Japan and ceded to Russia in 1875. The southern portion was returned to Japan by the Treaty of Portsmouth, in 1905. It would not be surprising if, under these circumstances, Japan should try to regain possession of the northern three fifths when the status of Siberia is finally determined.

CHAPTER XII

THE NEW FAR EAST

On the 18th of January, 1919, the delegates of the Allied and Associated Powers assembled in the Foreign Office at Paris to formulate the terms of peace which would be offered to Germany and her allies. In these discussions the representatives of the United States would be expected to play an important part. Not only had the American contribution of men and material brought about the unexpected termination of the war, but both Germany and her foes had accepted, as a basis for peace negotiations, the terms laid down by President Wilson in his address to Congress on the 8th of January, 1918, and in his subsequent addresses. And President Wilson himself was in Paris as the leader of the American delegation. The United States sought no territory and no indemnity. Its representatives were concerned solely with the preparation of a treaty which would bring about lasting peace and prevent a recurrence of the recent catastrophe.

Japan was represented by five distinguished statesmen and diplomats: Marquis Saionji, twice Prime Minister; Viscount Chinda, Ambassador to Great Britain; Baron Makino, formerly Minister of Foreign Affairs; Mr. Matsui, Ambassador to France; and Mr. Ijuin, Ambassador to Italy. In regard to the purely European settlements of the peace treaty, Japan took little interest. But two things she expected, as a matter of course: the cession to her of the German rights in Shantung and their possessions in the islands north of the Equator. And after the covenant of the League of Nations was under discussion,

230

she tried to have it include a recognition of the principle of racial equality.

China also appointed five representatives: Mr. Lou Tsengtsiang, Minister of Foreign Affairs; Dr. V. K. W. Koo, Minister to the United States; Mr. Alfred Sze, Minister to Great Britain; Dr. C. T. Wang, representative of the Canton Government; and Dr. W. P. Wei, Minister to Belgium, and also nominally representative of the South. The civil war, which had been in progress since June, 1917, had temporarily ceased during an armistice, and a peace conference was in session in Shanghai. At Paris, the representatives of both North and South worked unitedly and strenuously for China. A first disappointment was realized when, before the Conference opened, it was announced that China would be entitled to only two seats at the plenary sessions. In this respect she ranked below Belgium, Serbia, and Brazil, and on a par with Greece, Poland, Portugal, Czecho-Slovakia, Roumania, and the new Kingdom of the Hedjaz. China had three desiderata: the abrogation of the Japanese treaties of 1915, the direct restitution to herself of the leasehold of Kiaochow and other German rights in Shantung, and the readjustment of all treaty engagements which impaired her sovereignty. Under the latter head, China sought the abrogation of all foreign spheres of influence or interest, the withdrawal of all foreign troops and police, the withdrawal of foreign post-offices and wireless and telegraphic agencies, the abolition of consular jurisdiction, the restoration of the leased territories, the restoration of foreign concessions and settlements, and the establishment of tariff autonomy. It seems that China was injudiciously advised in bringing up these subjects for discussion. They had nothing to do with the purpose of the Conference, which was to formulate the terms of a treaty of peace with Germany, and they therefore were never taken into consideration. Nor was China able to estab-lish her claim that the 1915 treaties had arisen out of the war and thus should be reviewed at the Peace Confer-ence. She was therefore compelled to concentrate all her energies on the remaining desire, the direct restitution of the German rights.

The Japanese expected that there would be little diffi-culty about the German islands north of the Equator. Great Britain, France, and Italy had, in 1917, promised to support her claim at the Peace Conference. But, with the acceptance of the mandatory principle on January 29th, Japan was to receive a mandate rather than com-plete possession. As the United States did not agree to the terms of the mandate, as formulated by the Supreme Council on May 7, 1919, the United States later protested to the four powers then represented on the Council against the inclusion of the island of Yap in the Japanese mandate.

The next question in which Japan was concerned was that of racial equality. The original American plan of the League of Nations contained two articles, one protecting racial minorities, and the other guaranteeing religious freedom. On February 13th, Baron Makino presented an amendment: "The equality of nations being a basic prin-ciple of the League of Nations, the High Contracting Parties agree to accord, as soon as possible, to all aliens, nationals of all states, members of the League, equal and just treatment in every respect, making no distinction, either in law or in fact, on account of their race or na-tionality." In supporting his amendment, Baron Makino said: "You will permit me to say, for the sake of clear-ness, that the question being of a very delicate and com-plicated nature, involving the play of a deep human passion, the immediate realization of the ideal equality is not proposed. The clause presented to the Commission enunciates only the principle, leaving to the different governments concerned the actual working-out of the practice to be followed. In other words, the proposal is intended as an invitation to the governments and the peoples, who are to be associated in this great League, to examine the question more closely and seriously and to devise in a fair and accommodating spirit means to meet it." In spite of the strong hostility which the Chinese delegation held toward Japan, Dr. Koo rose and supported the proposal. "I fully realize," he said, "that the principle embodied involves a great number of questions, social and economic among others, which can be solved only in the fullness of time; but as a principle, I would like to see it given some recognition in this covenant." No vote was taken at this time, but a large majority of the League of Nations Commission expressed approval of the measure.

The Japanese amendment created much discussion. It was at once considered, in certain quarters, to be designed to remove all restrictions against Asiatic immigration, and Mr. Hughes, of Australia, opposed it on this ground. When the Commission assembled for its final session on April 11th, Baron Makino presented a compromise amendment, which asked for "equality of nations and just treatment of their nationals." Again the measure was strongly supported, although Greece, Poland, and Czecho-Slovakia, where racial minorities had created internal problems, opposed. When the vote was taken, eleven or twelve delegates voted for the amendment, and five against it. President Wilson, who was in the chair, ruled that such a motion required unanimity, and so it was lost. When the covenant was finally submitted to the Peace Conference, on April 28th, Baron Makino gave notice of the poignant regret of the Japanese Government and people at the failure of the Commission to approve of their just demand, and of their intention to insist upon the adoption of this principle by the League in the future.

The significance of the defeat of this amendment has not been properly understood in the West. It was looked upon by Japanese, and other thoughtful Orientals, as a fundamental principle of an association of nations. Japan had made a fight for equal treatment, which had been so long denied to Asiatics, and she had been defeated. And, in announcing that she would continue to press this matter, she assumed the leadership of Asia in this struggle, a contest in which sooner or later victory must rest upon her banners. The reasons for the defeat are not convincing. Only by a forced construction could the principle be applied to immigration. The control of immigration and naturalization are domestic matters, outside the jurisdiction of a League of Nations. But the just treatment of nationals who have been admitted to member states seems to be essential to the development of that good-will upon which international coöperation should rest. Japan herself could not relinquish the right to control immigration, else the cheap labor of China and India might be introduced to compete with her higher-paid workers. Nor are the Japanese less free from racial pride than Western peoples. The attitude of the average Japanese toward the Korean or the Chinese leaves much to be desired. But in advocating this great principle the Japanese won a moral advantage in spite of their defeat.

Having lost two of their desires, the Japanese were in no humor to abandon their claim to the German rights in Shantung. Their legal case was unassailable. They had actually taken the leasehold and the railroad and mines from Germany. China had agreed, in 1915, to accept the decision of the Peace Conference. Japan's allies had promised, in 1917, to support her claims. And China, in 1918, had again recognized her interests, by the secret treaty and the exchange of notes. The Chinese case was equally weak, from a legal standpoint, but it was morally strong. And for this reason it had the support of the American delegation, and to a great extent of the American people.

On January 27th, the Japanese presented their case before the Council of Ten, and the next day the cause of China was argued by Dr. Koo, in a brilliant address. In reply, Baron Makino cited the Agreements of 1918, which were unknown to the other members of the Council of Ten. On April 22d, Baron Makino presented Japan's reply before the Council of Four. Before doing so, he stated that the Japanese delegation had received instructions not to sign the treaty unless the Japanese claim to the German rights was sustained. That afternoon, Mr. Lou and Dr. Koo were again summoned to explain their case. And no further action was taken, apparently, until, on April 30th, it was announced that the Council of Three had decided to approve of the Japanese demands. The Chinese, who were not permitted to sign with a reservation, refused to attach their signatures to the treaty on June 28th.

The Chinese case rested on two main contentions. One was that the Shantung Treaty of 1915 was signed under duress, and that it and the Agreements of 1918 were merely temporary arrangements, subject to final revision by the Peace Conference because they dealt primarily with questions which had arisen from the war. The other was that, on declaring war upon Germany, she expressly stipulated that all treaties, agreements, and conventions between the two powers were abrogated. Thus the Germans possessed no rights in Shantung which they might cede to Japan. The first argument was favorably received by many, including the American commissioners and their Far Eastern advisers. But, as has been already remarked, if every treaty extorted by force from China could thus be annulled, foreigners would enjoy few treaty rights in that country. The railway agreement of 1918, and the notes then exchanged, after China entered the war, meant nothing unless the Treaty of 1915 were valid, and, in accepting an advance of 20,000,000 yen, the Chinese Government certainly assumed that the 1918 Agreement was not a temporary arrangement. And as to the effect of China's entrance into the war upon her treaty with Germany, this is still an academic question. Some authorities hold that a lease convention would be abrogated, and some do not. It should be noted, however, that, in the case of other Sino-German treaties and agreements, their abrogation was not taken as a matter of course, but was specifically declared in the text of the treaty, as a study of articles 128 and 132 would show. The strength of China's case was in its moral, rather than its legal, force. The restoration of the German rights would "comport to her national dignity and serve to illustrate further the principle of right and justice for which the Allies and Associates have fought the common enemy." To which the Japanese replied: "The impression derived from the examination of the Chinese memorandum is that Japan must bear the burden of all sacrifices, whilst China reaps all the benefits."

The Shantung controversy at Paris represented a conflict between the old order and the new. According to the standards which had prevailed in the past, the Japanese position was unassailable. And, when the decision was to be made, Japan could count upon two of the three votes, for Britain and France had promised to support her cause, and each held leaseholds and claimed spheres of influence in China. It was natural that the American delegates should have been impressed by the moral force of China's request, and should have attempted, as they did, to secure a decision in her favor. But only bitter partisanship could hold President Wilson responsible for not forcing his colleagues to break their plighted word to Japan. In this instance, as in 1915, Japan made a great mistake in following the old ways in dealing with China, rather than the dictates of reasonableness and concrete good-will. The German concessions in Shantung, valuable as they were, could never make up for the resentment aroused by Japan's possession of them. Outside of China and America, the Shantung decision was accepted as a matter of course. Europe saw in it nothing unusual or worthy of disapprobation.

The articles relating to Shantung in the Treaty of Versailles are articles 156, 157, and 158. Germany renounced to Japan all her rights acquired by the Treaty of 1898 — the leasehold of Kaiochow, the railways, mines, and submarine cables, and the movable and immovable property owned by her. And within three months she was to hand over to Japan all archives relating to the administration of the territory, and give particulars concerning all treaties, arrangements, or agreements relating to these rights, titles, and privileges. It should be clearly understood that the treaty transferred to Japan rights which Germany, and not China, possessed. It referred to a leasehold of some two hundred square miles — smaller than Weihaiwei and Kowloon, and slightly larger than Kwangchowwan, leased by Great Britain and France. The railway was two hundred and fifty-six miles long; two coal mines were in operation and an iron mine had been opened. In addition, Germany had secured loan options on certain railway lines, as recently as December, 1913, and June, 1914. Japan made no new promises as to the restoration of the leasehold. She announced that her promise of 1915 and the promise of 1918 to turn the railway into a Sino-Japanese enterprise would be observed. Later she offered to accept an international settlement at Tsingtao instead of a purely Japanese one.

From the very beginning of this discussion at Paris, the real facts were clouded by misrepresentation. On April 28th, Mr. Lansing, the American Secretary of State, recorded in his daily journal, in reference to the proposed transfer of the German rights to Japan: "It is a surrender of the principle of self-determination, a transfer of millions of Chinese from one foreign master to another." But he also spoke of the German treaties of 1898 as conventions "by which the sovereign authority over this 'Holy Land' of China was to all intents ceded to Germany." Dr. Koo, in presenting China's case, said that the people of Shantung "resented bitterly the German occupation of the Kiaochow Bay and the German penetration into the Province of Shantung." If that was the case, why did the Chinese Government encourage this penetration by granting additional railway loan options to Germany in 1913 and 1914? Dr. Hornbeck has clearly pointed out that, after the original seizure of Kiaochow, German policy became so moderate that "none of the powers holding bases on the China coast can offer better justification for its presence than could the Germans." It would have been absurd to say that the sovereign authority over Shantung was exercised by Germany in 1914, and it is just as absurd to say that the Versailles Treaty conferred upon Japan even "virtual sovereignty" over the 38,000,000 inhabitants of that province. If the railway and mining rights transferred to Japan should ever be extended into sovereign rights, it would be due to the absolute collapse of the Chinese nation. The way for China to avoid this calamity is through internal reorganization rather than by leaning upon foreign powers, no matter how well-intentioned they may be.

Because of the increasing criticism of Japan's foreign policies, her treatment of China, her uncertain course in Siberia, and her stern measures in Korea, and because of the misrepresentations of the real nature of the Shantung decision at Paris, the Shantung articles in the treaty received more discussion and unfavorable criticism than any portion of the treaty except the covenant of the League of Nations. In the United States Senate the subject was considered at great length, and among the fifteen reservations which were finally agreed upon was one which stated that the United States withholds its assent to these articles and reserves full liberty of action with respect to any controversy which may arise. That such a controversy could accomplish any good is not evident. The treaty had been ratified by enough of the powers to put it into effect. The German rights had actually been transferred to Japan, and there was no disposition on the part of the Senators to enter into a war to compel Japan to return them to China. So the hostile criticism embittered Japan and accomplished nothing for China. It would have been better to have expressed confidence in Japan and thus supported the efforts of that large group of Japanese who believe that their Government should deal generously with its neighbor. As the treaty failed of ratification in the Senate, the reservations, of course, had no effect.

American criticism of Japan because of her demand for the German rights in Shantung was intensified because of the reports which came out of Korea in the spring and summer of 1919. Stripped of the gross exaggeration which seems to be inevitable in much of the news from the Far East, it appeared that on the 1st of March, 1919, thirty-three Koreans assembled in a public park in Seoul, the capital, read a declaration of independence, and then waited to be arrested. This was followed by demonstrations for independence in many parts of the peninsula.

Although the Koreans used no force, the police, in many cases, handled the crowds roughly. Eventually fighting occurred and regular troops supported the police. The official report indicates that, up to October, — and by that time order had been restored, — 631 Koreans had been killed and 1409 wounded, while 9 Japanese policemen had been killed and 186 wounded. The burning of villages, churches, and homes as reprisals occurred too frequently during the early days. Reports were published abroad that from 20,000 to 40,000 Koreans had been killed, that native Christians were the especial object of Japanese brutality, and that a deliberate effort was being made to eradicate the Christian religion. It was the religious aspect of the movement which caught the attention of many Americans.

The unfortunate effect of the exaggerated statements has not yet been counteracted. Some Americans knew of the great contributions which Japan had made to the prosperity and welfare of the Korean people. They knew of the money which had been poured into the country to introduce public improvements of all kinds, schools, sanitation, and modern methods of administration. They realized some of the mistakes which the Korean Government had made — it had thought too much of material

betterments and had neglected the feelings of its wards.
And when the independence movement occurred they
remembered, with regret, that every ruling power be-
lieves that insurrection must be promptly suppressed
lest it spread so far that many thousands of lives would
be lost in the process. Just at this very time agitations
were sternly repressed in India and Egypt. The connection between Christian propaganda and the independence
movement was well understood by persons familiar with
conditions in Korea. Christianity is a religion of democracy. It stresses human rights, even though it admon-
ishes, "render, therefore, unto Cæsar the things which
are Cæsar's; and unto God the things that are God's."
In the Christian churches many Koreans received training in organization and leadership, and most of the Prot-
estant missionaries came from democratic countries. It
was natural, therefore, that from the very beginning
of Korean efforts for independence Korean Christians
should have been among the leaders of the movement,
and whenever the Government started repressive measures many Christians would be among the first to be arrested. These men were arrested because they were suspected political offenders, who happened to be Christians.
But it is easy to understand how many Japanese, such
as policemen and lesser officials, should have considered
them as offenders because they were Christians. There
is no reason to believe that the foreign missionaries gave
any encouragement to the independence movement, but
many of them were outspoken in indignant criticism of
the stern measures of the police and soldiers, and thus
they became associated with the cause in the minds of
many Japanese.

Happily, as soon as conditions in Korea became known
in Japan, the Government promptly moved to correct

some of the objectionable features of the administration. The military government came to an end, and a liberal retired admiral, Baron Saito, was appointed Governor-General. The police system was reformed, educational facilities were improved, discriminations were removed, and steps were taken looking toward greater Korean participation in the Government. No man who has the best interests of the Korean people at heart could sincerely advocate Korean independence at the present time. The people are still lacking in education and political experience. Japan has done much to improve the material welfare of her Korean subjects. She can do much more to further their intellectual and political development. There is no reason why Korea should not develop into an autonomous, prosperous, and contented part of the Japanese state, enjoying the advantages which come from membership in a strong and enterprising community.

If Americans, in many cases, were alienated from Japan in 1919 because of her conduct in Shantung, Siberia, and Korea, it must also be remembered that many Japanese were alienated from America because of her rejection of the treaty of peace, her refusal to join the League of Nations, and her adoption of a great naval programme. Early in 1919, the anti-Japanese agitation began in California which resulted in the passage of the Alien Land Law as an initiative measure in November, 1920. These events weakened the influence of Japanese liberals and gave aid and comfort to the military party. The noble words of President Wilson were apparently turned into mockery by sinister deeds. Against whom could the United States be preparing "the greatest fleet in the world," if not against Japan? Under these circumstances, it was natural that Japan should hurry her naval preparations, at the very time when liberal leaders in business and politics were advocating a reduction of armaments. In spite of the apparent justification for the Japanese interpretation of America's acts, few, if any, Americans thought of these measures as designed for aggression. Aside from the political aspects of the treaty discussion, the rejection of the League was primarily based upon the old American tradition of isolation. A host of forward-looking Americans, on the other hand, believed firmly that the time had come when America should join hands with the nations, of West and East, in the service of humanity and world peace. So if the Japanese, in so many cases, wrongly interpreted America's policy, it is quite as reasonable to believe that an equal misunderstanding prevailed in the United States as to the aggressive designs of Japan.

The people and Government of the United States desire to be on good terms with their neighbors across the Pacific, with Japan, China, and Russia. They believe in the principles of the Open Door and the independence and integrity of China. They seek no special privileges for themselves, and they resent any attempt to take advantage of the weakness of China to secure special favors for any country. Thoughtful Americans recognize the peculiar necessities of Japan — the pressure of a rapidly increasing population dwelling in a small area with limited natural resources. They welcome, therefore, any development of Japanese commerce and industry which will help Japan to provide for the economic advancement of her industrious people. But this development must not come at the expense of the rights and liberties of neighboring states. American capital has shown itself willing to coöperate with Japan in developing the resources of China, and the new consortium, if it can secure the coöperation of the Chinese people, will offer large opportunities for legitimate investment of American and Japanese capital in enterprises of great and permanent value in China. But if Japan should continue to follow the old precedents, should endeavor to extend her special interests in China by force or intrigue, then there need be no question that American public opinion will certainly support China, and the relations between Japan and the United States will be increasingly unsatisfactory.

From the point of view of Japan, it would seem to be the wisest public policy to do everything possible to regain and to hold the good-will of China. Good-will is an imponderable which is at the basis of good business. China possesses in large measure the raw materials, especially iron and food supplies, which Japan needs. She also should be the greatest market for Japanese goods. The geographical position of Japan gives her an advantage in Chinese commerce, which should make her a strong advocate of the Open Door. But age-long antipathy, in spite of a common culture, makes the establishment of cordial relations difficult. Ever since the days when Kublai Khan sent two armadas to conquer Japan, in the thirteenth century, the relations between the two countries have been generally hostile. After these attempts to conquer Japan, Japanese adventurers raided the coast of China for many years. Intercourse was suspended, save for a limited number of Chinese junks which were permitted to trade at Nagasaki, during the two hundred years of Japan's seclusion. Then, with the renewal of official intercourse in 1871, one episode after another served to endanger the peace — the Formosan expedition, the Korean controversy, the war between China and Japan. After the Russian War, many occasions for friction occurred in Manchuria, and then came the Shantung question, the Twenty-One Demands, and Japan's support of the Northern militarists. The relations between the Governments have been, therefore, constantly strained. And this has been true, also, of the popular feeling in both countries. Before the war of 1894, the Chinese looked down upon the Japanese as an inferior and barbarous people. After the war, they were forced to respect the power of Japan, but contempt only turned into resentment. And the Japanese, who had looked up to China as a great source of culture, began to hold her in contempt after her weakness and inefficiency became demonstrated in the nineteenth century.

Japan, therefore, must do something positive to improve these relations between the Governments and the peoples. It will not be an easy task as long as China is politically divided. If, after the revolution of 1911, China had advanced steadily in political organization, and in economic and educational development, the problem would be a much simpler one. China had a great opportunity during the European war, when the old pressure was removed, but that opportunity was lost through the selfishness of her political and military leaders. To-day China needs unselfish encouragement and support, and the three powers who have most at stake in rendering this are Japan, the United States, and Great Britain, and of these it means most to Japan. She should, therefore, be ready and willing to coöperate in all good works which will help China to regain her political union and independence. She should take the lead in offering to yield every special advantage which may hinder China's political and economic advancement. Japan knows, from bitter experience, the difficulties and dangers of extraterritoriality. She should lead in arranging for the restoration of these rights to China at the first possible moment. And in every proposal which will help China, Japan can count upon the cordial support of the United States and Great Britain.

It is true that there are some Japanese who hold most pessimistic views regarding China, who believe that only through foreign — and that is Japanese — control can China organize sound governmental institutions and proceed to the proper development of her great natural resources. Under the guise of a Monroe Doctrine for Asia, they would eliminate all European and American influence and then firmly establish Japanese control. They have little justification for their beliefs. However lacking in political solidarity the Chinese people may be at the present time, it is inconceivable that they would tolerate Japanese interference in their domestic affairs. The Monroe Doctrine, as Americans understand it, is a negative policy. It was designed to prevent European interference in the affairs of the American republics, but it created no special position for the United States in Latin America. The Japanese may properly look forward to the elimination of foreign special privileges in China, but they should not endeavor to supplant them by their own. Nor would it be wise for Japan to announce a real Monroe Doctrine for China until the Chinese people are willing to accept the assistance of Japan in this respect.

The problems of China — and of Asia for that matter — must be solved from within. As soon as education frees the latent capacity of the Chinese people, inefficiency in government and big business will give place to efficiency. All the friends of China should lend their aid to speed the coming of this day, but they must not expect it to come at once. And when that comes there will be no danger of foreign aggression. It should not tax the imagination to conceive of the time when all

THE NEW FAR EAST

European control of Asiatic peoples will come to an end —
when the people of India, Indo-China, the East Indies,
and the Philippines will be able to govern themselves
wisely and well. Then "Asia for the Asiatics" will be
a reality, but much harm may be done if the process
changes from evolution to revolution before the time is
ripe.

In spite of popular misunderstandings which have developed in the past fifteen years, the relations between
the Governments of Japan and the United States have
been uniformly friendly. But the increasing influence of
public opinion renders it essential that there should be no
misunderstandings. And the one remedy for misunderstanding is understanding. It is necessary, therefore, for
Americans and Japanese to know more about each other.
Each should know more about the historical development
and the present problems of the other people. Each
should recognize, not simply their own rights, but their
duties, and the rights and duties of their neighbor. And
each should try to appreciate the other's point of view —
but this, in turn, is possible simply through understanding. "I am glad to say," said Secretary Hughes, "that
the message of America is one of cordial friendship to all
nations. We have no questions which mutual good-will
and the processes of reason cannot solve." And this ap-
plies especially to Japan.

The immigration question has been settled by conference and mutual agreement and along lines which Japan
herself would use were she faced with a similar problem.
The Japanese in the United States will be protected in
their treaty rights and constitutional guarantees. As long
as racial antipathies exist, these questions must receive a
practical rather than a theoretical solution, but with the
passing of the years time will smooth away the occasions

for friction. For the present, each Government must observe its treaty obligations with unquestioned good faith.

And in the Far East, where in the last few years the most occasions for misunderstanding have arisen, the two Governments must coöperate cordially and sincerely to give reality to their announced principle of the Open Door and the integrity of China. The Japanese must realize that the United States is an American power with no desire or intention to interfere with the legitimate development of Japan or any other Asiatic nation. They must remember that an American concession to build a railway or a dockyard in China is a business transaction, pure and simple, with no political design in the background. And the American people must have the same confidence in Japan. They must free themselves from a state of mind which magnifies a Japanese fishing concession or a stranded cruiser in Lower California into a naval base. Japan is primarily an Asiatic country, and she should seek no special advantages in the Americas. But the right to invest her capital or engage in legitimate enterprises in Mexico should not be questioned. It would be too much to expect that the press in both countries would eliminate all alarming stories which are, on their face, preposterous. Bismarck once said "that every nation must pay in the end for the windows broken by its press," but with better understanding and mutual confidence fewer windows will be broken and the cost will be trivial.

There is no reason, therefore, why the people of Japan and the United States should not maintain unimpaired the traditional friendship. A war-weary world calls for the constructive services of all capable peoples. By wise statesmanship Japan can regain the confidence of America and the leadership of Asia, which she so nearly lost during the world struggle. But real leadership must be based upon service and not upon force, and no one could begrudge Japan such leadership in Asia. For a time it looked as if the lessons of the Great War had been unheeded, as if the old ways of national selfishness and rivalry and preparation for war still prevailed. But, although the deadly gas may linger over the silent battlefield, it is dissipated by the fresh winds of the morning; so may the days of readjustment result in a new resolve, on the part of both the American and the Japanese people, to live and work in harmony and to find a common field of service in helping the people of China help themselves.

CHAPTER XIII

THE JAPANESE IN AMERICA

THE so-called Japanese problem in America is simply one phase of an age-long and world-wide problem, the adjustment of human relations. If any one should be tempted to take a pessimistic view of the outcome of this effort, he need only remember that mankind has steadily progressed toward better human relations. Family and tribal wars have ceased, and, in spite of the terrible experience of recent days, the normal status of nations is that of peace. The last great adjustment which the human family is called upon to make is that between the races of different color, for the rank and file of mankind still classify men by color rather than by mental or moral attainments.

Oriental emigration developed with the improved means of transportation in the latter half of the nineteenth century. By that time the adventurous peoples of Europe, led by the Portugese and Spaniards, and then by the British, Dutch, and French, had taken possession of all the sparsely peopled regions of the Americas, Africa, and Australia, and ruled over hundreds of millions of Asiatic peoples. While Japan was still closed to foreign intercourse, the Chinese began to seek their fortunes far overseas, first in California and then in Australia as gold was discovered in both places. Later a large number of "coolie" or indentured laborers were shipped to Cuba, the West Indies, and South America. Japanese emigration developed later, and not until the eighties did any large number leave their homes.

The motives for this emigration were exactly the same

as those which attracted European emigrants to the
United States at the same time. They were primarily
economic, the desire to better one's self. Great opportunities existed in California, the land of gold, and every
Chinese hoped to make a fortune in a few years and then
return to his native district. For that reason very few
women accompanied the vigorous pioneers, whose stay,
it was hoped, would be but brief.

The United States, in those days, welcomed European
immigration. America was the home of the free and the
refuge of the oppressed, whether by religious, political, or
economic bonds. So millions of Europeans, first from
northern and then from southern and eastern Europe, entered her gates. Those who came from northern Europe
were easily assimilated by the old British stock, and in
comparison with the people of the colored races all the
Europeans were easily absorbed. If the parents held
to the old customs, the children, trained in the public
schools, grew up with few exceptions to be "real Americans." But the Chinese and Japanese usually remained
apart. They were different in color and in culture. For
mutual benefit and protection they tended to live together in groups, and thus cultural assimilation was
hindered. And coming from lands where the standard of
living was much lower than in America, they could live
on wages far below the prevailing rates. After the immigration question began to be studied, the dangers of mass
immigration were pointed out. By this was meant the
immigration of peoples from any part of the world in
such numbers that they would form homogeneous groups
or masses, which would maintain their national language,
customs, and standards of living. Such groups of European immigrants are found throughout the Atlantic
States, and have had much to do with the new immigra-

tion policy which has recently been adopted. Asiatic immigration, if unregulated, would tend to the mass type.

Chinese were the first Oriental immigrants to enter California after the American occupation. A few arrived before the close of 1848, sailing from Hongkong as soon as news of the discovery of gold reached there. Others promptly followed — several hundred in 1849, several thousand in 1850, and by the end of 1851 it was estimated that there were twenty-five thousand in the State. At first they were well received. They were peaceful, industrious, thrifty, and honest, and there was work enough for all to do and wages were high. But within a few years objections were raised against them, and local and State discriminations began which finally resulted in the passage of a Federal Exclusion Act in 1882. These objections may be summed up as: (1) social — they were said to be unassimilable, with strange and repellent manners, customs, and ideals; (2) economic — they were cheap labor, with a low standard of living, able and willing to work for less than a white man's wage; (3) moral — they engaged in opium-smoking, incessant gambling, and other vices; (4) political — if their numbers were not checked, they would soon overrun and control the whole Pacific Coast. These objections were cited, with varying emphasis upon one or another of them, throughout the whole campaign. There was some truth in them, but the truth was often concealed in a mass of exaggeration or falsehood. The desire of most Californians that Chinese immigration be restricted was a proper one, but the measures taken by the local officials and by many of the citizens were, in many cases, absolutely indefensible. The story of the mistreatment of the Chinese in California and other Western States is a discreditable page in American history.

THE JAPANESE IN AMERICA

Fortunately for the Japanese, their immigration to California did not develop until the anti-Chinese agitation had quieted down. For this reason they were not linked with the Chinese in the former brutalities, and when a Japanese problem arose it was promptly dealt with before popular ill-will had developed. On the other hand, some of the methods of the anti-Chinese agitators have been used effectively against the Japanese.

The first Japanese to visit California after the American occupation were shipwrecked seamen who were blown across the Pacific. In February, 1851, seventeen Japanese were rescued off the coast and brought to San Francisco, where they were kindly cared for. A few others arrived in this fashion. After the repeal of the seclusion laws, in 1866, a few Japanese came to the United States. In 1870, the census reported fifty-five persons of the Japanese race in the country; in 1880, the number was 148; and in 1890, 2039. In 1885, Japan permitted her laborers to emigrate, and an immigration convention with Hawaii was concluded the next year. This fact, coupled with the desire for labor in California to take the place of the unobtainable Chinese laborers, caused Japanese immigration to increase steadily after 1890. In 1891, 1136 entered the United States; in 1898, 2230; and in 1900, 12,628. The latter number has never been equaled since that time. After the annexation of Hawaii, a number of Japanese laborers passed to the mainland, but no figures of this domestic movement have been recorded. In 1900, the census reported 24,326 Japanese, and in 1910, 72,157.

The increase of Japanese immigration in 1900 and the following years alarmed some of the labor leaders in California. The Japanese, unlike many of the Chinese, were unwilling to remain as unskilled laborers, and many of them promptly changed their status from laborers to skilled workmen, small merchants, land renters and owners. On this account they began to compete with organized labor at first, and later with the farming class. In 1904, the American Federation of Labor met in San Francisco and memorialized Congress to extend the Chinese exclusion laws to Japanese and Korean laborers. The next year a bitter attack upon the Japanese was launched by an influential San Francisco newspaper, and the Japanese and Korean Exclusion League was organized, which for many years led in demanding the exclusion of these Orientals. Little popular interest was aroused, however, until the action of the Board of Education of San Francisco, of October 11, 1906, requiring Japanese school-children to attend the Oriental school, formerly used by Chinese alone. Although various explanations of this resolution were given at the time, the real reason was to start the process of discrimination which would eventually lead to the enactment of an exclusion law.

When the news reached Japan, great indignation was expressed. This was primarily due to regret that in the United States, a country which had been so uniformly friendly to Japan, such a discriminatory measure should be adopted. But, in addition, the blow fell at a most unfortunate time, for only a few months before the Japanese Red Cross had contributed to the relief of the earthquake and fire victims of San Francisco the sum of $244,960, an amount greater than the contributions of all the rest of the world, outside the United States. Japan had tried to demonstrate the traditional friendship, and the San Francisco School Board had replied in this regrettable fashion.

Throughout the United States there was widespread criticism of the action of the San Francisco officials.

sident Roosevelt instructed Secretary Metcalf, of the
)artment of Commerce and Labor, and a Californian
self, to visit San Francisco and report on the situation,
i number of assaults had been made upon Japanese by
less residents of the city. On receipt of this report,
President Roosevelt addressed a special message to Congress, on December 18, 1906, in which he said, in part:
"I authorized and directed Secretary Metcalf to state
that, if there was any failure to protect persons and property, then the entire power of the Federal Government
within the limits of the Constitution would be used
promptly and vigorously to enforce the observance of our
treaty, the supreme law of the land, which treaty guaranteed to Japanese residents everywhere in the Union full
and perfect protection for their persons and property;
and to this end everything in my power would be done,
and all the forces of the United States, both civil and
military, which I could lawfully employ, would be employed."

As there was a constitutional question involved, the
Federal Government brought two suits, one in the Federal Circuit Court and the other in the State Supreme
Court, to test the validity of the resolution. The issue
was never determined, for President Roosevelt had found
a better way to settle the difficulty. In a letter which he
wrote, two years later, he said that "the policy of the
Administration is to combine the maximum of efficiency
in achieving the real object which the people of the Pacific Slope have at heart, with the minimum of friction and
trouble." The real question was that of immigration, not
of the attendance of children at school. So he summoned
the Mayor of San Francisco to Washington and assured
him that the Nation and not the individual States must
deal with matters of such international significance, and

JAPAN AND THE UNITED STATES

must treat foreign nations with entire courtesy and respect; and that the Nation would at once, and in efficie
and satisfactory manner, take action that would meet t
needs of California. So, after a good deal of discussio
the objectionable measure was abandoned, and Preside
Roosevelt and Secretary Root made an arrangement with
Japan whereby the immigration of laborers was stopped.

This took the form of the "Gentlemen's Agreement."
Under it Japan agreed to give passports for America only
to non-laborers, such as merchants, travelers, students,
and officials. Laborers who had visited Japan might receive passports to return to the United States, and passports might be issued to the parents, wives, and children
of domiciled laborers, as well as to laborers who had already acquired an interest in a farming enterprise in that
country — only four of this class were admitted between
1909 and 1919. The United States, in turn, refused to
admit Japanese and Korean laborers who held passports
for Mexico, Canada, or Hawaii. The exact terms of the
agreement have never been made public, but the Japanese understood that, as long as they kept their part of
the agreement, the United States would not pass an exclusion law against Japanese. Such a law would have
been possible under the Treaty of 1894, but not under
the modified Treaty of 1911, but at the latter date Japan
renewed her pledge to maintain the immigration restriction.

There can be little question that the Gentlemen's
Agreement was a far more satisfactory way to meet the
question of Japanese immigration than an exclusion law.
Under the Chinese exclusion laws the American officials
had to pass upon the right of an immigrant to be placed in
the exempt class. This was a difficult thing to do, at an
American port, with inadequate sources of information.

THE JAPANESE IN AMERICA

Many grave abuses have developed under the method employed, Chinese of approved status have been badly treated, and others of the laboring class have been admitted by fraud or corruption. But, under the agreement, the Japanese Government scrutinized carefully every applicant for a passport. Its officials knew perfectly whether a man was a merchant or a laborer. There have been few if any cases of passports having been wrongly granted. Later criticisms arose from the nature of the agreement, rather than from its enforcement, and Japan then decided to bar out the so-called "picture brides," or women who had been married *in absentia* to Japanese residents of the United States. At the present time a question has arisen as to the right of adopted children to receive passports.

In considering this problem of immigration we must be guided by practical rather than theoretical considerations. Man for man, the Japanese immigrants compared very favorably with the European immigrants of this period. They were generally literate, almost always law-abiding, industrious, and ambitious to rise in the world. But, until the white residents of California were ready to receive the Japanese on terms of social and political equality, they would present all the undesirable aspects of mass immigration. Against them would be raised the old economic, social, and political objections, and these would be believed just as long as the people knew so little about the Japanese that they would not ignore them. In time, with the spread of more information and with more experience, racial antipathies will doubtless subside, but no good can be accomplished by forcing this process too speedily. It was much better to restrict the immigration of Japanese laborers until their presence would not be considered a problem or a menace.

And this restriction should carry with it no implication that the Japanese are inferior to the Americans or undesirable as residents. It merely means that they are different, and that the time is not ripe for mingling large numbers of people of very different race and culture. If the conditions were reversed, and Japan were threatened with the immigration of a considerable number of white laborers who would, because of racial and cultural conditions, tend to form mass settlements, Japan would be equally justified in protecting her own people by similar arrangements.

The immigration question is the fundamental question concerning the Japanese in the United States. It has been settled by an agreement which has worked satisfactorily since 1908. If at any time it should fail to operate, and Japanese laborers should enter the country in violation of its terms, some other method should be considered and adopted. But, on the other hand, the question has been complicated by various attempts to discriminate against Japanese who are lawfully resident in the United States. In so far as these measures are discriminatory they are indefensible. The Fourteenth Amendment to the Constitution of the United States declares that no State shall "deny to any person within its jurisdiction the equal protection of the laws." In addition to their treaty rights, therefore, the Japanese residents are protected by this strong constitutional provision, which breathes the American spirit of justice and fair play.

The more recent questions at issue have been concerned with these discriminatory laws. In 1913, the California Legislature passed an act which denied to aliens ineligible to citizenship the right to own land or to lease agricultural land for more than three years. When this measure was under consideration, President Wilson sent Mr.

Bryan, the Secretary of State, to oppose its passage, but he was unsuccessful. The measure received some support from the farming interests, but its passage was primarily due to the unwillingness of local politicians to oppose any measures which restrict the privileges of Orientals. This is largely a result of the anti-Chinese agitation days, and it may be taken as a matter of course that, as long as public opinion is hostile to Oriental immigration, the representatives of the people will vote for practically any measure of this kind which is proposed. If Japanese laborers were still entering the country in large numbers, then it would be wise for the State, in which most of them settled, to prevent its land from falling into their possession. But such was not the case. The act cleverly threw the responsibility upon the Federal Government, because it made the basis of discrimination the naturalization law of the United States, which denied citizenship to persons who were not free white persons or persons of African nativity or descent.

. In spite of the irritation and resentment aroused in Japan by this discrimination — which was directed against her nationals, although they were not directly named — the Government and business men determined to prove their good-will for the United States, and especially for California, by preparing a notable exhibit for the Panama-Pacific Exposition which was held in San Francisco in 1915. The Great War had caused most of the European belligerents to abandon their exhibits, so that of Japan was the most elaborate national contribution to the exposition. This act of good-will was properly appreciated by thoughtful Californians, many of whom had opposed the Alien Land Law.

On this account, and because of the unsettled conditions caused by the war, no anti-Japanese measures were advocated in California between 1913 and 1919. Students of the question, who realized how well the Gentlemen's Agreement was operating, believed that all occasion for agitation and misrepresentation had passed, and that the resident Japanese could now be judged on their merits as individuals rather than as representatives of an unpopular race.

Unfortunately, early in 1919, the old agitation against the Japanese was renewed. Its origin was purely political, for an important election was to be held in 1920, and a prominent candidate desired to make his campaign as the defender of California against the Japanese invasion. Under his leadership a number of organizations, hostile to the Japanese, began a widespread agitation. The political aspects of the case are interesting. The State Legislature, controlled by members of the party opposed to the candidate seeking reëlection, refused to pass the laws he demanded, lest he secure the credit for them. The Governor also refused to call a special session of the Legislature to pass a more effective Alien Land Law than that of 1913. Thwarted in this way, the advocates of the measure succeeded in placing it on the election ballot by means of the initiative. As soon as this was done, all the politicians hastened to support the measure, including the Governor who had so recently opposed it. Naturally, the proposal carried, by a large but not an overwhelming majority, but the candidate who had proposed the measure was defeated at the polls.

During the discussion, which raged with considerable warmth during 1919 and 1920, it was alleged that large numbers of Japanese were entering the United States in violation of the Gentlemen's Agreement; that the amazing birth-rate among the resident Japanese threatened to produce a Japanese majority in the State within ninety years; that the Japanese had secured possession of much of the best farm land of the State and would soon monopolize the agricultural industry; and, finally, that the Japanese were absolutely unassimilable, and therefore they and their children should be denied forever the rights of citizenship.

It seems hardly necessary to discuss these extravagant statements, which were given the widest publicity and which were rarely discussed dispassionately in the local press. Between July, 1908, and July, 1919, 79,738 Japanese entered the continental United States, but 68,770 departed, so the net increase was only 10,968, or an average of less than a thousand a year. Yet, in spite of these official figures, the average Californian believed that Japanese laborers were pouring into the State. And, when the alarming statements regarding the Japanese birth-rate were tested by the actual facts, the conditions were found to be perfectly reasonable. The proportion of Japanese births to total births was high simply because the Japanese settlers, to an unusual degree, were recently married men and women in the prime of life. As a matter of fact, the birth-rate reached its peak in 1917, and has steadily declined — as every student of the problem predicted. The 1920 census figures reported a Japanese population of 70,707 out of a total of 3,426,861. The increase in the past decade had been, of Japanese, 29,351, and of the entire population, 1,049,312, so only the most inveterate opponents of the Japanese continued to predict a Japanese domination within the next few years. Japanese landholding had, however, largely increased within the decade. At the end of 1919, Japanese owned 74,769 acres of land, and leased 383,287 additional acres. This was due to the change in status of Japanese farm laborers to renters and, in some cases, to landowners. The high prices of farm products and the scarcity of white labor during the war had caused white owners to lease large amounts of land to Japanese tenants. After these unusual conditions had passed, it might be expected that the acreage used by Japanese would decrease, or at most increase slowly, especially as there were not enough Japanese laborers to meet the requirements of the Japanese farmers. Many white men are employed by Japanese farmers in California.

Remembering the powerful forces which supported the initiative measure, and the unlimited publicity which their arguments received, it is a matter of some interest that 222,086 voters opposed the measure; and although it was carried by 668,483 affirmative votes, these did not number one half of the registered voters in California. Chambers of commerce, representatives of the churches and universities, opposed the measure, and it is reasonable to believe that, if the real facts in the case could have been presented to the people, the opposing vote would have been much larger. Thus, for a second time, a measure was passed which reversed the wise policy of President Roosevelt, for it combined a maximum of friction with a minimum of efficiency. The act made it more difficult, but not impossible, for Japanese to own land. But it did not prevent them from using land, as its advocates had alleged, for crop contracts would take the place of leases, as had frequently been done in the past. Several features of the law were of doubtful constitutionality, and the courts will pass upon them as soon as cases are brought before them.

It should be said, in this connection, that the renewal of the anti-Japanese agitation coincided with the widespread criticism of Japan because of her actions in China, Siberia, and Korea. It also was a part of the political campaign in which ratification of the Versailles Treaty was the leading issue, and in which the Shantung articles were bitterly criticized. For these reasons the Japanese in California suffered to some extent because of the acts of their Government.

After the election, the discussion in California rapidly subsided. In spite of many of the bitter things which had been said during the campaign, no Japanese was in any way molested in person or property, which indicates a great improvement over the old anti-Chinese demonstrations. And when, in the summer of 1921, a gang of lawless white men drove some Japanese laborers away from their work near Turlock, on the ground that they were accepting less than the customary wage, prompt measures were taken to protect the Japanese and to punish the offenders, while on all sides the press and the leading citizens announced that the treaty and constitutional rights of the Japanese must be scrupulously protected.

The Japanese question in California, and in other Western States, consists of two elements, which should not be confused. One is the question of immigration, the other is the treatment of Japanese who are lawfully resident in the United States. The restriction of Oriental immigration is an American policy, as the Chinese exclusion laws, the General Immigration Act of 1917, and the Gentlemen's Agreement with Japan, all testify. The policy is a wise one, and is so considered by thoughtful Japanese and Chinese. But it should be carried out in a way which should give the least offense. The method adopted for controlling the immigration of Japanese laborers is the best which has yet been devised. Eventually Oriental as well as European immigration will be subject to uniform regulations. As soon as modifications were considered necessary in the Agreement, the Japanese

Government promptly adopted them, as in the case of refusing passports to "picture brides." And if other changes should be deemed desirable, there is no question but that it would promptly undertake them. But, on the other hand, Japanese of the exempt classes should be, and are, welcomed in the United States. In fact, the Japanese Government should be requested to modify its regulations regarding students' passports, so that more young men and women may come to American institutions of learning. In order that no professed students might enter the United States and then become laborers, the Japanese Government has established rigid qualifications, especially of a financial nature, which have debarred many students who sought passports. There is no more effective agency for good understanding than the movement of students from one country to another. During their student days they are representatives and interpreters of their home land, and after their return they are interpreters of the land where they have studied. Students, business men, and travelers are representatives of the best Japanese types; they have no difficulty in meeting and associating with Americans of their class. It is unfortunate that the average Californian knows of Japan only through dealings with the laborers who entered the State before the passport agreement was in force.

On the other hand, the Japanese in the United States must be protected in every treaty right and constitutional guarantee. Under the American system of government the States may take actions regarding aliens which may involve the whole nation in serious foreign complications. This is unwise, and it should be made impossible. The Federal Government should act promptly whenever any State action contravenes a treaty or a constitutional right. Discrimination is a dangerous game to commence, for both sides can play it. The United States can hardly stand for the principle of equal opportunity in the Orient, and permit its component States to deny equal opportunity to Orientals within their limits.

The Federal Government should also make a positive contribution to the solution of this problem by adopting a new naturalization law which will make the basic qualification for citizenship something besides color. It seems almost unbelievable that the great democracy of the West should deny the suffrage to all save free white and negro adults. Only trained ethnologists should administer such a law, for there are many people who pass as white who are descended from a yellow race. The Chinese are denied naturalization by a special act of Congress, but Japanese formerly were admitted to citizenship by judges who stressed the status of freedom rather than the accident of color. In recent years, however, the rulings in the lower Federal courts have been opposed to the naturalization of Japanese. The question has never come before the Supreme Court. But it should not be left to judicial determination. The present statute is an absurdity. In 1906, President Roosevelt recommended to Congress that it provide for the naturalization of Japanese, but instead of such a special law a general one should be substituted for the present act, one which will set high qualifications of residence, education, and character, but which will apply to all aliens irrespective of color or race. And, on the other hand, Japan, as well as certain European countries, should permit expatriation without any troublesome formalities. At present American-born Japanese are subject to military duty in Japan, unless, before the age of seventeen, they have renounced their Japanese nationality. Some European countries do not recognize expatriation under any circumstances, and Japan, having adopted the European system of conscription, followed the European practice of demanding the allegiance of the foreign-born children of her nationals, but modified it in 1916, to permit voluntary expatriation. As very few American-born Japanese have formally renounced their Japanese nationality, most of them, therefore, possess a dual nationality— American citizens by birth and Japanese by descent. This has been used as an argument in favor of withholding citizenship from Japanese native-born, for it has been alleged that, as a class, they would be loyal to the country of their ancestors rather than to the country of their birth. Of course, this is one of the many statements regarding the Japanese which is not susceptible of proof. It seems more reasonable to believe that, if the native-born Japanese are protected in their constitutional rights and given equal opportunities with their fellow citizens, they will, like all other descendants of aliens, become loyal citizens of the country in which they were born, where they have lived and toiled, and where they hope to end their days. One reason why the Japanese question has lent itself to exaggeration and misunderstanding is because it is such a recent question. The bulk of the Japanese adults in California entered the State between 1900 and 1908. Very few native-born Japanese have grown to manhood, although a few were able to play their part creditably in the Great War. A few children of the second generation probably exist, but they must be very few. It would be well to suspend judgment regarding cultural assimilation, good citizenship, and the effects of the language schools, until there are a considerable number of native-born Japanese of the first and second generation who have grown up under American cultural conditions.

In fact, it was very unfortunate that the agitation

should have been renewed in 1919. At that time there were few reliable statistics available to refute the current exaggerations. The Federal census was not taken until 1920, and the report of the State Board of Control on Oriental immigration, population, and land-ownership was not submitted until June of that year. The Gentlemen's Agreement had been in operation since July, 1908, so the Japanese laborers and farmers had, with few exceptions, entered the State before that date. Some had certainly crossed the borders illegally, but that was due to no fault of the Japanese Government, for the responsibility rested upon the United States to police its borders and enforce its immigration laws. In the absence of authentic statistics, it was easy to make extravagant guesses as to the number of Japanese in the State. These ranged from 100,000 to 150,000. The census finally reported only 70,707. This figure is probably somewhat below the actual numbers, for the enumerators failed to report some of the residents of the State. But it is the only figure, based on an enumeration, which is available, and it must stand as correct until a more careful census is taken. In opposition to those who take an alarming view of the situation in California are others who have studied the subject carefully, and who believe that in time the relative number of Japanese will steadily decrease, although the actual number will increase, because the population of California will be augmented by both immigration and natural increase, while the Japanese population will increase almost wholly by births. They believe also that the birth-rate of the resident Japanese will steadily decline and tend to approximate that of the white residents, as the age-groups become normal and the Japanese yield to the social and economic influences which effect the birth-rate. And they also believe that, although the Jap-

267

anese will always play a prominent part in agriculture, because of their skill in intensive farming, their relative importance will also decline as the immigrant stock dies out and their children move to the cities as other native-born children tend to do. In other words, a careful study of all the facts available would encourage one to believe that the excuse for anti-Japanese agitation in California is rapidly passing away, and that no real problem exists in the State so long as immigration is controlled as effectively as at present.

One of the encouraging lessons of the past may be found in the remarkable change which has taken place in the attitude of many Californians toward the Chinese. In the early days the Chinese were the victims of mis-representations far worse than the Japanese have had to endure. In addition, many of them suffered grievously at the hands of lawless white men, and there was little re-dress. But after the cessation of Chinese immigration, and as the Chinese population steadily declined, the agitation, with its appeal to racial passions, ceased. The Chinese could then be judged on their merits, and most Californians are ready to say a good word for the Chinese residents, in spite of the criminal deeds of some of their "highbinders." A similar change may be expected in the local attitude toward the Japanese as soon as little excuse remains for a campaign of misrepresentation. When the old laboring stock, speaking little or no English, and cling-ing to alien customs, is supplanted by native-born Japa-nese, the product of American public schools, it will be difficult to arouse much popular opposition to men of this type.

With the immigration question satisfactorily settled, until such time as Oriental immigration can be dealt with by a general law affecting all immigrants, the next problem, as we have said, is the problem of protecting the Japanese and other Orientals, who are admitted, from any discrimination in the eyes of the law. This can be prevented largely by Federal action, through the maintenance of treaty and constitutional guarantees, and through the right of naturalization. But a fundamental way of preventing discrimination is by furthering assimilation. By this we do not mean biological assimilation or intermarriage, for, however desirable this may be from a biological point of view, the fact remains that it is rarely successful from a social or cultural standpoint. But intermarriage is not essential to cultural assimilation. What is necessary is for the native-born children to enjoy the opportunities of the American public school, where they will learn, not merely the language, but the ideals, of their native land. The State should take care to offer every facility for preparing these young people for lives of usefulness and good citizenship.

Although in the past the Japanese have had cause for resentment because of the treatment of their nationals in some of the American States, there should be little occasion for this in the future. The real harm has been done by words rather than deeds. Except for the right to own land and to acquire citizenship, Japanese nationals are subject to no disabilities. But in the heat of political campaigns many things have been said which have grievously hurt a self-respecting people. The immigration question certainly should give no further cause for offense, for it is settled exactly as Japan would wish to settle it if the conditions were reversed. And as the years pass by, and Americans understand the Japanese residents better, it is reasonable to believe that the desire for political or economic restrictions will cease. The Japanese remember what a serious domestic crisis was precipitated when a few foreigners were admitted to Japan in 1857. They can afford to be patient while the white countries, around the Pacific, learn how to receive and treat fairly the representatives of a very different race and culture. Time is the great solvent of present problems. And contact between the races presents no insoluble difficulties, none which time and a mutual desire to be reasonable and fair cannot remove.

THE END

INDEX

INDEX

Aguinaldo, Emilio, 166.

Ainu, primitive people, 4, 5.

Alcock, Sir Rutherford, British Minister to Japan, 44, 48, 49, 53, 65, 67.

Alexieff, Admiral, 177.

Alien Land Law, Californian, 242, 259, 260–62.

American Federation of Labor, the, 254.

American legation at Yedo burned, 58.

American students should study in Japan, 105.

Anglo-Japanese Alliance, the, 179, 202, 203, 206.

Annam, and France, 146.

Antung-Mukden Railway, the, 192, 216.

Arbitration, principle of, introduced to Japan by Minister Pruyn, 70. *See also* Mediation.

Arthur, President Chester A., 149.

Asia for the Asiatics, 247.

Aulick, Commodore John H., 22.

Bayard, Thomas F., Secretary of State, 126.

Belgium, invaded by Germany, 208.

Bell, Admiral, 138.

Bellecourt, M. de, French Minister to Japan, 44.

Biddle, Commodore James, 18; sent to Japan, 19.

Bingham, Hon. John A., Minister to Japan, 117; his views on tariff and extraterritoriality, 118–20, 123; on quarantine regulations, 120, 121; proposes a separate treaty, 126; his action in regard to the Formosan expedition, 141–43.

Bismarck, Prince, quoted, 248.

Blaine, James G., Secretary of State, 129.

Boissonade, M., helps draft penal code for Japan, 124.

Bolsheviki, 228, 229.

Boxer outbreak in China, 172–76; indemnity, 176; remitted by United States, 112, 194.

Brest-Litovsk Treaty, 226, 227.

Brinkley, Capt., quoted, 5.

British legation in Yedo invaded, 54.

Brooks, Charles Walcott, first Japanese consul at San Francisco, 104.

Brown, Dr. S. R., missionary in Japan, 102.

Bryan, William J., Secretary of State, 259.

Buchanan, President James, receives first Japanese mission, 47.

Buddhism, 7; Zen sect of, 13.

California, annexed to the United States, 22; Japanese in, 242, 253–68; Chinese in, 250–52, 268.

California school case, the (1906), 195, 254.

Capron, Gen. Horace, 102.

Cassel, Lieut. Commander Douglas, in expedition to Formosa, 141–43.

Cassini, Count, and Li Hung-chang, 161.

Chaffee, Gen. Adna R., in the Boxer uprising, 175.

China, early civilization in, 5; influence on Japan, 6; toleration of Christianity in, 93; claims suzerainty over Korea, 106, 107; enters into treaty with Japan, 137; conflict with Japan over Formosa, 138–44; and over Korea, 145,

273

INDEX

INDEX

Fish, Hamilton, Secretary of State, on Japanese rights, 118, 119.

Foote, Gen. Lucius H., American Minister at Seoul, 150.

Formosa, island of, 137; Ryukyu natives murdered on, 138; Japanese expedition against, 140–44; ceded to Japan, 158.

Foster, John W., at Treaty of Shimonoseki, 156.

France, action in the Shimonoseki affair, 61, 66, 68; treaty with Annam, 146, 150; acts with Russia against Japan and China, 158–60; demands lease of the Bay of Kwangchow, 164; sphere of interest in China, 164; Franco-Russian Alliance, 178, 180.

French sailors killed near Osaka, 88.

Fujiwara, the, 9.

Fujiyama, the sacred mountain, 3.

Fukuzawa Yukichi, 47.

Geisinger, Commodore David, and shipwrecked American seamen, 20.

General Sherman, American merchant ship, destroyed by Koreans, 135.

German propaganda in the United States, 196, 223.

Germany, disregards Japanese quarantine regulations, 121; joins Russia and France against Japan, 158, 159; gets lease of Kiaochow, 161–63; invades Belgium, 208; rights of, in Shantung, 209, 215, 217, 219, 227, 230–32, 234–39.

Glynn, Commodore James, sent to Nagasaki, 20, 21.

Good-will, at the basis of good business, 244.

Goto, Baron, Minister of Foreign Affairs, 226.

Goto Islands, arrest of Christians at, 97.

Grant, Gen. U. S., visits Japan, 105; arbitrates Ryukyu dispute, 106, 107, 145; quoted, 108, 109, 117, 121, 159.

Great Britain, legation in Yedo attacked, 49, 54; paramount influence in Japan, 52, 53; the Richardson murder case, 54–59, 63; the Shimonoseki affair, 64–68; revision of Japanese tariff, 76, 77, 130, 131; action in the Boxer uprising, 174–79; Anglo-Japanese Alliance, 202, 203, 206.

Gresham, Walter Q., Secretary of State, 153.

Griffis, Dr. W. E., in Japan, 102.

Hakodate, 27, 30; Americans permitted to reside at, 35.

Hanabusa, Mr., Japanese Minister at Seoul, 149, 150.

Harriman, E. H., tries to form a round-the-world transportation system, 190, 197.

Harris, Townsend, early life, 33; consul at Shimoda, 33, 34; negotiates new convention with Japan, 35; has audience with the Shogun, 36; arranges a commercial treaty, 36–41, 134; at variance with his colleagues, 44, 48; refuses to leave Yedo, 48, 49; asks to be called home, 50; friend and counselor of the Japanese, 51; tries to secure religious toleration, 93; on extraterritoriality, 116.

Hawaiian Islands, annexed to the United States, 169.

Hay, John, Secretary of State, and the Open Door in China, 169–71.

Hepburn, Dr. J. C., missionary in Japan, 102.

Heriero, Captain, of the *Maria Luz,* 100.

Hesperia, German steamer, quarantined, 121.

Heusken, Mr., Townsend Harris's secretary, assassinated, 47–49.

Hideyoshi, greatest of Japanese generals, 10, 12.

Higashikuze, representative of the Mikado at Hiogo, 86, 87.

275

INDEX

Hiogo, opened for commerce, 38, 84.

Hioki, Mr., Japanese Minister at Peking, 209, 210.

Hitotsubashi, Lord, 79.

Hokkaido, island of, 1, 17; American whaler wrecked off, 20, 21.

Honshiu (Hondo), island of, 1, 4.

Hornbeck, Dr., quoted, 238.

Hotta, Lord, Minister for Foreign Affairs, 36–41.

Hsu Shi-chang, Viceroy of Manchuria, 193.

Hubbard, Richard B., American Minister to Japan, 126; signs new treaty of amity and commerce, 129.

Hughes, Charles E., Secretary, quoted, 247.

Hughes, Rt. Hon. William M., Premier of Australia, 233.

Iemochi, chosen Shogun, 40; dies, 79.

Ieyasu, founder of the Tokugawa Shogunate, 10.

Ii Naosuke, Lord, appointed regent, 40; works for treaty with the United States, 40–43; creates a new port at Yokohama, 45; assassinated, 46.

Ijuin, Mr., Japanese Ambassador to Italy, 230.

Immigration, Japanese, 183, 201, 253–68; European, 251; Chinese, 252.

Inouye, Marquis, 66, 147, 150; tries to regain sovereignty for Japan, 125, 127, 128.

Ishii, Viscount, sent on mission to the United States, 224.

Ito, Prince, 66, 87, 104, 107, 150, 151, 158; opposes expedition against Korea, 140; offers aid to United States in the Philippines, 168; killed by a Korean fanatic, 200.

Iwakura, Lord, mission to the treaty powers, 98, 104, 106, 110,

122; opposes expedition against Korea, 140.

Japan, area of, 1; situation, 2; compared with Great Britain, 2; climate, soil, natural beauty, 3; racial origins, 4, 5; language, 5; influenced by China and Korea, 5, 6; oldest books, 6, 7; art, 7; religion, 7–9; political organization, 9–12; a hermit nation, 9, 14, 15; diplomatic relations with the United States, three phases, 16; early relations with Russia, 17; mission of Commodore Biddle, 18, 19; of Commodore Glynn, 20, 21; of Commodore Perry, 22–29; treaty with United States signed, 27; ports opened, 27, 30, 31, 84, 124; equal terms granted to other nations, 29, 30, 32; Townsend Harris received as consul at Shimoda, 33; new treaties, 35; first treaty of commerce, 37–41; tariff modified, 42, 74–77, 123; the currency question, 45; first mission to a foreign country, 46, 47; assassination of Mr. Heusken, 47–50; growing differences between Mikado and Shogun, 53; murder of Mr. Richardson, 54–59; expulsion of foreigners decreed, 57–60; Choshiu tries to enforce the decree and is punished, 61–69; Shogun withdraws notice of expulsion, 64; Mikado ratifies treaties of 1858 (1865), 69, 71; Japanese permitted to visit the treaty powers, 74; the rise of New Japan, 80; religious intolerance, 81, 82, 93–98, 99; office of Shogun abolished, 82–85; the Mikado receives foreign representatives, 88; restoration of the Emperor completed, 91; feudalism abolished, 99; friction with Peru, 100, 101; universal education planned, 102; American advisers, 102, 103; students sent to America, 104,

INDEX

105; visit of Gen. Grant, 105–109; dispute over the Ryukyu Islands, 106–108, 137–44; the Shimonoseki indemnity, 109–12; contends for tariff autonomy and against extraterritoriality, 114–25, 127; hunting regulations, 118, 119; quarantine troubles, 120, 121; makes extradition treaty with the United States, 127; constitution promulgated, and Imperial Diet summoned, 130; treaties revised (1894), 130–32; offers to mediate between the United States and Korea, 135, 136; negotiates treaty with China, 137; sends an expedition against Formosa, 138–44; the Korean problem, 145–47, 149–54; war with China, 154–57; Treaty of Shimonoseki, 158, 159; joins other powers against the Boxers, 173–76; the Anglo-Japanese Alliance, 179, 202, 203, 206; war with Russia, 180, 181; Treaty of Portsmouth, 182; emigration to the United States, 183, 201, 247, 253–68; change in public opinion about the United States, 188, 189; operations in Manchuria, 189–93, 197; Russo-Japanese treaty and treaty with Korea (1910), 199; annexation of Korea, 200; new commercial treaty with the United States (1911), 201; enters the World War, 206, 207; claims former German rights in Shantung, 209, 219, 220, 230; presents the Twenty-One Demands, 209–14; treaties with China (1915), 215–17; hostile criticism, 218; exchange of notes between Viscount Ishii and Secretary Lansing, 224, 225; makes large loans to China, 225, 226; sends troops to Siberia, 227, 228; representatives at the Paris conference, 230; urges her claims to former German possessions, 232, 234–39; contends for racial equal-

ity, 232–34; severity in Korea, 240, 241; anti-Japanese agitation in California, 242; the wisest policy towards China, 243–46.

Japanese and Korean Exclusion League, the, 254.

Japanese art, 7.

Japanese immigration, 183, 201, 253–68.

Japanese in America, the, 250–70.

Japanese Red Cross, 254.

Japanese students in America, 104, 105, 264.

Kagoshima, shelled by British fleet, 63.

Kanagawa, opened for commerce, 38, 44.

Kaneko, Baron, 184.

Kang Yu-wei, 172.

Kato, Baron, Minister of Foreign Affairs, 210.

Katsu Awa, Count, organizer of the modern Japanese navy, 47.

Katsura, Count, and E. H. Harriman, 190.

Keiki, popular name of the Shogun Yoshinobu, 79. *See also* Yoshinobu.

Kiaochow, the finest port in North China, 161; leased to Germany, 162; restoration promised by Japan, 217.

Kirin-Changchun railway, the, 211, 216.

Knox, Philander C., Secretary of State, proposes international railway administration in China, 198, 199.

Kojiki, the, 6.

Kolchak, Admiral, 228.

Komei, Mikado, death of, 80.

Komura, Baron, opposes E. H. Harriman, 190, 191.

Koo, Dr. V. K. W., Chinese Minister to the United States, 231, 233, 235, 238.

Korea, early influence on Japan, 5; Chinese claim suzerainty over, 106,

277

INDEX

107; Japan remits indemnity to, 112; case of the *General Sherman,* 135, 136; refuses diplomatic intercourse with Japan, 136; conflict with the United States, 136, 137; makes a treaty with Japan, 145, 146, 149, 150; treaty relations with the United States, 147–50; independence acknowledged by China, 160; Japanese occupation, 240–42; her present needs, 244–46.

Kowloon Peninsula, leased to Great Britain, 164.

Kublai Khan, 244.

Kung, Prince, 106, 107, 142, 143.

Kurile Islands, 1, 17.

Kuroda, General, 146.

Kwangchow, Bay of, leased to France, 164.

Kyoto, the Emperor's capital, 10.

Kyushiu, island of, 1, 4.

Lagoda, the, deserters from, 21.

Lansing, Robert, Secretary of State, and Count Ishii, 224, 225; quoted, 238.

Lawrence, the, American whaler, wrecked off Hokkaido, 20, 21.

Le Gendre, General, American consul at Amoy, advises Japan about Formosa, 138; accompanies Lord Soyeshima to Peking, 139; and the expedition against Formosa, 141–44.

Li Hung-chang, 103, 106, 108; signs treaty with Japan, 137; and Commodore Shufeldt, 148; action in regard to Korea, 146, 150, 151, 153; sues for peace, 156, 158; turns to Russia, 161.

Liaotung Peninsula, ceded to Japan, 158; relinquished, 159; lower part leased to Russia, 163.

Lloyd George, Premier, quoted, 207, 221.

Lobanoff, Prince, 161.

Loochoo Islands, *see* Ryukyu Islands.

Lou Tsengtsiang, Mr., Chinese Minister of Foreign Affairs, 231, 235.

Low, F. F., American Minister to China, sent to Korea, 136.

Loyalty, Japanese, 83.

Lungkow, 208, 215.

McDougal, Commander, attacks Shimonoseki, 62.

McKinley, President William, 167.

Maine, the, American battleship, sunk at Havana, 166.

Makino, Baron, at the Paris conference, 230, 232, 233, 234, 235.

Manabe, Lord, aids in treaty negotiations, 43.

Manchuria, overrun by Russia, 177, 180; Japan in, 189–94.

Maria Luz, Peruvian coolie ship, 70, 100, 101.

Matsui, Mr., Japanese Ambassador to France, 230.

Mediation, by Emperor of Russia between Japan and Peru, 101; by Gen. Grant in Ryukyu Islands case, and Chinese claim on Korea, 106, 107; offered in United States treaties with China and Japan, 134; offered by Japan, 135.

Megata, Mr., Japanese financial adviser to Korea, 199.

Metcalf, Victor H., Secretary of Commerce and Labor, 255.

Mexico, and Japan, 128, 129; German alliance with, proposed, 223.

Mikado (Emperor), Lord of Heaven, 9; long without real power, 10; ratifies foreign treaties, 69; regains full power, 83–86; assumes the treaty-making power, 87; receives Gen. Van Valkenburgh, 88; adopts sound foreign policy, 91, 92.

Missionaries, in Japan, 8, 9, 94, 97, 98, 102.

Monroe Doctrine, the, 246.

Mori, Lord, tries to enforce the expulsion decree, 61.

INDEX

Mori Arinori, 146; first Japanese Minister Resident at Washington, 104.

Morse, Hosea B., on Col. Shiba, 173.

Muneki Date, 137.

Muravieff-Amursky, Count, 46, 177.

Murray, Dr. David, establishes public schools in Japan, 102.

Mutsu, Count, Minister of Foreign Affairs, arranges treaties, 130, 131, 158.

Mutsuhito, Prince, becomes Mikado, 80.

Nagasaki, the Dutch at, 19, 20, 30; Commodore Glynn sent to, 20; opening of, 26, 27, 30, 35.

Nariaki, Lord of Mito, 80.

Naturalization, in the United States, 265.

Neale, Colonel, British Chargé, 56, 58, 59, 63.

Neesima, Joseph Hardy, founder of the Doshisha, 104.

Nihongi, the, 6.

Niigata, opened for commerce, 38.

Nobunaga, 10.

Ogasawara, Mr., Japanese Foreign Minister, 59.

Okuma, Marquis, 102, 141; Minister of Foreign Affairs, 128; attempt on his life, 130; Chinese policy, 209, 210.

Open-Door policy, in China, 158–82.

Opium, banned, 35, 38, 39.

Oriental emigration, 250; motives for, 251.

Osaka, opened to foreigners for residence, 38, 84.

Panama Canal, the, 186.

Panama-Pacific Exposition, the, 259.

Paris, peace conference at, 230–39.

Parkes, Sir Harry, British Minister to Japan, 68, 71, 76, 84; his party

attacked in Kyoto, 88; received by the Mikado, 88; supports the Emperor, 91; tries to secure religious toleration, 96, 98; on Gen. Grant, 109.

Peking, siege and relief of, 173–76; Treaty of, 190, 191, 193.

Pembroke, the, 70.

Penal code compiled for Japan, 124, 125.

Pennock, Rear Admiral Alexander M., 143.

Perry, Commodore Matthew Calbraith, 1; sent to Japan, 22; his first visit, 23, 24; his second visit, 25–29; insists upon a treaty, 26.

Peru, and Japan, 100, 101.

Pescadores Islands, ceded to Japan, 158.

Philippine Islands, acquired by the United States, 166–69.

Picture brides, 257.

Port Arthur, leased to Russia, 163; in the Russo-Japanese War, 180.

Portman, Mr., American Chargé, 73.

Portuguese, the, in Japan, 8, 14.

Poutiatine, Admiral, negotiates treaty with Japan, 30.

Pratt, Zadock, M. C., 18.

Press, the, inaccuracy of, 184–86, 189, 261.

Printing, early, in Japan, 7.

Pruyn, Robert Hewson, second American Minister to Japan, 51–53; tries to prevent reprisals, 57, 58; proposes joint naval demonstration, 60; sends the *Wyoming* against Shimonoseki, 61, 62, 67; appealed to by the Shogun's government, 64; returns home, 68; friendly relations with the Shogun's representatives, 70; retires from diplomatic service, 78.

Public opinion, power of, v; changing in Japan and the United States, 183–89; in the World War, 220.

INDEX

Quarantine regulations, 107, 120, 121.

Racial equality, 232–34, 250.

Railroads in Japan, 99.

Red Cross, Japanese, aids San Francisco, 254.

Reed, William B., arranges a commercial treaty with China, 134.

Richardson, Mr., British subject, killed near Yokohama, 54–56, 63.

Roberts, Edmund, American Minister to Siam, 18.

Roches, M., French Minister, 84, 95.

Rockhill, W. W., on the Open Door, 170.

Roosevelt, President Theodore, and the Portsmouth treaty, 182, 183; sends battleship fleet round the world, 195, 196; refuses to intervene in behalf of Korea, 199, 200; action in the California school case, 255, 256; on the naturalization of Japanese, 265.

Root, Elihu, Secretary of State, 256; exchanges notes with Baron Takahira, 194, 195.

Russell, Lord, demands indemnity from Japan, 54, 56, 57; disapproves Alcock's plans, 65; approves later, 67.

Russia, early interest in Japan, 17; secures treaties, 29, 30, 32, 35, 42; seeks Saghalien, 46; Emperor of, arbitrates between Japan and Peru, 101; and Korea, 160; seeks harbor of Kaiochow, 161; gets lease of Port Arthur, 163; overruns Manchuria, 176, 177; Russian diplomacy, 177, 178; war with Japan, 180–82; in Manchuria, 197, 198; Russo-Japanese Treaty, 199.

Ryukyu Islands, 1; Commodore Perry at, 24; Gen. Grant arbitrates dispute over, 106, 107; Chinese claims, 137, 138; treaties with, 137; obtained by Japan, 144.

Saghalien, island of, 1, 2, 17; desired by Russia, 46; Japanese interest in, 229.

Saigo, Gen. Takamori, Minister of War, 139; killed, 140.

Saigo, Gen. Yorimichi, in Formosa, 143.

Saionji, Marquis, 230.

Saito, Baron, Governor-General of Korea, 242.

Sakai, French sailors killed at, 88.

Salisbury, Lord, and the Boxer outbreak, 174.

Samurai, the, 13.

Sanjo, Lord, Prime Minister, 139, 140.

Sanmen Bay, lease to Italy refused, 164.

Saris, Captain, English envoy, 36.

Satsuma, *daimyo* of, and the murder of Mr. Richardson, 55, 56, 63; and the Ryukyu Islands, 137, 138.

Seward, Consul-General George F., 143.

Seward, Secretary William H., 65, 89, 136; proposes naval demonstration in Japanese waters, 49; persuades Mr. Pruyn to accept Japanese mission, 52; tries to secure repeal of laws against Christianity, 82, 95, 96; and the Shimonoseki indemnity, 111.

Shantung Province, German missionaries murdered in, 161; Germany demands concessions, 162; treaty about, 215; at the Paris conference, 234–40.

Shepard, C. O., American Chargé, 100.

Sheppard, Eli T., adviser of Japanese Foreign Office, 103.

Shiba, Colonel, in the Boxer outbreak, 173.

Shikoku, island of, 1, 4.

Shimada, Hon. Saburo, on American missionaries, 98.

Shimadzu, Saburo, and the murder of Mr. Richardson, 55.

Shimoda, opening of, 27, 30, 35;

INDEX

Townsend Harris sent as consul to, 33.

Shimonoseki, straits of, closed by Choshiu, 61, 64; attacked by Commander McDougal, 62; straits forced, 65, 66; indemnity paid, 67–69, 109–12; opened to Americans, 124; treaty of, 156, 158.

Shinto, the Way of the Gods, 7, 8.

Shipwrecked men, American, 19, 20, 21, 27.

Shishido, Mr., Japanese Minister at Peking, 145.

Shogun, the, 9; administrative head of Japanese state, 10; power of, 11; gives audience to Townsend Harris, 36; surrenders all power to the Mikado, 83, 85, 89, 90; office abolished, 84.

Shufeldt, Commodore Robert W., in Korea, 147–49.

Siam, treaty with, 33.

Sill, Mr., American representative at Seoul, 152, 154.

Silver coins, Japanese, 45.

Smith, E. Peshine, adviser of Japanese Foreign Office, 103, 122.

South Manchurian Railway, the, 190, 216.

Soyeshima, Lord, mission to Peking, 103, 139.

Spain, war with the United States, 165–68.

Spaniards, the, in Japan, 8, 14.

Spheres of interest in China, 164, 165, 170.

Steam power, importance of, 14.

Stevens, Durham W., diplomatic adviser to Korea, 199.

Stirling, Admiral, negotiates treaty with Japan, 29.

Stonewall, ironclad ram, bought by Japan, 89.

Straight, Willard, American Consul-General, 193, 197.

Suyemitsu, Baron, 184.

Swift, Mr., American Minister to Japan, 132.

Sze, Alfred, Chinese Minister to Great Britain, 231.

Tai Wen Kun, 136.

Taiping Rebellion, the, 24.

Takahira, Baron, Ambassador at Washington, 194.

Tang Shao-yi, Governor of Mukden, 193, 194, 197.

Tariff, Japanese, 38; modified, 42, 74–77; Japan seeks to control, 114, 115.

Telegraph lines in Japan, 99.

Terashima, Tozo, Foreign Minister, 87, 121, 142.

Terauchi, Count, 225.

Territorial integrity of China, 176, 177.

Thomson, H. C., on the Japanese soldiers, 175.

Tientsin, in the Boxer outbreak, 174, 175.

Tokugawa Shogunate, the, 10, 11; weakening of, 25, 41, 43, 53, 55; Keiki surrenders all power to the Mikado, 83–85.

Tokyo (formerly Yedo), made one of the imperial capitals, 91.

Trans-Siberian Railway, 160, 228.

Treaty revision, 99, 114–33.

Tseng Chi, Tartar general, 177.

Tsingtao, 206–208.

Tsung-li Yamen, 139, 155.

Tsushima, island of, 2, 75.

Tuan, General, Chinese premier, 222, 223.

Turlock, California, Japanese laborers driven from, 263.

Twenty-One Demands, the, of Japan on China, 209–14.

Tycoon, *see* Shogun.

United States, opening of diplomatic relations with Japan, 16; mission of Minister Roberts, 18; of Commodore Biddle, 19; of Commodore Glynn, 20, 21; of Commodore Aulick, 22; of Commodore Perry, 22–29; sends Townsend

281

INDEX

Harris as consul at Shimoda, 33; new treaty with Japan (1857), 35; first commercial treaty, 37–41; Japan sends first mission, 46, 47; assassination of Mr. Heusken, 47–50; tries to act as mediator in the Richardson case, 57; American legation in Yedo burned, 58, 59; strikes first blow in defense of treaty rights, 62; second and last hostile action, 66, 67; American teachers and advisers in Japan, 101–103; Japanese students in America, 104, 105; Shimonoseki indemnity returned, 109, 111, 112; upholds Japan in regard to extraterritoriality, 118–20, 126, 133; a good friend of Eastern nations, 134; trouble with Korea, 135–37; treaty with Korea secured, 147–49; sends a Minister to Seoul, 150; friendly offices in the Chino-Japanese War, 154–57; becomes an Asiatic power, 165–68; annexes the Philippine and Hawaiian Islands, 169; urges the Open-Door policy for China, 170–72; attitude in the Boxer outbreak, 173–76; change in public opinion about Japan, 183–88; new commercial treaty with Japan (1911), 201; enters the World War, 220, 221; German propaganda, 223; exchange of notes between Secretary Lansing and Viscount Ishii, 224, 225; her great contribution to the Allied cause, 227; European immigration, 251; Chinese immigration, 252, 268; Japanese immigration, 183, 201, 247, 253–68; Japanese population in California, 261, 267; need of a new naturalization law, 265.

Urakami, arrest of Christians at, 94–97.

Van Valkenburgh, General R. B., third American Minister to Japan, 78; has private audience with the Shogun, 81; visits west coast of Japan, 81, 82; goes to Hiogo for the opening of the port, 84; invited to visit the Mikado, 88; refuses to deliver the ram *Stonewall*, 89; tries to secure release of Christians, 94–96; in the *General Sherman* case, 135.

Verbeck, Rev. Guido, missionary in Japan, 102.

Vladivostok, Japan takes control of, 228.

Von Eisendecker, Mr., in the *Hesperia* affair, 121.

Von Richthofen, Baron, 161.

Wade, Sir Thomas F., British Minister to China, 144.

Wang, Dr. C. T., of Canton, 231.

Wasson, Lieut. James R., in expedition to Formosa, 141, 142.

Watson, R. G., British Chargé, 100.

Webster, Daniel, 22.

Wei, Dr. W. P., Chinese Minister to Belgium, 231.

Weihaiwei, leased to Great Britain, 163.

Whalers, in the North Pacific, 18, 21.

Williams, Dr. S. Wells, Perry's interpreter, 26, 29; on extraterritoriality, 115, 116; appealed to by Prince Kung, 142, 143.

Wilson, President Woodrow, 258; idealistic utterances of, 221, 242; at the Paris Conference, 230, 233, 237.

Winchester, Mr., British Chargé, 68.

Witte, Count Sergius, Russian Minister of Finance, 159, 161; Memoirs of, 184.

World War, the, 206–29.

Wyoming, the, at Shimonoseki, 62.

Yamaguchi, Marshal, at Tientsin, 175.

Yap, island of, 232.

282